Seneca

Greek and Latin Studies
Classical Literature and its Influence
Editors
C. D. N. Costa and J. W. Binns
*School of Hellenic and Roman Studies
University of Birmingham*

Greek and Latin Studies
Classical Literature and its Influence

Seneca

Edited by
C. D. N. COSTA

Routledge & Kegan Paul: LONDON AND BOSTON

*First published in 1974
by Routledge & Kegan Paul Ltd
Broadway House, 68–74 Carter Lane,
London EC4V 5EL and
9 Park Street,
Boston, Mass. 02108, USA
Set in Garamond 11 point, 1 point leaded
and printed in Great Britain by
The Camelot Press Ltd, Southampton
© Routledge & Kegan Paul Ltd 1974
No part of this book may be reproduced in
any form without permission from the
publisher, except for the quotation of brief
passages in criticism
ISBN 0 7100 7900 1
Library of Congress Catalog Card No. 74-79358*

Contents

	Introduction	vii
	C. D. N. COSTA, *University of Birmingham*	
	Abbreviations	ix
I.	*Imago Vitae Suae*	1
	MIRIAM T. GRIFFIN, *University of Oxford*	
II.	Form and Content in the *Moral Essays*	39
	J. R. G. WRIGHT, *University of Edinburgh*	
III.	Letters to Lucilius	70
	D. A. RUSSELL, *University of Oxford*	
IV.	The Tragedies	96
	C. D. N. COSTA, *University of Birmingham*	
V.	Seneca's Philosophical Influence	116
	G. M. ROSS, *University of Leeds*	
VI.	Seneca and English Tragedy	166
	G. K. HUNTER, *University of Warwick*	
VII.	Seneca and Neo-Latin Tragedy in England	205
	J. W. BINNS, *University of Birmingham*	
	Subject Index	235
	Name Index	241

Introduction

C. D. N. Costa

Few writers have experienced in themselves and in their work such extremes of favour and disfavour as Seneca. Certainly no other single writer of the ancient world has exercised a comparable influence on both the prose and the verse of subsequent literatures. Both for what he said and for the way he said it Seneca was for centuries a household name in literary and philosophical circles, and the magnitude of this achievement cannot be denied even by those who find his thinking trite and his style insufferable. Perhaps it would be rash to claim that today there are a great many more people who enjoy him than there were a generation ago. But at least greater efforts are now being made to establish clearly the texts of what he wrote, to go beyond facile comparisons between his preaching and the practice of his life, and to sort out what is really valuable in the Senecan heritage. Major critical texts of the prose treatises and the tragedies are in hand, the Loeb Seneca is now complete, and recent published work shows some concern for getting to grips with the complexities of his life and writings. The present volume is offered as a tributary to this stream of activity, containing as it does a selection of modern views on most aspects of his work.

Seneca is tailor-made for the series *Greek and Latin Studies*, in which some stress is laid on a writer's subsequent influence, and consequently a larger proportion than usual of the book is devoted to *Nachleben*. For this reason and because of his very large output there are inevitable gaps in the discussions of his works themselves: the prose treatises had to be examined selectively, and very little is said of the *Natural Questions*. Otherwise, the contributors here assembled should offer food for thought to the interested amateur, and material for discussion and controversy to the Senecan specialist; the book will be justified if it achieves even one of these aims.

Finally, it should be acknowledged that some overlap may be seen here with two chapters on Seneca which appeared in the recent volume of this series, *Neronians and Flavians*, edited by D. R. Dudley. No apology is offered for this: the volumes were planned separately and can supplement each other, as no two viewpoints really coincide regarding this many-faceted writer.

Abbreviations

AE	L'Année Épigraphique
AJP	American Journal of Philology
BICS	Bulletin of the Institute of Classical Studies
CP	Classical Philology
CQ	Classical Quarterly
CW	Classical Weekly
DNB	Dictionary of National Biography
HSCP	Harvard Studies in Classical Philology
ILS	Inscriptiones Latinae Selectae
JHS	Journal of Hellenic Studies
JRS	Journal of Roman Studies
OCD[1]	Oxford Classical Dictionary, first edition
PIR[2]	Prosopographia Imperii Romani, second edition
RE	Pauly-Wissowa, Realencyclopädie der classischen Altertumswissenschaft
REA	Revue des Études Anciennes
REL	Revue des Études Latines
RhM	Rheinisches Museum
SIG[3]	Sylloge Inscriptionum Graecarum, third edition
TAPA	Transactions of the American Philological Association

I

Imago Vitae Suae

Miriam T. Griffin

Although Seneca's immortality derives mainly from the style he created and the philosophy he transmitted, his conduct as a man has also earned him fame, and notoriety. Ring-burdened Seneca, 'in his *books* a philosopher', fawning while praising liberty, extorting while praising poverty, is one of literature's great hypocrites.[1] To a more sympathetic eye, he has been 'the sage tossing on his couch of purple' as he struggles with the temptations of a decadent age and a tyrannical prince.[2] Then again, approached in a spirit of robust common sense, he has had his genius diagnosed as a mere gastric disorder or a paranoiac abnormality.[3] This enduring biographical concern with Seneca is only fair, for he himself adopted, as a stylist, the maxim 'talis hominibus oratio qualis vita', and, as a moralist, the rule 'concordet sermo cum vita'.[4]

In his own lifetime, Seneca's moral and political behaviour won him admirers and disciples, but critics and slanderers as well. The historian Tacitus records a diatribe directed against him at the height of his power alleging sexual licence and the accumulation of excessive wealth by dubious means, all belying his philosophical pretensions. Seneca had a philosophical defence to hand: *De Vita Beata* gives the sort of arguments he used against this attack by the notorious informer Suillius Rufus and against other such attacks.[5] Some must have found his case convincing, for, in addition to the inevitable crowd of political associates and dependants that he owed to his position close to the Emperor, Seneca had a more intimate circle of friends who believed in him as a moral teacher. To these men he offered not only encouragement and the lessons of his own struggle for moral improvement, but himself as a model, such as Socrates had been to Plato. It is thus with some verisimilitude that Tacitus makes Seneca offer on his deathbed, as his most precious legacy to his friends, the 'imaginem vitae suae'.[6]

What picture of his life has Seneca left?[7] The historical tradition about him was formed by his own younger contemporaries. Among these was probably the author of the *Octavia*, a historical tragedy in which Seneca appears as the brave and virtuous adviser of a tyrant who will not listen.[8] That assessment is also found in Juvenal, who celebrates, in addition, Seneca's generosity as a patron. Thirty years after Seneca's death, the poet Martial, who had come to Seneca as a poor client from a less civilized part of his native province, was still expressing his gratitude.[9] Another literary protégé, Fabius Rusticus, produced a history of the period that gave Seneca special prominence and credit.[10] But other historians produced more qualified portraits, recording the sordid charges of Suillius and others (that Seneca provoked Boudicca's rebellion in Britain by his usury, that he encouraged his wife's suicide attempt) that we find preserved in the third-century historian Dio Cassius.

The definitive account of his period of power under Nero was produced by Tacitus, who was a child when Seneca died. In using his literary sources, the historian had to look out for the various types of bias we have mentioned. In evaluating oral tradition, he had in addition to reckon with a change in literary fashion that branded Seneca's style as corrupt. The chief exponent of that view was the Flavian professor of rhetoric, another Spaniard, Fabius Quintilianus. Tacitus, as is clear from the *Dialogus de Oratoribus*, thought that Quintilian went too far in blaming Seneca for the decline of Latin eloquence, but he shared the change in taste and had to allow for it in his own reading of Seneca's works.[11] Suetonius, a less conscientious writer, made no attempt to escape the current prejudice.[12] It is not surprising that Tacitus's portrait of Seneca in the *Annals* is at times agnostic or equivocal. What is more interesting is that this acute and cynical judge, well aware of literary pose and moral falsity, but knowing also the hazards and temptations of imperial politics, delivered on balance a favourable verdict.[13]

Even if Seneca had not been a moralist, his great political standing as one of the most influential *amici principis* in the reign of Nero would still have attracted sharp criticism. For, like

'IMAGO VITAE SUAE'

Maecenas and Agrippa before him, Seneca was a new man of non-senatorial family but personal talent who thereby rose to power under the Principate. The Civil Wars had been, as such periods tend to be, a time of social mobility, but even afterwards the new imperial system offered rapid promotion to those who could impress the Emperor and his favourites with their abilities. Yet Maecenas, eccentric and effete as he was, and Agrippa, who preferred not to use his undistinguished *nomen*, were at least born in Italy; Seneca was 'equestri *et provinciali* loco ortus'.[14]

His birthplace was the Roman colony of Corduba in Baetica,[15] the richest and most peaceful of the Spanish provinces. But, according to a distinction that apparently mattered to the Romans (though it cannot in fact have been rigidly maintained or in particular cases proved), he was not of Spanish blood, but of Italian immigrant stock, *Hispaniensis* not *Hispanus*. His family name Annaeus proclaims an ultimate ancestry in north-eastern Italy,[16] but there is no telling when the family emigrated. From the beginning of the second century B.C., when the Spanish provinces were organized, Italian veterans, traders, mine speculators and political refugees settled there in considerable numbers. Corduba had been founded early as a community of Roman *émigrés* and was later reinforced by Augustus, who settled veterans there and gave the town the status of a Roman colony, with the grand title Colonia Patricia.[17] Seneca's lost biography of his father probably had something to say of his earlier ancestors;[18] without it, we know only that the first member of the family of literary consequence, Seneca's father, L. Annaeus Seneca, was himself born in Corduba and was well established there.[19]

Father Seneca was a Roman *eques*, hence a man with a substantial census rating and the high social standing in his native city that normally went with it. It is likely that the principal source of his wealth was agricultural land, for the banks of the Guadalquivir on which Corduba stood were covered with olive groves and vineyards; and the *patrimonium* of his sons was administered by their mother Helvia during their long absences from Spain, a situation easiest to imagine if their wealth consisted of landed estates. He probably held no municipal office, nor did he avail himself of the opportunities created by the first Princeps for *equites* to serve Rome in a financial or administrative capacity.

Nor, though he devoted a good deal of his life to the study of rhetoric, was he ever a teacher or practising advocate. The epithet Rhetor by which he is sometimes known has no ancient authority behind it, but derives from the work of a humanist scholar who realized, as many before him had not, that the works of the father and the son, transmitted together in the manuscripts, were in fact composed by different Senecas. To mark the distinction, he called the author of the works we call the *Controversiae* and *Suasoriae*[20] Seneca Rhetor.

Born between 55 and 50 B.C., the Elder Seneca was prevented from going to Rome for his very early education by the dreadful Civil Wars started by Caesar and Pompey and continued by their followers throughout the decade of the forties (*Contr.* 1, pref. 11). Corduba, the effective capital of the province of Hispania Ulterior, wavered between the two sides, trying to save its wealth and status. Even after the battle of Philippi, Sextus Pompey menaced the sea between Spain and Italy until 36 B.C., so that it was somewhat belatedly that this ambitious provincial finally found himself in Rome studying under an insignificant teacher from Spain called Marullus (*Contr.* 1, pref. 22). By that time he had been through his preparatory education with a *grammaticus* in Corduba, at whose school he exhibited the outstanding powers of memory to which we owe our most detailed knowledge of the declamatory schools (*Contr.* 1, pref. 2). As a schoolboy, he could repeat in reverse order single lines of verse recited by his more than two hundred fellow-pupils; in old age he was able to recall word for word many of the *sententiae* of famous declaimers that he had heard even on his first visit to Rome, including some by the boy Ovid.

Training in rhetoric was essential to a political career at Rome, and it is possible that Father Seneca already harboured those ambitions to be a Roman senator to which he confesses in the *Controversiae* (2, pref. 4). The impetus may be traceable to his early acquaintance with the great general, orator and historian Asinius Pollio, for Seneca tells us that he was admitted to Pollio's private declamations in the 30s B.C. (*Contr.* 4, pref. 2–4). This acquaintance could go back to the days when Pollio was governing Spain for Caesar and spending much of his time on literary pursuits in Corduba.[21] The senatorial career never materialized, but Father Seneca's eventual decision to write history may owe something to Pollio, whose history he admired (*Suas.* 6.25), and whose *veritas* he apparently emulated. The son describes his father's work as 'a history running from the start of the civil wars, when truth was first put to flight, almost up to the day of his own death'.[22] The wars meant are doubtless the great civil upheavals of his childhood. The history probably ended with the reign of Tiberius, for its author died in 39 or 40,[23] leaving the manuscript for his son to publish. He may never have done so, for we have no certain fragment of that work.

The Elder Seneca had returned to Spain around 8 B.C., where he married a certain Helvia, who bore him three sons: Annaeus Novatus, known after his adoption many years later by his father's friend, the senator L. Junius Gallio, as L. Junius Gallio Annaeanus;[24] L. Annaeus Seneca, born in 1 B.C. or shortly before;[25] and M. Annaeus Mela, father of the poet Lucan. By A.D. 5 the father had returned to Rome with his sons and was continuing his visits to the rhetorical schools and supervising their education. He wished his sons to have the senatorial career he had once desired, but he regarded the study of rhetoric as essential to the pursuit of any art, even philosophy to which, by the time the *Controversiae* and *Suasoriae* were being composed, his youngest son was wholly devoted (*Contr.* 2, pref.). That was after 37, and the old man was nearly ninety when he acceded to his sons' request to recall and compile for them the best *dicta* of the declaimers that they had been too young to hear, giving his judgment of each (*Contr.* 1, pref.). By that time his sons were adult and the two oldest embarked on their careers as orators and senators; yet such was the *antiquus rigor* of the old man[26] that in this work, intended from the start for publication, he scolds them for preferring rhetorical bagatelles to solid historical matter (*Suas.* 6.16) and castigates the laziness and effeminacy of their whole generation whose standards of eloquence were consequently in decline (*Contr.* 1, pref.).

A man of strong character and married to a woman from a strict old-fashioned provincial home,[27] Father Seneca maintained that same atmosphere in his. Helvia was discouraged from pursuing a natural taste for literature and philosophy because he thought these pursuits inappropriate for women, and young Seneca was successfully deflected from a youthful passion for a fashionable brand of ascetic philosophy involving vegetarianism.[28] For the youngest son Mela, Father Seneca had the typical weakness of the patriarchs, openly proclaiming him the cleverest of the three and indulging in him a taste for philosophy and a lack of ambition he would have found intolerable in the older ones. But his devotion to them all was undeniable, and his second son was to describe him in old age as *pater indulgentissimus*, recalling how filial affection had deterred him from committing suicide in youth when he despaired of recovery from consumption (*Epist.* 78.2). Seneca was also indebted for his style to his father's training and example: he took over many of his turns of phrase and his literary judgments.[29] Finally, the sons were prevented from losing all feeling for their native Corduba when they moved to the capital. Father Seneca himself died in Spain despite long years spent in Rome, and, in the collection of declamatory material he made for his sons, he expresses his delight in writing about Spanish declaimers and especially in rescuing from oblivion those who had practised their art only in the province (*Contr.* 1, pref. 13, 20; 10, pref. 13). His sons were educated at Rome along with the son of one of these, a certain Clodius Turrinus (*Contr.* 10, pref. 16). The youngest son Mela married in Corduba and his son Lucan was born there;[30] his more successful brother when imperial adviser extended his patronage to several young hopefuls from the province.[31]

To his mother Helvia, Seneca owed his early taste for philosophy, and to her family the start of his political career (*Cons. Helv.* 15.1; 19.2). For Helvia had a stepsister whose husband, C. Galerius, was one of the new imperial brand of *equites* and rose to be Prefect of Egypt,[32] the highest post then open to a non-senator and one which put him above many senators in power and influence. This aunt had brought Seneca to Rome as a child and now, towards the end of her husband's sixteen-year term of office under Tiberius, she invited him to travel to Egypt for his health. The voyage and the climate were reputed good for tubercular cases. He returned with his aunt in A.D. 31, an eventful voyage on which they were nearly shipwrecked, and his uncle died (*Cons. Helv.* 19). Seneca was then past thirty, five years older than the minimum age for holding the quaestorship, the first magistracy that carried senatorial rank. He records gratefully how, some time after their return from Egypt, his aunt canvassed all of her influential connections to secure his election to that office, presumably having first obtained from the Emperor for him the grant of the *latus clavus* which gave him the right to stand. To judge from their father's description of them shortly after 37 as preparing for the forum and magistracies (*Contr.* 2, pref.), neither Seneca nor his older brother Novatus had advanced beyond the quaestorship by Gaius's reign, so that it is possible that they were both around forty when they entered the senate.

Ill-health may have played some part in this slow beginning, for both brothers were tubercular. A temperamental distaste may also be involved: Novatus was a gentle man with little taste for flattery, according to his brother (*Nat. Quaest.* 4, pref. 10ff.), while Seneca was profoundly absorbed in natural science and moral philosophy. Before his visit to Egypt, he was drinking in with rapture the lectures of the Stoic Attalus, whose ascetic recommendations he put into practice. By A.D. 19 he was an enthusiastic adherent of the only philosophical school to originate in Rome (*Epist.* 108.13–23), a basically Stoic sect with ascetic neo-Pythagorean elements. It may be significant for Seneca's late start that the founder, Q. Sextius, had himself been offered a senatorial career by Caesar the Dictator and refused (*Epist.* 98.13). After his return from Egypt in 31, any new ambitions Seneca may have had failed to flourish in the new political situation following the fall of Sejanus. The recall of his uncle Galerius precisely in 31 and his hasty replacement by a freedman suggests that, like that long-standing friend of the family Junius Gallio, the Senecas were somehow involved with the fallen praetorian prefect.[33] But it is also well to remember Tiberius's neglect of government in his last years: not many young *equites* were given the *latus clavus* in the last years of that bitter recluse's government.[34]

Seneca's works give, on the whole, a low estimate of Tiberius, showing him as a proud, ungrateful man, whose meanness was unworthy of a ruler and whose policy degenerated into a judicial reign of terror.[35] Seneca's youthful spell of vegetarianism, inspired by Sotion, a follower of the Sextii, had been brought to a hasty finish early in Tiberius's reign in A.D. 19, when abstinence from pork, on whatever grounds, was being construed as conversion to Judaism, and persistence in vegetarianism might have led to his being expelled from Rome as a proselyte.[36] Yet his references to Tiberius are moderate, especially when compared with what he has to say of his successor.

It was probably in the reign of Gaius that both Seneca and

Novatus reached the next step on the *cursus honorum*, the aedileship or tribunate, of which Seneca tells us nothing. He was becoming a successful orator, enough, it was said, to provoke the Emperor's jealousy and his very unflattering criticism of his style as 'sand without lime'.[37] In addition, Seneca had already published at least one scientific work, on earthquakes (*Nat. Quaest.* 6.4.2) and he was beginning to find favour in high places. Various shreds of evidence suggest an early connection with the sisters of the Emperor and with Cornelius Lentulus Gaetulicus, an aristocrat, a writer of history and poetry, and, by virtue of his ten-year governorship of Upper Germany, a political power.[38] In 39, a conspiracy to put Aemilius Lepidus on the throne was exposed. As a result, Gaetulicus was killed and Gaius's three sisters sent into exile. Seneca may well have been casting about for new friends when he wrote the first of his Consolations, the one addressed to Marcia, a well-born woman of senatorial family and connections who carried on the literary interests of her father, Cremutius Cordus. His works, burned in the reign of Tiberius, had been republished with Gaius's permission, as a demonstration of his belief in freedom of speech, though the republication was a censored version.[39]

At last, in January 41, the tyrant was dead, murdered by a tribune of the praetorian guard with the co-operation of many senators and *equites*, but not, apparently, of Seneca. He may have been in the theatre on the fateful day and he published his approval of the deed years after, without however betraying any intimate knowledge of the assassination, and in fact implying the reverse by speculating at a distance about the motives of the conspirators (*Const. Sap.* 18; *Ira* 1.20.9). Seneca's friends Gaetulicus and Julius Graecinus were avenged (*Ben.* 2.21; *Epist.* 29.6), Gaius's two surviving sisters were recalled, but Seneca's misfortunes were only beginning. On the throne now was a better Emperor, but one less in control of what happened.

Seneca was now middle-aged, and not yet praetor, hence of little standing in the senate. He had given up oratory, perhaps at first to avoid the consequences of Gaius's jealousy, but finally for more fundamental reasons: his weak chest had probably always made speaking an effort and he no doubt realized, like his father (*Contr.* 1, pref. 7), that the virtual monarchy by which Rome was governed had diminished the importance of oratory as a source of power or a form of public service. Like one of his

Sextian teachers, Papirius Fabianus, a declaimer turned philosopher, Seneca concentrated on natural science and took up the challenge set by Cicero to write philosophy in Latin. His talents as an orator he was learning to employ as a *vitiorum insectator*; the spiritual comfort of Stoicism he was to administer to others – and himself. For in 41, Seneca lost a son, the only child he was to have, and, probably, his wife as well.[40] Towards the end of the year, he was relegated to the island of Corsica and deprived of some of his property on a charge of adultery with Gaius's sister, Julia Livilla. Seneca himself tells us that he was tried before the senate, which declared him guilty and prescribed the death penalty; but that Claudius asked that his life be spared (*Cons. Polyb.* 13.2). Yet Tacitus says that Seneca was thought to nourish a grudge against Claudius *dolore iniuriae*.[41] These statements can only be reconciled by assuming that Claudius's clemency counted for little with Seneca because he felt that his conviction had been altogether unjust and would not have happened under a better Emperor. In his Consolation to his mother Helvia, Seneca offers the comforting picture of himself as an innocent victim sustained by his virtue and his philosophical beliefs. Even in the other Consolation he wrote from exile, that addressed to Polybius, he asks that the Emperor recall him as an act of *iustitia* or *clementia*.

It would seem then that Seneca was either innocent or at least not manifestly guilty; otherwise these works designed to win him sympathy would instead have exposed him to ridicule. The historian Dio Cassius makes out a plausible case for his being an innocent victim of Claudius's young wife Valeria Messalina, who was envious of Livilla and determined to be rid of her.[42] Seneca himself alludes in a later work to some victims of Messalina and Claudius's most powerful freedman Narcissus, friends of Seneca's addressee Lucilius, who proved loyal to them under questioning (*Nat. Quaest.* 4, pref. 15). The passage is general but he may be including himself among the victims. Allegations of immorality involving royal princesses were a favourite weapon in the struggles concerning the succession. Reasonably, as actual liaisons of this kind could support or create claims to the throne, given a system of government that was in fact a hereditary monarchy, but could not be described as such and therefore could not rely on a law of succession or any other fixed system for deciding claims. In 41 Messalina had just produced an heir, and she may well have feared the influence on the susceptible Claudius of attractive nieces with the blood of Augustus in their veins. Julia Livilla she removed, but she met her match in Julia Agrippina, who may already have had enough sway over the uncle she was later to marry to cause his mitigation of Seneca's sentence: Tacitus says that she later recalled Seneca expecting him to be loyal *memoria beneficii*.[43]

Seneca spent nearly eight years on Corsica, reading works on natural history and the masterpieces of consolation literature (*Cons. Helv.* 1.2; 8.6). He analysed the native dialect (*Cons. Helv.* 7.9) and brooded on Ovid's last works,[44] doubtless drawing parallels between his own fate and the poet's eight years in dismal Tomis. Bidding for the sympathy of Polybius, he complains, like Ovid, that his Latin is becoming rusty (*Cons. Polyb.* 18.9); yet there were two Roman colonies on Corsica and he may have been accompanied into exile by a loyal friend,[45] surely enough to keep him in practice. In any case, Seneca kept his style fresh by writing. To mention only works that survive, he composed or at least planned much of *De Ira*, and he applied his reading of consolations to the composition of two such works: one addressed to his mother Helvia, the other to the 'insolent and pampered freedman of a tyrant' (in Macaulay's words), Polybius, at the time serving Claudius as *a libellis* and *a studiis*. In the guise of a work consoling Polybius on the death of his brother, Seneca made a transparent appeal to be recalled to witness Claudius's imminent British triumph (13.2). The work that has come down to us contains praise of Polybius and of Claudius so exaggerated that some scholars have construed it as satire, intended or unconscious.[46] Such an apology overlooks both Seneca's important lapse from good taste in the funeral eulogy of Claudius, and the standards of adulation of his time, standards that already seemed shocking to Pliny half a century later.[47] One of the indictments that Dio Cassius brings against Seneca is the composition of a book sent from exile praising Messalina and Claudius's freedmen, a book Seneca afterwards suppressed or repudiated. Dio's meaning, as transmitted through an excerptor, is not clear.[48] Though the extant Consolation does not contain praise of Messalina, the identification with the work mentioned by Dio is hard to challenge: the opening chapters of the extant piece were lost early and may have been flattering to Messalina, and Dio's excerptor may have transmitted inaccurately some phrase of Dio's meaning that Seneca tried to suppress the work. In any case, Polybius was unmoved or already experiencing that decline in influence with Messalina that ended in his death. Other exiles came home for Claudius's triumph,[49] but Seneca had to wait until Messalina was dead and Agrippina married to Claudius.

The year 49 opened with the imperial nuptials, followed soon after by the recall of Seneca and his designation as praetor for the next year. Both improvements in his fortunes Seneca owed to Agrippina, though they were formally carried through by Claudius and the senate.[50] Agrippina, according to Tacitus, thought an act of mercy towards a promising writer, who was widely regarded as an innocent victim of the previous wife, would divert attention from the sinister circumstances of her own marriage to Claudius. For it was an incestuous union by Roman law and darkened by the suicide of L. Junius Silanus, a descendant of Augustus betrothed to Claudius's daughter Octavia.[51] Silanus was surely not alone in seeing what Agrippina intended and would certainly achieve, namely, the betrothal of her son to Octavia as a first move towards his ultimate replacement of Claudius's son Britannicus as heir apparent. Seneca had never been a man of rigid principle: he had given up his asceticism to avoid prosecution and crawled to Polybius for recall from exile. He must have known that the price for his return to the literary life of the capital and the restoration of his property and status would be collaboration in the schemes of his benefactress. He must have known and accepted it. A late source records that he was hoping to go to Athens on his return.[52] At most this reflects a vain wish at the time or a later defence of his motives for accepting recall, but it might simply be an attempt to explain why such an educated man had never been to Athens.

Seneca's older brother did go to Greece, probably as a result of Seneca's change of fortune, for he is attested by an inscription at Delphi as proconsul of Achaea in 51/2. He is called there by his adoptive name, and it is likewise as 'careless Gallio' that he has been immortalized by *Acts* because of his reluctance to be embroiled in the religious quarrels of the Jews.[53] It may also have been at this time that the youngest brother Mela gave up his single-minded devotion to philosophy to become a procurator of the imperial estates, a 'praepostera ambitio' in Tacitus's view, leading not only to wealth but to political power equal to that of consular senators by the safer route of remaining an *eques*.[54]

Seneca and Gallio went on to become suffect consuls in successive years early in the reign of Nero (Gallio, the older, fittingly holding the office in 55, Seneca in 56); but then, as under Claudius, Seneca's power and significance owed little to his place in the senate. He became a courtier, exercising for the rest of his life those qualities that he himself describes in *De Tranquillitate Animi* (6) as necessary to life at court: control of one's temper, one's words and one's wit. In particular, that trait so often ascribed to senators of Stoic sympathies had to be controlled: 'contumacia non facit ad aulam'.[55] At the same time, Seneca was an extremely productive and popular author, developing the new anti-Ciceronian style whose roots are apparent in the pieces of declamation preserved by his father. From now on, the philosophical sentiments in his treatises laid him open to charges of hypocrisy, while the extreme reticence he preserves in them about his activities and position makes it tempting to think that he kept his life and his literary work rigidly separate. But the historical evidence we have about life at the court of Claudius and Nero does explain, at least in part, his preoccupation with the fragility of power and wealth, the possibility of sudden punishment and death, the appropriate time and reasons for committing suicide, and the right reasons for undertaking or abandoning a public career.

His immediate task was to instruct Agrippina's son Domitius. By his adoption as Claudius's son in February 50, Seneca's pupil became Nero Claudius Drusus Germanicus, and, by the three-year advantage in age he had over Britannicus, he became the expected heir to the throne. Seneca was to teach him rhetoric and, no doubt, to impart some of his own charm and polish. It was a difficult task. In his treatise *De Ira*, already complete or near completion in 49, Seneca shows his awareness of the difficulties involved in educating the children of wealthy and powerful families: such children will have their passions inflamed by flattery and indulgence if they are not disciplined and made to live on terms of equality with their peers (2.21.7–11). The mixture of praise and admonition with which Seneca was to address the eighteen-year-old Nero (now Princeps) in *De Clementia* shows what psychological skill he must always have needed in teaching his royal pupil. Tacitus makes Seneca claim to have exercised *libertas* in his dealings with Nero, but the historian's own phrase *honesta comitas* is probably nearer the truth.[56]

Nero declaimed in Greek and Latin and acquired some skill in *ex tempore* speaking, but his artistic and athletic interests never allowed him to reach the standard of eloquence required for major speeches as Princeps. Seneca was generally believed to have written these.[57] According to Suetonius, Agrippina banned philosophy from Nero's curriculum, but she could not have included in that ban the practical moral instruction traditionally associated with teaching in rhetoric.[58] In fact, an anecdote in Plutarch shows that Seneca was thought to have given his pupil counsel of this sort, teaching him on one occasion to bear the loss of a costly and irreplaceable marquee with self-restraint.[59] Seneca was adaptable. Stoicism, he explains in *De Clementia* (2.5.2), is not, as widely believed, a harsh doctrine unsuitable for rulers. What advice he gave Agrippina and her son on practical politics no doubt represented a considerable bending of Stoic doctrine.

Until Nero's accession in October 54, Seneca was simply his *magister* or *praeceptor*; from then on he was also one of the principal *amici principis*. In fact, he never held any official position apart from the magistracies and senatorial seat which, as we have said, were not the source of his power. No historian mentions any occasion on which Seneca spoke in the senate or was even present, and the unwillingness of the Neronian senate to vote on measures put to them by the consuls without prior reference to the Emperor suggests that Seneca, whose views would be taken to carry imperial sanction, rarely attended meetings.[60] One of his enemies, it is true, accused him of sponsoring the first *senatus consultum* of the reign (one cancelling an edict of Claudius that had encouraged informers),[61] but it is likely that even this showpiece of senatorial liberty was supported from behind the scenes. It was, in fact, from the equestrian order that most of Seneca's political associates and the friends to whom he addressed his essays were drawn. In some cases, the two categories just mentioned overlap, for many of Seneca's friends were favoured with governmental positions. To Pompeius Paulinus, the father of his second wife (whom he probably married on his return from exile) and *praefectus annonae* from about 49 to 55, Seneca addressed *De Brevitate Vitae*. To Annaeus Serenus, who held the important command of the night-watch from about 54 until some time before 62, Seneca dedicated a group of three dialogues in which Serenus is depicted as a pupil in three stages of moral development: a sceptic in *De Constantia Sapientis*, a struggling convert in *De Tranquillitate Animi*, and a confident Stoic in *De Otio*. To the obscure Lucilius Junior, who attained the unimportant post of procurator in Sicily shortly before 62, Seneca sent more works than to anyone else: some are lost, but *De Providentia*, the *Naturales Quaestiones* and the great *Epistulae Morales* survive.[62]

Seneca's most important political associate was an *eques* who received no philosophical treatise and needed no patronage. Sextus Afranius Burrus from another civilized western province, Gallia Narbonensis, was, like Seneca, a protégé of Agrippina. Though the inscription recording his career, found at his home town of Vaison, gives as his earlier posts only a military tribunate followed by procuratorships of the properties of Livia, Tiberius and Claudius,[63] Burrus had apparently acquired a considerable military reputation before he was elevated by Claudius in 51 to the sole command of the praetorian guard. According to Tacitus, this step consolidated Agrippina's power, for she, at one stroke, secured control of the guard and rid herself of two allies of Britannicus who shared the post before.[64]

The harmony of Seneca and Burrus was as fortunate as it was remarkable. Tacitus's description of their collaboration in handling Nero recalls Seneca's argument in *De Ira* that spoiled and well-born pupils must be alternately goaded with the spur and held in with the reins: 'They were in their different ways equally influential, Burrus through his military position and his strict morality, Seneca through his instruction in rhetoric and his agreeable, though upright, personality, supporting each other so as to be able to restrain the Emperor's susceptible youth by licensed pleasures should he spurn virtue.'[65] But Burrus was more than Nero's reins: of the two advisers he alone had the chance of building up considerable independent power which the Princeps needed and feared. It was he, for example, who calmed the praetorians and the urban populace after Nero's murder of Agrippina, thereby removing the threat of a popular rising.[66] Therefore it is not surprising to find that Tacitus dated the serious decline in Seneca's influence to the death of Burrus.[67]

Tacitus is our most detailed source for the activities of Seneca and Burrus. His account was based on three contemporary sources who could survey their doings from close-range but different standpoints: the senior senator Cluvius Rufus, the equestrian officer and procurator Pliny the Elder, and the young protégé of Seneca, Fabius Rusticus.[68] Tacitus and Dio both credit the two *amici* with virtual control of imperial policy in the early years, but they differ on the nature of the control and the policy. According to Dio, Seneca and Burrus sponsored reforms through legislation;[69] according to Tacitus, they worked behind the scenes, so much so that Seneca could be credited by some with all of Nero's good actions, by others with all of his crimes,[70] and their work concerned not so much the substance as the manner of government. Dio presents no example of a reform carried out to support his view and, in an attempt to give it any plausibility, he has to make Seneca and Burrus give up their interest in government impossibly early, in 55.[71] Tacitus, on the other hand, can offer a picture of their role that he illustrates and that fits the political character he attributes to Nero's early reign, i.e. *civilitas*, a return after Claudius to proper forms and procedure, particularly as regards relations with the senate. There is no doubt that Tacitus's picture must be preferred, with due allowance for the possibility that he has exaggerated the importance of Seneca and Burrus. For Tacitus was clearly fascinated by Seneca, largely because Seneca displayed that combination of talent and flexibility, that exercise of political skill without display that always attracted Tacitus.[72] But Seneca is far more prominent in Tacitus's writing than other mixed characters like Marcus Lepidus, Petronius, Otho, or Lucius Vitellius. A family connection goes some way towards explaining this. Seneca's works show him to have been an admirer and possibly a friend of Julius Graecinus, the grandfather of Tacitus's wife. But there was also the Senecan style which had captivated his generation in youth. For Seneca's doctrine, however, Tacitus cares nothing – only the philosopher's enemies allude to that in the *Annals* – but, despite the reaction in taste, Tacitus shows his thorough knowledge of Seneca's works by his deliberate echoes of their language and thought.[73]

One of the scenes in which these allusions are particularly apparent is the dialogue between Seneca and Nero in *Annals* 14.53–56. The year is 62. Seneca, his power broken by the death of Burrus and the growing influence of one of the new praetorian prefects, Ofonius Tigellinus, asks for permission to surrender some of his wealth to Nero and to retire from life at court. Seneca is made to compare his services to Nero with those of Agrippa and Maecenas to Augustus. Now Seneca himself, in a work written during his period of greatest influence with Nero, makes some significant remarks about the relations of these two *seniores amici* with the Princeps. Augustus, in a fit of temper, reported to the senate all the sordid details of his daughter Julia's erotic adventures, then repented, saying, 'None of these disasters would have happened to me, had either Agrippa or Maecenas been alive.' Seneca comments bitterly, 'There is no reason to believe that Agrippa and Maecenas regularly told him the truth; had they lived, they would have been in the ranks of those who concealed it. It is a custom of kings to praise those absent in order to insult those present, and to attribute the virtue of free speech to those from whom they no longer have to hear it' (*Ben.* 6.32, 2–4). This anecdote, like the parallel drawn by Nero in the retirement dialogue between Seneca and Lucius Vitellius, suggests that one function of Seneca and Burrus was to counsel the Princeps on his personal affairs where they touched politics, and to invent and impose on the public an official version of such events.

This side of Seneca's and Burrus's activity is abundantly illustrated by Tacitus. Their first task was to curb the political influence of the overbearing Agrippina and to end the Claudian pattern of excessive influence by wives and freedmen, while publicly showing honour and respect to the dead Emperor and his widow in order to quiet the anxieties of those who had flourished under the old régime and were worried by Nero's succession. In controlling the adolescent Princeps, Seneca and Burrus, somewhat indulgent and detached, had an unwilling ally in Nero's aggressive and tactless mother. She humiliated him by the respect she showed to the freedman Pallas, and by her assertion of equal imperial authority. She thwarted his youthful impulses by confining him to an unloved wife selected by her for political reasons. She tried to bully him by threatening to support his rivals to the throne. It was Seneca who, with great presence of mind, averted Agrippina's design of mounting Nero's tribunal to receive ambassadors, prompting Nero to rise and descend the dais with a courteous gesture of welcome. It was Seneca who covered up Nero's affair with the freedwoman Acte by inducing his protégé Annaeus Serenus to act as a decoy. Seneca and Burrus averted a complete break between mother and son in 55, when Agrippina, having stampeded Nero into murdering Britannicus by supporting his claim to the succession, was reported to have put her influence behind another rival. Seneca warned Nero against incestuous relations with his mother and, with Burrus, managed public opinion after the clumsy matricide which they had refused to execute.[74] Their innocence of the murder is clearly attested by Tacitus and is more credible than the story in Dio Cassius making Seneca an accomplice.[75] For Seneca and Burrus must have appreciated that their power depended on the continued existence and influence of Agrippina, from whom they provided a refuge. It was a dangerous game they played, and her ultimate destruction in 59 considerably diminished their control over the Emperor, who found others more polite about his chariot-racing, singing and poetry.

Throughout the period ending with Burrus's death, and even for some time afterwards, Seneca had an opportunity to exercise patronage. We have already mentioned some of the friends who may have achieved office through him. The careers of his brothers Gallio and Mela continued; his nephew Lucan was recalled from his university course in Athens to assume the quaestorship five years before the legal age.[76] His brother-in-law Pompeius Paulinus reached the consulship and went out to govern Lower Germany.[77] The young relative of Seneca's uncle, P. Galerius Trachalus, was launched on a senatorial career.[78]

But Seneca was also thought to have a hand in appointments that were made for reasons of state rather than for the gratification of his dependants. In Nero's very first winter as Princeps, there was a crisis in Armenia. Once again the mountainous buffer state between Rome and the Parthian Empire had lapsed from Roman control. Nero's appointment of Cn. Domitius Corbulo, an able general whose military ambition had been thwarted by the cautious or jealous Claudius, pleased the senate and was traced by one popular rumour to the influence of Burrus and Seneca.[79] As a step towards removing the abuses of the Claudian régime, Nero demanded Pallas's retirement from his post *a rationibus*, and Agrippina held Seneca and Burrus responsible.[80] It was Seneca, according to Plutarch,[81] who decided on the appointment of the future Emperor, L. Salvius Otho, as governor of Lusitania, in order to free his wife Poppaea for Nero. These examples make it likely that Seneca and Burrus were often consulted in the allotment of imperial posts.

The advisory functions so far described were shared by Seneca with Burrus. But it fell to Seneca alone, if not always to invent, then at least to advertise the formulae justifying what was done. Lucius Vitellius had persuaded the senate, not merely to accept but to advocate Claudius's marriage to Agrippina, and he may well have influenced that Emperor's pronouncements on the Jews, for he was experienced in Eastern politics.[82] Seneca went farther and actually wrote Nero's official speeches: a funeral eulogy of Claudius; an accession speech addressed to the praetorian guard and one to the senate; speeches to the senate on clemency in 55;[83] and perhaps the humiliating letter to the senate in which the Emperor spun a tale of remorse and suicide to explain his mother's end, but, by including a list of her crimes in justification, virtually confessed to her murder. Tacitus notes that Seneca was generally thought to be the author of this letter, and that it brought him no credit.[84] Certainly, it accords ill with Seneca's own condemnation of Augustus's unrestrained communication to the senate on the subject of Julia, and it forms a contrast to the brief edict issued by Nero on the death of Britannicus, which simply expressed grief and excused the haste with which the obsequies were performed. But whoever wrote that edict – and it might have been Seneca – had an easier task. For the murder of Britannicus was carried out secretly and could be dissimulated. But Nero's ex-teacher Anicetus, prefect of the fleet at Misenum, had bungled Agrippina's death. The ship carrying her home from an affectionate meeting with her son was to have collapsed entirely, killing her in the process. But she survived the shipwreck, which attracted spectators who also saw guards surrounding the villa afterwards.[85] Some explanation had to be offered. Even so, Seneca may have chosen words that were inappropriate to the occasion; he had already done so in writing the funeral encomium on the dead Claudius. Here Seneca had proceeded according to the traditional formula, praising Claudius's ancestors and his scholarly talents, turning then to his achievements as Princeps, first in foreign policy, then in governing the Empire. But here apparently he chose to attribute to Claudius qualities (*providentia, sapientia*) that could only remind the audience of the deceased's absent-mindedness and gullibility, thereby inadvertently raising a laugh.[86]

The funeral speech must have seemed particularly absurd to those of the inner court circle who had heard Nero's own jokes about Claudius's stupidity and cruelty, particularly after they attended the recitation of Seneca's *Apocolocyntosis*, in which all of Claudius's vices and weaknesses were exposed to ridicule. We will return to Seneca's speech-writing, but something must first be said about this cruel satire that has offended the taste of modern readers, more than it offended or even interested his ancient or post-classical critics.[87] Some have even tried to deny that the work we have is by Seneca, but the manuscripts all attribute it to him and the arguments against his authorship are very weak. Although the humour may seem in conflict with Seneca's usual philosophical or tragic solemnity, we know from a letter of Pliny that he wrote light verse and from Tacitus that he was believed to put on comic imitations of Nero's singing.[88] Even the dialogues we have contain satirical descriptions of current *mores*. Moreover, Dio affirms that Seneca wrote a farce on Claudius's consecration called the *Apocolocyntosis*, the title being, he explains, a pun on the word for consecration. A description similar to Dio's, i.e. 'Divi Claudi apotheosis per satiram', is prefixed to our best manuscript of the work, so that, although the title 'Apocolocyntosis' is not preserved there nor in the other manuscripts (which call it 'Ludus de morte Claudi'), the identification with the skit Dio mentions can hardly be doubted. The title 'Transformation into a Gourd' is probably a pure play on the word *apotheosis*, with perhaps additional comic overtones because gourds may have been used as dice-boxes and Claudius was addicted to the game: the fact that no actual transformation of this kind takes place can hardly seem an argument against identification to anyone with enough humour to enjoy the piece.[89] Finally, the contrast with Seneca's earlier praise of Claudius in the *Consolatio* to Polybius and the funeral *laudatio* may not be morally edifying, but it is all too explicable and Seneca alludes to it himself. Before the other courtiers who had themselves laughed in private at the consecration they solemnly celebrated in public, Seneca enjoyed parodying his own work from exile: there (15–16) Claudius had been made to complain of the misfortunes of Augustus and his own relatives; in the *Apocolocyntosis* (10.4–11.1) Augustus blames Claudius for the sufferings of his. In the *Consolatio* (17.4) the thought of Caligula moves Seneca to exclaim 'pro pudore imperii'; in the satire (10.2) the thought of Claudius moves Augustus to say 'pudet imperii'. Seneca even makes a joke of his well-known hostility to Claudius, through whom he had lost not only his integrity but also nine years of his cultured and witty life. He piously borrows the historians' cliché: 'There will be no concession made to resentment or partiality' (1.1).

Claudius died on 13 October 54 and was probably buried soon after. But the consecration need not have followed immediately.[90] Seneca may have taken advantage either of the abandoned mood that accompanied imperial funerals or of that traditional at the Saturnalia in December, for the presentation of his farce. The criticism of Claudius includes those charges mentioned in earnest in Nero's accession speech to the senate: the power of his freedmen, the venality of his court, the monopoly of jurisdiction by the Princeps, and his neglect of proper procedure. The highpoint of the indictment of Claudius is a speech by Divus Augustus who vetoes his deification at the council of the gods on the grounds of his folly and cruelty. But there are also trivial criticisms: Claudius's voice, his walk, his pedantry. The ridicule of Claudius is relieved principally by the praise of Nero, which similarly combines the serious promises of a new type of government with trivial praise of Nero's good looks and voice.

Many scholars have thought that the *Apocolocyntosis* has a serious political aim, that by attacking Claudius's deification Seneca either made an attack on Agrippina, who was the priestess of Claudius's cult and the obstacle to the reform of his methods of government, or on Britannicus whose claim to the succession was inadvertently strengthened by his father's elevation.[91] There are difficulties in seeing the work as aimed at Agrippina: whereas at court Claudius's poisoning was the subject of jokes, the *Apocolocyntosis* seems to credit an official version of his death as being due to fever (6) and taking place at the time Agrippina had announced (2.2; 4.2) and not earlier as some said it did – which seems odd in a work attacking Agrippina. But then Messalina is treated surprisingly charitably,[92] and that is odd for an attack on Britannicus. Is it likely, in fact, that the farce is a serious attack on the consecration? Coins show *divi Cl. f.* still advertised in 55 (and on one rare one of 56), while official inscriptions carry the filiation even later. The spirit of amnesty advertised by the deification was carefully preserved. Of the men whom Claudius had made patricians, L. Salvius Otho had a younger son who prospered at court, Q. Veranius was chosen to initiate an aggressive policy in Britain. Claudius's prefect of the city from 42, L. Volusius Saturninus, was retained by Nero until his death. These examples can easily be multiplied. The mistake is to take a work in which almost nothing is serious too seriously. Even Augustus is laughed at here for the self-magnification of the *Res Gestae* and his obsession with his family (10). It is probably more appropriate to laugh than to read between the lines.

The policy of civil harmony without reprisals was stated explicitly in Nero's opening speech to the senate. There too Nero promised to follow the example of his predecessors, notably Augustus, and sketched his formula for government. He repudiated the worst Claudian abuses (judicial irregularities, control by freedmen, venality of the court) and stated the principle of divided responsibility between Princeps and senate.[93] That must not be taken too literally: similar promises were regularly made by new Principes. Since Tacitus tells us that Nero was true to his promises in his early years, we can tell from his account of those years what was being promised: not, clearly, a true constitutional dyarchy with the Emperor running the army and military provinces and the senate in sole control of Italy and the public provinces. That was in practice impossible, given the financial and military system which was retained. Nero was promising merely to accord the senate and its members as much responsibility as was possible given the system, and to show that body the kind of respect it had not known under Claudius. More things were done *arbitrio senatus*, and the Princeps exercised the virtues of *liberalitas*, *comitas* and *clementia*: he was generous, approachable and merciful.[94]

This speech to the senate was clearly designed to fit the ideology of that body: a resigned acceptance of the Principate as the only form of government that could ensure peace. The Republic, which had perished in the great Civil Wars it had generated, remained the ideal; but, after the weak attempt to restore it on the death of Caligula, champions of liberty concentrated on ensuring as important a role as possible for the senate in selecting and advising the Princeps.

A year or two after Nero delivered his accession speech, at the end of 55 or in 56, Seneca published his only work of political philosophy. Dedicated to the Princeps and containing a discussion of the qualities necessary in a ruler, *De Clementia* must have seemed a public, if not an official, statement. The author says that his purpose is to delight Nero by holding up to him a mirror in which he can see his virtue. Yet this is a eulogy that is also an exhortation: the Emperor is warned that his clemency must be maintained and his own security and glory are adduced as incentives. There are lessons for the reading public too: the blessings of the *laetissima forma rei publicae* are enumerated and Seneca explains that the Principate is indispensable to the survival of Rome. The Roman people will avoid disaster, he says, 'as long as it can bear the reins; once it breaks them or refuses to submit to them again after they have given way, this unity and the structure of this great Empire will shatter into pieces' (1.4.2). Seneca also reassures the public and defends himself by denying the common view that Stoics disapprove of clemency (2.5ff.).

The mixture of eulogy, admonition, and reassurance found in this work is perfectly intelligible in the contemporary political context. For it was widely believed that Nero had arranged the death of Britannicus in 55. Many were prepared to justify the murder on the ground that rule was indivisible; some *potentissimi amici*, who probably included Seneca, were bribed to acquiesce in the killing. Seneca would probably have practised dissimulation in any case, seeing that his own retirement would certainly mean the domination of Agrippina and perhaps his own death. More important, Nero's general political behaviour was still up to the standards of his early promises: his relations with the senate were good, and he had only just started the unconventional behaviour that was to offend all but the Roman *plebs* and his Greek subjects. *De Clementia* was designed to commit Nero to the clemency he had so far shown outside the palace, and to reassure the literate public that the murder of Britannicus and the tensions at court between the Princeps and his mother, the Princeps and his advisers, did not foreshadow a change in the character of the government.

Clemency had first become a mainstay of political propaganda with Julius Caesar, and Augustus and his successors had adopted it as an imperial virtue. The elevation of clemency to the position of chief imperial virtue by Seneca suits the political climate after Britannicus's murder, but the quality had received emphasis from the very start of the reign because of the cruelty of Nero's predecessor. It figured prominently in the accession speech to the senate and in that announcing the restoration to the senate of Plautius Lateranus.[95] Yet *De Clementia* does not simply repeat the principles of the accession speech. Seneca presents a picture of the state as an organism whose soul is Nero, and he constantly uses the words *princeps* and *rex* interchangeably. In one passage (1.8.1), Nero is called king by implication. Much of the counsel Seneca offers was found in the Hellenistic treatises on kingship that were written by philosophers of all schools. But the Romans were for historical reasons sensitive to the word *rex*, which they regarded as synonymous with the Greek word for tyrant rather than that for king.[96] Seneca's use of it here can hardly be due to carelessness in translating from or thinking in Greek. Rather he is outlining a political ideology more realistic and more positive than the negative resignation of the senate: the Principate should not be regarded as a second-rate Republic, but as the ancient and venerable institution of monarchy; there can be no constitutional safeguards, for the only guarantee of good rule is the character of the ruler; his education and his advisers are vitally important, and his subjects have a clear duty to obey him as long as he looks after their welfare.

Seneca was a realist in the realm of political practice as well as in theory. His advice resulted in the maintenance of the forms and authority the senate valued, and champions of *libertas senatoria* were well satisfied while his influence lasted.[97] According to Tacitus, the turning point of Nero's reign came early in 62[98] with the death of Burrus and the consequent loss of influence by Seneca. In the popular view, the death of Agrippina marked the turning point,[99] when Nero, with two murders to his credit, and the check of maternal discipline gone, gave free rein to his artistic and sporting enthusiasms, even cultivating *doctores sapientiae* other than Seneca. Certainly, from 59 on, Seneca and Burrus found it harder to discipline Nero, and there were men who encouraged his emancipation. Ofonius Tigellinus, Nero's evil genius (according to Tacitus) now came into his own. A friend of Nero through his breeding of racehorses, Tigellinus became prefect of the night-watch after Seneca's protégé Annaeus Serenus died with his officers at a banquet featuring poisonous mushrooms.[100] Among the new favourites were such senior senators as Aulus Vitellius, who inherited his father's talent for *obsequium*, Petronius, who became Nero's *elegantiae arbiter*, and born courtiers like Cocceius Nerva and Eprius Marcellus.

Burrus's control of the praetorian guard had given the advice of both Seneca and himself persuasiveness and weight. When he died early in 62, he was succeeded by Tigellinus and Faenius Rufus, but the power lay with the first. Seneca now asked leave to withdraw from court and to surrender a large part of his property and money. Nero refused, and Seneca remained, to outward appearances, a favoured *amicus*. His friends continued to profit from his position: his brother-in-law was appointed by the Princeps to a special financial commission;[101] his younger brother continued to manage imperial estates; his friend Lucilius did the same in Sicily and was hoping in 64 for later employment at Rome (*Epist.* 19.8). But Seneca no longer had a say in important appointments or in Nero's conduct; and he reduced his style of life and his public appearances, pleading ill-health and devotion to study.[102] He represents himself in his Letters to Lucilius as travelling in Campania and Latium. Yet the Campanian trip in the spring of 64 might be more official that it at first appears, for Seneca makes vague allusions in these letters to his involvement in *occupationes* and *officium civile* (*Epist.* 62; 72; cf. even later 106). Nero was at that time performing at the theatre in Naples, and Seneca may have been perforce among the crowd of courtiers that Nero brought in with him to fill the seats.[103]

Seneca knew that appearances had been sufficiently preserved for him to be blamed for Nero's crimes. After the great fire in July of 64 – which is not mentioned in Seneca's letters covering that period, perhaps because of the danger involved in mentioning or seeming to mention its cause – Nero pillaged temples in Greece and Asia to replace the treasures lost in the fire. Seneca was concerned to avoid all implication in this sacrilege, according to Tacitus, and so once more asked to retire, this time into the country, and to be allowed to return the greater part of his wealth. This time Nero's financial difficulties induced him to accept the money, but he again refused leave to retire.[104] Seneca then withdrew to his room and lived like an invalid. But not permanently, for, though his own letters covering this last period of his life are lost, Tacitus notes that he was again in Campania in the spring of 65.[105]

That April, Seneca died by imperial command, though he was

allowed, as were most men of his rank, to take his own life. Officially, he was punished as one of the participants in the conspiracy against Nero's life, whose head, or figurehead, was C. Calpurnius Piso. The question of his guilt or innocence is one that can hardly be answered conclusively, but it nevertheless merits consideration, for it clearly affects the picture we have of him. Here, as so often, our historical sources do not agree. Dio Cassius, according to his Epitomator, asserted confidently that Seneca and the praetorian prefect Faenius Rufus were members of a plot to murder Nero, the other participants including a centurion of the guard, Sulpicius Asper, and a military tribune, Subrius Flavus. He does not say what man or what system was to replace Nero.[106] Tacitus states that Nero had no evidence that Seneca was in the Pisonian conspiracy. He simply used the story of an exchange of letters between Seneca and Piso (the only evidence he could collect even under threat of torture) to rid himself of a man whose disapproval he resented. For Tacitus, the death of Seneca was to be counted among Nero's crimes.[107] Writing between Tacitus and Dio, Polyaenus records that Epicharis, whose role in the conspiracy is also recorded by Tacitus, was persuaded to join the conspiracy by Seneca and was the mistress of his brother Mela.[108]

No one doubts that Tacitus's account is not only the most copious and detailed but also the most well-informed – he could still profit from discussions with eye-witnesses[109] – and careful. But, despite his belief in Seneca's innocence, Tacitus transmits evidence that has led readers to be dissatisfied with his verdict. He himself suggests that Seneca may have known the conspirators' plans, for he says that he returned to his villa near the city on the very day set for the murder of Nero 'forte an prudens'.[110] Tacitus also allows that the conspirator Antonius Natalis who accused Seneca may have been a go-between for Piso and Seneca.[111] Seneca admitted, on Tacitus's evidence, to an exchange of messages with Piso that prove at least that they were normally on friendly visiting terms, for Piso had complained through Natalis at not being permitted to call on Seneca. The reply he was accused of giving – that their mutual interests would not be served by frequent meetings but that his safety depended on that of Piso – Seneca denied, for it could be construed as treasonable: the phrase about safety was reminiscent of the oath of loyalty taken to the Princeps by soldiers and civilians.[112] If Seneca did actually use these words, however, he could at least have been trying to discourage Piso's attempt by warning him against taking risks. Again, Seneca's presence in Campania could have given him information, for it was there that Epicharis tried to corrupt the commander of the imperial fleet at Misenum.[113] (If even part of Polyaenus's account is right and Epicharis was connected with Mela, then the possibility of Seneca's knowledge is even stronger.)

Finally, Tacitus's account includes two remarks which were widely circulated at the time and which bear on Seneca's involvement. Subrius Flavus, one of the praetorian officers who was most active in the conspiracy, was quoted as saying that it would not remove the disgrace to replace a lyre-player with a tragic actor, alluding to Piso's stage performances.[114] That suggests that he had someone other than Piso in mind to succeed Nero. Tacitus reports the rumour that the candidate was Seneca and that he knew of the plan, a rumour echoed in Juvenal's 'Libera si dentur populo suffragia, quis tam/perditus ut dubitet Senecam praeferre Neroni',[115] and receiving some support from the last words of another praetorian as reported in Suetonius and Tacitus: Sulpicius Asper was asked by Nero why he wished to kill him and replied that there was no other way in which he could help the Emperor's vices. This idea that it is justified to kill a man vicious beyond redemption occurs at least twice in Seneca's works (*De Ira* 1.6.3; *Ben.* 7.20.3).

On the basis of these pieces of evidence, it has been claimed that Tacitus was wrong to deny Seneca's guilt. Seneca was at least the ideological inspiration behind the conspiracy, if not ambitious on his own behalf: it was by prior arrangement that he arrived in Rome on the day when Nero was to be killed, coming from Campania where he had worked with Epicharis. But none of this evidence is conclusive. Seneca could have known of Piso's plans through Piso himself, or through Faenius Rufus with whom he probably had a connection going back to the early days of his co-operation with Burrus.[116] He may have come to his villa fearing for the safety of his property and his household in the turmoil he expected. The praetorian officers in the conspiracy may well have found some of the effete members of the conspiracy uncomfortable partners and have hoped some other man than Piso could be put in to replace Nero: perhaps the praetorian prefect Fabius Rusticus or Lucius Silanus whom Piso feared. The echoes of Seneca's philosophy need not mean much: the idea that the death penalty is the only remedy for incurable vice is found in Plato and was doubtless a philosophical cliché by the time of Seneca.[117] Moreover, other ideas of Seneca's do not fit the picture of Seneca the tyrannicide: he regarded the murder of Caesar as a folly, yet the whole plan of the conspiracy was modelled on that assassination;[118] as we have seen, he took no part in the murder of Gaius though he regarded it as justified; finally, he had a horror of civil war (*Ben.* 1.10.2; *Epist.* 73.9-10), which was always a risk in such plans.

We have then no evidence strong enough to invalidate Tacitus's belief in Seneca's innocence. How strong are the reasons for trusting it? Tacitus claims to have ascertained from documents and eye-witnesses of the events that there really was a conspiracy.[119] In addition to the *acta senatus*, he had read at least two historical accounts of the conspiracy, those of the Elder Pliny and Fabius Rusticus. He seems to have scrutinized his sources with care, rejecting a story in Pliny about the involvement of Claudius's daughter Antonia (perhaps wrongly), and refusing to swallow stories, perhaps similar to what we find in Polyaenus, about how Epicharis was brought in.[120] Nor does he manifest prejudices strong enough to explain his acquittal of Seneca. His sympathy for Nero's adviser would not, in any case, have ruled out a portrayal of him as a conspirator, even one who falsely protested his innocence, for Tacitus, though he disapproved of Piso, apparently approved of the plan to remove Nero, and even of one of the conspirators who at first lied and declared his innocence.[121]

But, in fact, Tacitus in this part of his work is not uniformly favourable to Seneca; he is more shocked about a rumour attributing weakness to Seneca's wife than the one attributing callous ambition to Seneca.[122] He testifies to Seneca's courage and freedom of speech and to his simple funeral instructions, but Seneca's end is, for all that, shown up as pretentious. In his last moments, he has time for the high-flown style, and his death is a deliberate imitation of Socrates's, down to the hemlock.[123] What Tacitus feels about Seneca's death (and about the later imitation of it by Thrasea Paetus) comes out clearly in his account of the ironic death of Petronius. He too opened his veins and addressed his friends, but not with solemn sentiments designed to earn him a reputation for *constantia*, the great Stoic virtue, nor with stage directions borrowed from the *Phaedo*.[124] Still, without any strong prejudice of his own, Tacitus could be said to have been taken in by a prejudiced source, for he himself tells us that Fabius Rusticus was inclined to laud his patron. Yet Tacitus must have been on guard against what he recognized as bias, and, in any case, a partial historian could have given a favourable picture of Seneca as a brave tyrannicide rather than as an innocent victim. There are features of Tacitus's narrative that are best explained, not by the determination of his source or himself to tell one story rather than another, but by the source's need to put a favourable interpretation on the true story, i.e. the fact of Seneca's non-participation, which would be well-known to Fabius and to Seneca's other friends whom he must have counted as his most devoted readers. Thus those members of Seneca's family who were implicated, Lucan and his father, emerge disgracefully from Tacitus's account: Lucan bargains for his life with that of his mother and then goes on to supply other names; Mela provokes Nero by greedily trying to recover Lucan's estate and then tries to incriminate another man in his will. By contrast, Seneca's older brother Gallio is treated sympathetically.[125] A simpler explanation could be found for this contrast by supposing a split between Lucan and his uncle which involved their intimate friends, Fabius Rusticus taking one side, the poet Persius and doubtless more taking the other.[126] Yet it is likely that a split between Seneca and Lucan, however temperamental in origin, would involve differences on a political issue like the conspiracy, for their works show Lucan as a great admirer of Brutus and Cassius while Seneca deplored Caesar's murder. Rusticus's troubles may again lie behind the savage way in which Faenius Rufus, a protégé of Agrippina like Seneca and Burrus and probably a political associate, is handled by Tacitus: he could hardly be right to join the conspiracy if Seneca stayed out.

Tacitus points out that Seneca's will showed the contempt for wealth and pomp that he preached. His death too fits his teaching: he had long been prepared for it, keeping a supply of hemlock by him (cf. *Epist.* 70.18); he showed no fear or undue haste and, like Socrates, he waited until the order was given (cf. *Epist.* 70.8-12). His last words that he dictated were widely circulated and known to Tacitus's readers. They were probably, like Thrasea's later on, philosophical in content, to judge from the contrast Tacitus draws between them and the blunt reproach of Nero's vices uttered by

'IMAGO VITAE SUAE'

Subrius Flavus.[127] Seneca's suicide was certainly theatrical, but in the atmosphere of Nero's later years it was a source of inspiration to courage. Thrasea copied it, likewise pouring a libation to Jupiter Liberator, for death was, according to the Stoics, the avenue to freedom provided by Providence.[128] Thrasea, like Seneca, offered himself as an *exemplum* to his friends. Over four centuries later, the philosopher Boethius in prison found Seneca's end an inspiring example and paid him the honour of comparing his death to that of other philosophical martyrs including Socrates himself. But what of his life?

'Aliter loqueris, aliter vivis': this is the charge that Seneca tried to answer in *De Vita Beata* and that which his biographers and readers have been pondering ever since. Seneca's literary activity, except for minor works such as an essay on earthquakes, belongs to his mature years. From the publication of the *Consolatio ad Marciam*, probably in 39, he poured out a tremendous quantity of prose and verse. Because of his reticence about everything but his spiritual life and philosophical ideas, most of his works can only be dated within broad limits, but we do know that, aside from his two overtly political works (*Apocolocyntosis* and *De Clementia*), many of the tragedies with their hatred of tyranny and cruelty belong to his period of political power, as well as many of the shorter dialogues (*De Brevitate Vitae, De Constantia Sapientis, De Tranquillitate Animi, De Otio, De Vita Beata*), and probably part of *De Beneficiis*. All of these works, like those written when Seneca was losing or had lost power in 62 and later (*Naturales Quaestiones, Epistulae Morales*), are full of condemnations of flattery and collaboration with tyranny, and of diatribes against sexual licence, wealth and luxury. Yet Seneca's enemies claimed that he was guilty of all of these vices.

We have already discussed the servile adulation of Emperor and freedmen in the *Consolatio ad Polybium*. It is perhaps fair to Seneca to remember that Ovid had appealed to Augustus at greater length and that both he and Seneca showed some courage in claiming innocence, particularly as they were subjected to greater suffering than Cicero, whose laments from exile were more querulous and pathetic than theirs. On the other hand, Cicero did not publish his own laments and Seneca did, whether or not he later tried to withdraw the work from circulation. The flattery of *De Clementia* can be excused as the only vehicle of instruction possible under an autocracy,[129] but that in the *Apocolocyntosis* exceeds this purpose, while that in the *Naturales Quaestiones* (7.21.3; 7.17.2; 1.5.6) does not serve it at all. Yet Seneca, in his philosophical works, while certainly expressing admiration for those who exercise freedom of speech before rulers (*Tranq. An.* 14.3; *Ben.* 5.6.2–7) and claiming to use it himself before Nero (*Clem.* 2.2.2), never demanded, and, in fact, condemned the ostentatious provocation of those in power. He stated that *contumacia* was a quality incompatible with life at court (*Tranq. An.* 6.1). For him, what counted was the giving of honest advice where it was needed (*Ben.* 6.29–30). As a good Stoic, he thought that personal humiliation did not touch the soul and was sometimes acceptable as a means to an end (*Const. Sap.* 14.2; 19.3), and, as a shrewd critic of facile heroics, he advised against offending rulers, even to the point of disguising political withdrawal as retirement for health reasons (*Epist.* 14.7; 19.2, 4; 68.1, 3–4; 73). The last he certainly carried into practice.

Equally pragmatic was his willingness to compromise with evil during his years of influence. Some might have thought the balance between the good he could do and the evil he must countenance had tipped with the murder of Britannicus or – where popular opinion put the turning point of the reign – with Agrippina's murder. But Tacitus agreed with Seneca: it was 62, with the return of *maiestas* trials and the perversion of Seneca's doctrine of clemency that mattered more. Yet Seneca should at least have realized that the lesson of *De Clementia*, that the Princeps was absolute in power and controlled only by self-restraint, was a dangerous one for a Princeps like Nero. To that extent, Seneca was, as Dio called him, a *tyrannodidaskalos*, an instructor in tyranny.

In his writings, Seneca condemned adultery by the husband or wife. For his sexual life, we have no evidence aside from the charges of adultery and pederasty traceable to Suillius Rufus. These were based on Seneca's conviction for adultery in 41, and were probably no more than slander. It is notable that most of Agrippina's political protégés were alleged to have enjoyed her favours.[130] Otherwise, Seneca's Letter 104 (1–5) proclaims a deep affection for his wife Pompeia Paulina, which accords well with the value he set on marriage in *De Matrimonio* and appears to be confirmed by his wife's wish to die with him and her later devotion to his memory.[131]

'IMAGO VITAE SUAE'

The principal reason for regarding Seneca as a hypocrite has always been that he enjoyed great wealth while praising poverty. As Suillius Rufus asked: what philosophical doctrines had taught him to amass 300 million sesterces in four years of friendship with the Emperor? Tacitus makes Seneca offer to surrender his wealth in 62 because it brought him a bad name and gave the lie to his claim to be satisfied with little. Undeniably, Seneca was very rich. He inherited a respectable fortune from his father, and he received from Nero estates in Egypt, capital that earned him interest, and money to buy at least one extra villa.[132] His position of influence brought him substantial legacies. Nor was he entirely passive in acquiring wealth: his skill in viticulture and the profits he thereby derived are well attested,[133] and the stories that were told of a financial killing in Britain suggest, at least, that he was a cunning investor. Seneca was accused of a luxurious style of life, and it is more than likely that he lived up to his position at court. Tacitus notes that, like other great men, he was greeted and escorted each day by a crowd of clients and dependants. These he treated generously, dining them well and sending them gifts, as Juvenal and Martial attest, comparing him with Calpurnius Piso and Aurelius Cotta.[134] Seneca was on friendly terms with Piso, whose taste for high living and culture he may well have shared, in the period before his retirement. The general picture is clear, though one need not accept details like the five hundred tables of citrus wood that Dio says graced his banquets. Finally, he probably acquired some of his wealth by acquiescing in crime, especially if he was among those whom Nero bribed into silence after the murder of Britannicus.

There are obvious things that can be said in Seneca's defence. First, that he was generous with his own wealth, and probably encouraged Nero's liberality. Next, that he kept to certain ascetic habits acquired (under the influence of Attalus) in youth (abstinence from oysters, moderation in wine, rejection of soft mattresses)[135] and was able to practise extreme frugality in his food after 64. That he requested a simple funeral in a will written when he could have afforded an ostentatious one.[136] Finally, that Seneca did actually hand over a large part of his wealth to Nero to help in the reconstruction of Rome.[137]

And yet, the discrepancy between words and deeds remains, and an even more interesting problem. For Seneca could have justified almost all of his actual practices in Stoic terms, and, in doing so, have strengthened the moderate view of Stoicism he advertised in *De Clementia*. In fact, he did so in one work, *De Vita Beata*. For all Stoics, although virtue was the only good and vice the only evil, some positive value attached to such things as health, beauty and wealth, and some undesirability to their opposites. Though none of these 'indifferents' affected a man's happiness, which was acquired by virtue alone, it was emphasized by some Stoics, notably Panaetius, that wealth was useful as the material of virtuous acts, and that it could add a certain joy to life. This view Seneca took over in *De Vita Beata*, going as far as to say that even the wise man would actually prefer to have some wealth with his virtue, providing it was not acquired at another's expense or by sordid methods. The wise man would like to have a splendid house and ample resources for generosity to individuals of every degree (23.5–24.3). There are traces of this positive view in Seneca's other works, and in *De Beneficiis* (5.4.2–3; 1.15.5–6; 2.18.5; 2.21.5) he specifically allows gifts from men in power if they are of good character, explaining that under duress even that condition is waived (2.18.7; 5.6.7). Tacitus used this argument in composing Seneca's request to retire in *Annals* 14.53.

But the usual attitude to wealth in Seneca's works is more negative. In addition to spiritual detachment from it (which he could claim to have demonstrated by its surrender), Seneca often praises poverty in itself, declaims against efforts made to acquire wealth, and suggests that men would be better off without it (notably, *De Tranquillitate Animi* 8). He constantly urges the need to prepare for poverty by frugal living, and inveighs at excessive length against luxury as an unnatural outgrowth of the passions. The problem is twofold, for the well-attested popularity of Seneca's works suggests that not only Seneca, but his readers as well, preferred to write and talk about wealth in this negative way. Many of his readers were men of considerable property, but they felt bored with or guilty about it, or anxious under a régime which required the Emperor to spend a lot of his personal fortune and did not authorize him to tax wealthy citizens in Italy.

Perhaps an even more important consideration was the opportunity offered by the theme of the evils of luxury – for so long a standard *topos* in the rhetorical schools – to a virtuoso preacher like Seneca. Even Quintilian, who disliked his style and its influence, had to admit that Seneca was an exquisite lambaster of vice. He added that a more disciplined style would have earned the author the admiration of the learned rather than the love of boys (10.1.130), a point to which Seneca had already supplied the answer in Letter 108 to Lucilius. There he recalls how, even in the theatre, verses condemning avarice and urging contempt of wealth win applause, because people accept the condemnation of vice if put with poetic or rhetorical effect and not in coldly analytic argument. The most promising pupils, he adds, are the young, who are easily roused to love of virtue by an effective speaker, learn most readily, and are most easily persuaded to put what they have learned into practice. Seneca then strengthens the case for rhetorical teaching aimed at the young, by recounting the tremendous impact made on him by the first philosophy lectures he heard and by testifying to the lasting effect some of them had on him.

But in this same Letter, Seneca also admits to his swift return from the more extreme ascetic practices to ordinary life (*Epist.* 108.15). This frankness and modesty about his own moral achievements throughout his works is the only effective answer to the charges of hypocrisy and the only one Seneca himself ever offered. In *De Vita Beata*, for example, he says of the Middle Stoic views he presents: 'I do not offer this defence for myself, for I am sunk in vice, but for a man who has achieved something' (17.4). In the Letters, he hopes for a place among those on the lowest level of spiritual progress (75.15), and he describes the Letters themselves as conversations between one moral invalid and another (27.1). Accordingly, when Seneca urges Lucilius to moderate his grief at the death of a friend, he confesses to his own weakness on a similar occasion and explains what self-examination has taught him (63). Again, in the famous Letter 47 advocating kind treatment of slaves, Seneca criticizes men who seize every pretext for being angry with their slaves. Lucilius, he says there, is a good master, but Seneca shows himself, in an earlier Letter (12), to be guilty of just this fault: he visits his suburban villa after a long period of absence and, noting signs of decay which remind him of his own advanced age, relieves his irritation by scolding his slaves for neglecting the property. But he recognizes and admits his error, and incidentally reveals his former and customary kindness to his slaves and their habit of speaking frankly to him. It was this tenderness, this insight into weakness, this awareness of how hard it is to be good, that doubtless made Seneca an effective teacher for those who, once stirred by his style, tried to follow the Stoic way. The opening chapters of *De Tranquillitate Animi* show him administering moral therapy to a friend who came and described the symptoms of his relapse and wished to try once more to be cured. For his disciples, contemporary and later, Seneca's power as a healer of souls has more than made up for his shortcomings as a model of virtue. The literary portrait of himself as a moral teacher that Seneca has left in his essays and letters [138] is rightly judged a more precious legacy than the historical *imago vitae suae*.

Notes

1. W. S. Landor, 'Epictetus and Seneca', *Imaginary Conversations*; Macaulay, 'Lord Bacon' (1837).
2. S. Dill, *Roman Society from Nero to Marcus Aurelius* (London, 1904), p. 13.
3. The first view is that of T. S. Jerome, *Aspects of the Study of History* (London, 1923), pp. 79ff.; the second that of E. Phillips Barker in *OCD*[1], s.v. 'Seneca'.
4. *Epist.* 114.1; 75.4.
5. Tacitus *Ann.* 13.42; cf. Dio Cassius 61.10.
6. *Epist.* 6.5; cf. Tacitus *Ann.* 15.62.1.
7. Much material relevant to the verdict on Seneca as a man, in antiquity and the Middle Ages, can be found in W. Trillitzsch, *Seneca im literarischen Urteil der Antike, I* and *II* (Amsterdam, 1971). The collection starts with Seneca's autobiographical references and ends with Erasmus.
8. On the problem of authenticity and date see M. Coffey, 'Seneca, Tragedies (1922–1955)', *Lustrum*, 2 (1957), pp. 174ff.; C. J. Herington, 'Octavia Praetexta: a survey', *CQ* 14 (1961), pp. 18ff.
9. Juvenal 8.211–14; 5.108ff.; 10.15–18; Martial 4.40.1; 12. 36.
10. Tacitus *Ann.* 13.20.
11. Quintilian 10.1.125ff.; Tacitus *Ann.* 13.3: Seneca had a 'charming talent and one suited to the taste of his time'.
12. Suetonius *Nero* 52.
13. I. Ryberg, 'Tacitus' art of innuendo', *TAPA*, 73 (1942), pp. 383ff.; R. Syme, *Tacitus* (Oxford, 1958), pp. 551ff.; Trillitzsch, *Seneca im Literarischen Urteil*, pp. 94ff.
14. On Agrippa's *nomen*, Elder Seneca *Controversiae* 2.4.13; Tacitus *Ann.* 14.53.
15. Martial 1.61.7ff.; cf. 'Seneca' *Epigram* 3 (Prato, p. 18).
16. Syme, op. cit., App. 80.
17. The date when Corduba acquired colonial status and other points of detail and dispute on pp. 3–6 I have discussed in *JRS*, 62 (1972), pp. 1ff.

'IMAGO VITAE SUAE'

18 Haase frags 98–9.
19 Martial 1.61.
20 The actual title is *Oratorum et Rhetorum sententiae, divisiones, colores.*
21 Cicero *Ad Fam.* 10.31–3.
22 Haase frag. 99: 'historias ab initio bellorum civilium, unde primum veritas retro abiit, paene usque ad mortis suae diem.'
23 Seneca *Cons. Helv.* 2.4–5.
24 His full name after adoption is given by an inscription at Delphi, SIG^3 801D, and one at Rome, *AE*, 1960, no. 61.
25 Seneca *Tranq. An.* 17.7; *Epist.* 108.22 (cf. Tacitus *Ann.* 2.85.4).
26 Seneca *Cons. Helv.* 17.3.
27 Ibid. 16.3.
28 Ibid. 17.4; *Epist.* 108.22.
29 For a collection of parallel passages see E. Rolland, *De l'Influence de Sénèque le père et des rhéteurs sur Sénèque le philosophe* (Ghent, 1906).
30 Vacca, *Life of Lucan* (Rostagni, pp. 176ff.).
31 Syme, op. cit., 591–2.
32 Seneca *Cons. Helv.* 19.2–7; PIR^2 G 25.
33 Tacitus *Ann.* 6.3. The family connection with Sejanus was suggested by Z. Stewart, 'Sejanus, Gaetulicus, and Seneca', *AJP*, 74 (1953), pp. 70ff.
34 This is an inference from Dio 59.9.5.
35 E.g. *Ben.* 2.7.2–8; 3.26.1; 5.25.2.
36 Seneca *Epist.* 108.22; cf. Tacitus *Ann.* 2.85.4; Josephus *AJ* 18.84; Suetonius *Tiberius* 36; Dio 57.18.59.
37 Suetonius *Gaius* 53; cf. Seneca *Epist.* 49.2.
38 Notably, Seneca *Nat. Quaest.* 4, pref. 15; Dio 59.19 (a story of dubious truth and significance); Dio 60.8.5–6; Tacitus *Ann.* 12.8.2.
39 Suetonius *Gaius* 16; Quintilian 10.1.104.
40 Seneca *Cons. Helv.* 2.5. The death of his wife is suggested by the fact that she is not mentioned in this work written from exile and containing a considerable amount of detailed information about his family.
41 Tacitus *Ann.* 12.8.8.
42 Dio 60.8.5.
43 *Ann.* 12.8.2.
44 The end of the *Consolatio ad Polybium* is a distinct echo of such Ovidian lines as *Ex Ponto* 4.2.15ff.
45 Martial 7.44; cf. Seneca *Epist.* 87.
46 Intended satire: W. H. Alexander, 'Seneca's *Ad Polybium De Consolatione*, a reappraisal', *Trans. Royal Soc. Canada*, ser. 3, 37 (1943), pp. 33ff. Unconscious satire: A. Momigliano, *Claudius* (Oxford, 1834), pp. 75–6.
47 Tacitus *Ann.* 13.3 where 'quamquam' shows that Tacitus thinks that Seneca did not intend the laughable effect produced by his exaggerated praises of Claudius; Pliny *Epist.* 8.6.
48 Dio 61.10.2.
49 Suetonius *Claudius* 17.3.
50 Tacitus *Ann.* 12.8; Suetonius *Claudius* 12.
51 Tacitus *Ann.* 12.2–4; 8.

52 Scholiast on Juvenal 5.109.
53 *Act. Ap.* 18.11–17.
54 *Ann.* 16.17.
55 'Stubborn arrogance renders men unfit for court.'
56 Tacitus *Ann.* 13.2.
57 Tacitus *Ann.* 13.3; 13.11; 14.11.
58 Suetonius *Nero* 52; Pliny *Epist.* 3.3.4.
59 Plutarch *De cohibenda ira* 461F.
60 Tacitus *Ann.* 13.26; 14.49; 15.22.
61 Tacitus *Ann.* 13.5; 13.42.
62 The table of contents of the Codex Ambrosianus (on which the text of the dialogues principally depends) starts 'In primis ad Lucilium De Providentia.' Rossbach plausibly suggested that the 'in primis' was copied inadvertently from a longer table of contents prefixed to a lost complete collection of the dialogues where it signified that Lucilius was the principal addressee. It would follow that Lucilius was the addressee of a large number of dialogues from which the Codex A selected one. Some of these are lost; others may be among those surviving in a fragmentary state with the name of the addressee missing.
63 *ILS* 1321.
64 Tacitus *Ann.* 12.42.
65 *Ann.* 13.2.
66 Tacitus *Ann.* 14.7; cf. 14.13.
67 *Ann.* 14.52.
68 *Ann.* 13.20.
69 Dio 61.4.2.
70 *Ann.* 14.52; 15.45.
71 Dio 61.7.5.
72 Syme, op. cit., p. 545.
73 E.g. *Ann.* 13.27 echoes Seneca *Clem.* 1.24.1; *Ben.* 3.16.1; 3.14.1–2. *Ann.* 14.53–4 echoes *Ben.* 2.18.6ff.; 1.15.5; 2.33.2.
74 Tacitus *Ann.* 14.2; 14.10–11.
75 Tacitus *Ann.* 14.7; Dio 61.12, noting his reliance on authorities that he regards as trustworthy.
76 Suetonius *Lucan*, 11.2–3; 11–12 (Rostagni, pp. 143, 145).
77 Tacitus *Ann.* 13.53.
78 *PIR*[2] G 30.
79 Tacitus *Ann.* 13.6.
80 Tacitus *Ann.* 13.14.
81 Plutarch *Galba* 20.1.
82 Tacitus *Ann.* 12.5–6; Josephus *AJ* 20.12.
83 Tacitus *Ann.* 13.3; Dio 61.3.1.
84 Tacitus *Ann.* 14.11. Quintilian 8.5.18 confidently attributes the letter to Seneca.
85 Tacitus *Ann.* 13.17.1; 14.8.
86 Tacitus *Ann.* 13.3.
87 Note that Pliny (*Panegyricus* 11.1) seems to blame Nero alone for the ridicule of Claudius's consecration.

'IMAGO VITAE SUAE'

88 Pliny *Epist*. 5.3.5; Tacitus *Ann*. 14.52.3.
89 An excellent summary by M. Coffey of the problems concerning authorship, date, title and purpose of the preserved work can be found in *Lustrum*, 1961, pp. 245ff.
90 Furneaux *ad loc*. rightly pointed out that the notice of the vote of *caelestes honores* to Claudius immediately after his death, in Tacitus *Ann*. 12.69, is proleptic, the real notice of *consecratio* coming in 13.2.
91 For earlier discussions, see Coffey (above, n. 89). Since then, a powerful if ultimately unconvincing case for the work being an attack on Britannicus and his party has been argued by K. Kraft in *Historia*, 15 (1966), pp. 96ff.
92 This point was made forcibly by D. Baldwin in *Phoenix*, 18 (1964), pp. 39ff. who used it as a point against Senecan authorship. But Messalina was old news in late 54.
93 Tacitus *Ann*. 13.4.
94 Tacitus *Ann*. 13.5; Suetonius *Nero* 10.
95 Tacitus *Ann*. 13.11.
96 Cicero *Rep*. 2.47–9; 52. For the survival of this sentiment under the Principate, see, for example, Seneca *Ben*. 6.34.1; Lucan 7.440ff., 643; Tacitus *Ann*. 3.56.2; Pliny *Pan*. 55.7.
97 Tacitus *Ann*. 13.49 (A.D. 58): Thrasea Paetus regards a modest role in the Neronian senate as compatible with his policy of *libertas senatoria*.
98 Tacitus *Ann*. 14.51–2. The time of year is inferred from the number of incidents that Tacitus shows must be fitted between Burrus's death and the death of Octavia on 9 June 62 (Suetonius *Nero* 57).
99 Tacitus *Ann*. 15.67. Tacitus opens Book 14, Dio Book 61 with the murder of Agrippina.
100 Pliny *NH* 22.96.
101 Tacitus *Ann*. 15.18.
102 Ibid. 14.56 *ad fin*.
103 Ibid. 15.33–4.
104 Ibid. 15.45.3; Dio 62.25.3; cf. Tacitus *Ann*. 15.64.4.
105 Ibid. 15.60.
106 Dio 62.24.1.
107 Tacitus *Ann*. 15.61.
108 *Strateg*. 8.62.
109 Tacitus *Ann*. 15.73.
110 Ibid. 15.60. For the day, see P. Treves in *Studia Florentina Alexandro Ronconi Sexagenario Oblata* (Rome, 1970), pp. 507ff.
111 Tacitus *Ann*. 15.56.
112 Ibid. 15.60: 'respondisse Senecam sermones mutuos et crebra conloquia neutri conducere; ceterum salutem suam incolumitate Pisonis inniti.' Compare *ILS* 190; Suetonius *Gaius* 15.3; Epictetus 1.14.15. W. H. Alexander in *CP* 47 (1952) pp. 1ff. tried to show that Seneca's reversal of the terms *salus* and *incolumitas* in his paraphrase of Natalis's charge against him (*Ann*. 15.61) was designed to make his message to Piso seem less treasonable. But the two terms seem to be used almost interchangeably of the Princeps. In fact, the parallels just cited use

salus (which Alexander thought more innocuous), and a temple of Salus was dedicated after the detection of the conspiracy. We probably have to do with a mere verbal variation by Tacitus.

113 Tacitus *Ann.* 15.51.
114 Ibid. 15.65; cf. 15.67.1.
115 Juvenal *Sat.* 8.211–14: 'If a free vote were given to the people, who would be so depraved as to waver in his preference for Seneca over Nero?'
116 Faenius Rufus, like Burrus and Seneca, was originally a protégé of Agrippina.
117 Plato *Gorgias* 473–80; 525b and elsewhere in *Republic* and *Laws*. Compare Cicero *De Finibus* 4.56.
118 Seneca *Ben.* 2.20; Tacitus *Ann.* 15.53.
119 *Ann.* 15.73.
120 Ibid. 15.51: 'incertum quonam modo sciscitata'.
121 Ibid. 'neque illi ante ulla rerum honestarum cura fuerat' 15.67.1.
122 Ibid. 15.60; cf. 15.65.
123 Ibid. 15.61–2. Is Tacitus's remark in 15.67 that Nero was not accustomed to being reproached with his crimes an implicit denial of Seneca's claim to have treated Nero with *libertas*?
124 Ibid. 16.19.
125 Ibid. 15.56–7; 16.17; 15.73.
126 Persius, according to the *Life* by Valerius Probus (Rostagni, pp. 167ff.), was educated with Lucan, but only met Seneca once and thought little of him.
127 Tacitus *Ann.* 15.67.
128 Ibid. 16.34–5.
129 The method is avowed in *Clem.* 2.2; cf. Thrasea's use of the technique in Tacitus *Ann.* 14.48.
130 Tacitus *Ann.* 12.7; 12.65; 15.50.5.
131 Ibid. 15.64.
132 Ibid. 13.42; Seneca *Cons. Helv.* 14.3; *Epist.* 77; Tacitus *Ann.* 14.53.5–6. Pliny *NH* 14.49ff. shows that the villa at Nomentum was acquired between 61 and 64.
133 Seneca *Nat. Quaest.* 3.7.1; *Epist.* 86.14ff.; Pliny *NH* 14.51; Columella *RR* 3.3.3.
134 Martial 12.36; Juvenal 5.109.
135 Seneca *Epist.* 108.15–16, 23.
136 Tacitus *Ann.* 15.45.3; cf. Seneca *Epist.* 83.6; 87.1–5; 123.3; Tacitus *Ann.* 15.64.
137 Dio 62.25.3; cf. Tacitus *Ann.* 15.64.4.
138 For the place of the *Epistulae Morales* in the development of autobiography see G. Misch, *A History of Autobiography in Antiquity* (English translation, 1950), vol. 2, pp. 418ff.

II

Form and Content in the Moral Essays[1]

J. R. G. Wright

I

Seneca's manner of writing has not lacked critics. The line begins with Caligula.[2] We shall never be able to tell the precise context of his two comments (though presumably they refer to Seneca's speeches), or even whether they are part of a single remark,[3] but their general tendency is clear. *Senecam commissiones meras componere*: Seneca's compositions were mere exhibition pieces, declamations fitted for performance in the theatre; [*Senecam*] *harenam esse sine calce*: he was sand without lime, cement lacking the necessary constituent to bind it together and prevent its fragmenting into a myriad of separate parts. Professional jealousy may be alleged,[4] but the Emperor was not without insight.[5]

It has always been a criticism of Seneca that his work does not hold together. At the stylistic or verbal level the straining for 'point' and rhetorical effect breaks up the flow of the writing. At the wider level of the structure of whole works there is no discernible pattern, no organized shape which could give unity to the plethora of highly contrived individual passages. Another aspect of this weakness is the absence of consistency between one part of a work and another. Seneca is quite happy to contradict what he has said earlier,[6] or to repeat the same arguments over and over again with little or no variation.[7] The conclusion to which even a sympathetic critic is liable to be driven is well expressed by Justus Lipsius in the final words of his *Argumentum* to Book 1 of *De Ira: Libri in partibus pulchri et eminentes sunt, in toto parum distincti, & repetitionibus aut digestione confusi.*

That is the case against Seneca. Is any defence possible, or even worthwhile? If so, do we deny the charges, or admit them but attempt to show that they are not crimes? Perhaps both methods may be appropriate. At all events the effort will compel us to try to understand more fully what he was about, and is likely to be more illuminating than abrupt and unthinking dismissal.

The first question that we must ask is what Seneca conceived of as the purpose of his writings. For on this depends the form which he would be likely to regard as appropriate. The answer is clear. His aim in writing was a practical one. The philosopher is *generis humani paedagogus*,[8] the teacher of mankind. He is, in an endlessly repeated comparison, the physician who can heal the ills in man's soul as a doctor heals those of the body.[9] The method of cure is not, as it had been for Plato and Aristotle and perhaps for the earlier Stoics, an arduous intellectual progress towards the truth. The traditional liberal arts are at a discount,[10] and the syllogistic subtleties of traditional school philosophy may lead us astray from the main task.[11] What is required, rather, is an act of faith. 'Believe me', is the demand made by an Epicurus, a Seneca, or an Epictetus.[12] Where man's salvation[13] is at stake abstract reasoning is not enough.

This has important consequences for our appreciation of Seneca's *Moral Essays*. Every one of them is an answer to a moral problem or dilemma posed by or arising in the life of one of his friends or relations.[14] Although they do not entirely eschew theory their basic purpose is practical, to clarify for the addressee the points at issue and tell him how he must conduct himself if he is to fulfil the obligations of a good Stoic.[15] What we expect, then, is an appeal to the emotions as much as to the intellect. The development of a continuous argument will be less important than the immediate impact of individual passages. Syllogizing will take second place to precept and example.[16] All this is no mere special pleading. If Seneca had attended more to the overall form of his work and less to each separate part he might well have pleased his critics but failed to affect his audience. Thus one can argue that he may be more or less successful in what he attempts, but the nature of that attempt must be clearly understood.

If a knowledge of his philosophical purpose helps to clarify his literary aims, so, too, will his educational background. The family came from Córdoba in Spain, a famous home of rhetoricians, and his father was an enthusiastic amateur of that art.[17] It is a commonplace that Seneca is an intensely rhetorical writer – what

Latin author was not? – and his skill as a speaker was noted from an early age.[18]

A student of the great rhetorical works of Cicero or Quintilian encounters a tradition which placed great emphasis upon formal organization of material under clearly indicated headings, and there is no reason to doubt that these played an important part in basic rhetorical education at this time. Did this have any effect on Seneca? Can these principles be detected in his work? The answer is that they can, and have until recently been unduly neglected.[19] This can easily be seen by selecting a few technical terms and considering Seneca's performance in the areas to which they refer.

1 *Exordium*: the treatment of the opening of each work follows in one way or another the accepted procedures. They either contain vivid or striking passages to arouse the reader's (or listener's) interest (e.g. *Prov.*), statements of the problem designed to attract the reader's attention (e.g. *Tranq. An. Brev. Vit.*), or attempts to engage the reader's sympathy on behalf of the author (e.g. *Const. Sap., Clem., Cons. Helv.*).

2 *Propositio*: the formal statement of the point at issue prior to discussing them is so common as to be hardly worth illustration. One example will suffice: *ergo quaerimus quomodo animus semper aequali secundoque cursu eat propitiusque sibi sit et sua laetus aspiciat et hoc gaudium non interrumpat, sed placido statu maneat nec adtollens se umquam nec deprimens. id tranquillitas erit* (*Tranq. An.* 2.4).

3 *Divisio*: the formal division of the subject-matter into the various categories under which it will be treated is very frequent.[20] For my present purpose it is beside the point that this plan which he announces may be lost sight of, or may be interrupted by digressions. What I am arguing for at the moment is an awareness on Seneca's part of these modes of organization of a work and his conscious intention to use them on many occasions. It is noteworthy that on one occasion when he is specifically not making a full-scale *divisio* he finds it necessary to comment upon this and to justify it: *quod proposui*[21] *si in partes velim et argumenta diducere, multa mihi occurrent per quae probem brevissimam esse occupatorum vitam. solebat dicere Fabianus, non ex his cathedrariis philosophis, sed ex veris et antiquis: contra adfectus impetu non subtilitate pugnandum*, etc. (*Brev. Vit.* 10.1). Seneca does argue for some modification of

Fabianus's position. To cure their misapprehension the victims *docendi, non tantum deplorandi sunt*, and a brief *divisio* follows, but it is pursued only for the remainder of chapter 10 and the essay takes a new course after that. There is thus a tension, felt by the author, between certain accepted ways of setting out the material and his moral purpose, and it is a tension which he will sometimes resolve in one way and sometimes in another.

4 *Peroratio:* the emotional appeal to the jury so beloved of the forensic orator naturally has its counterpart in these works whose object is to capture the hearts of men as much as their minds. Notable are the noble prosopopoeia of God with its fine exposition of the Stoic disregard for death which concludes *De Providentia*, and the impressive description of the invulnerability of the *sapiens* at the end of *De Constantia Sapientis*.

5 *Tractatio per utile atque honestum:* after these divisions of the work itself it is worth looking at one of the traditional ways of handling material. The contrast between utility and moral worth (the latter sometimes expressed by such words as *decere* or *magnitudo animi*) was attractive for a philosopher. It was often important for him to show that the two, far from being opposed, in fact coincided, that what was bad could have no utility and that what was good was useful. Yet, however relevant to his own special purposes, this technique[22] must have been first learned by Seneca as part of his rhetorical education and would be built into his intellectual equipment when he started writing.

The formal techniques of traditional rhetoric were thus present in Seneca's mind and used by him, but he did not feel bound by them. His remark *quoniam liberaliter agere coepi* (*Vit. Beat.* 5.1) may seem all too accurate a description of his procedure.[23] The fact was that there were developments[24] in rhetorical studies pulling in the opposite direction from the old formalism, and to these we must now turn.

The use of declamation[25] as a means of training in youth, combined with the habit of public recitation of works of literature, tended to focus attention upon the particular passage at the expense of the whole work. The listener must be stimulated by arresting examples or anecdotes, dazzled by epigrams, and compelled to sustain his interest by a constant stream of new and unexpected ideas. All this does not conduce to painstaking development of a lengthy argument. Yet it is the degree of employment of these techniques rather than their mere existence which is inimical to ordered exposition. They were familiar enough to Cicero, but used only in moderation. By Seneca's time every chapter, almost every paragraph, must be worked round to an epigrammatic ending. Example must be piled upon example till the work virtually ceases to be anything more than a collection of examples. Consider the long passage on anger and kingship at *De Ira* 3.16.2–23. The point could have been made without the long list of eleven protagonists, some of them appearing more than once. The section on Caligula in particular (18.3–19) assumes an independent existence of its own and is expanded in a lurid and dramatic way far beyond the real needs of the argument.[26]

There is, too, the brilliantly related story of Augustus and Cinna (*Clem.* 1.9). Its length is quite disproportionate to its importance in the argument, a fact which is recognized by Seneca when he stops himself short with the words: *ne totam eius orationem repetendo magnam partem voluminis occupem* (*Clem.* 1.9.11). More explicitly irrelevant (since it is inserted as a *praeteritio*) is the elaborately worked account of the argument from design at *De Providentia* 1.2–4. *Supervacuum est in praesentia ostendere* . . . , says Seneca (1.2), and *suo ista tempori reserventur*, he concludes (1.4), but the passage is there to form a striking opening to the work and to predispose the reader's mind to accept that Divine Providence exists and is beneficent. Thus the contemporary move away from large formal structures in rhetoric towards a greater emphasis upon immediate effect fitted very well with the type of writing which Seneca's philosophical aims required. The old formalism was not wholly abandoned, but the spirit of the work was that of the declaimers.

The development of the forms of philosophical literature had moved in the same direction. The earlier Platonic dialogues had represented a search for the truth. They claimed to reproduce conversations which proceeded by way of genuine give and take and a series of successive approximations as far as human knowledge could go. But the Stoic philosopher already knew the truth. What he has to say is an exposition of a dogma that cannot be refuted. The dialogue can still exist as a formal device. Objections can be made to the master's teaching, but they exist only to be knocked down and by their fall to clarify and confirm the doctrine.

All this leads to a style of writing which owes less to reasoned argument than to vigorous rhetoric. The most influential of the early Stoics, Chrysippus, gave an excellent precedent for this. As Fronto tells Marcus Aurelius: 'Wake up and hear what Chrysippus himself aims at. Is he content with giving information, expounding the facts, making definitions and laying things before you? Certainly not. He expands things as much as possible, he exaggerates, he forestalls objections, he repeats himself, he puts things off, he goes back on his tracks, gives descriptions, makes divisions, introduces characters and puts what he has to say in other people's mouths.'[27] This could stand as a description of Seneca's procedure. He himself cites Posidonius as a model which he can follow: *Posidonius non praeceptionem ... sed etiam suasionem et consolationem et exhortationem necessariam iudicat* (*Epist.* 95.65). So he had more than mere contemporary rhetorical justification for his way of writing.

Stoic theory,[28] too, as well as practice could be enlisted on his side. Originally its basic aims were clarity and naturalness, by which was meant a simple and straightforward style. Unvarnished truth was to be presented to the reader without rhetorical embellishment. The orator should aim to instruct the mind, not move the emotions. Seneca was not averse to professing these views. Thought is more important than form, truth than style.[29] Eloquence may even be harmful to the young if it is sought for its own sake and at the expense of the subject-matter.[30] A natural word order is best.[31] The ideal can be expressed thus: *magnus ille remissius loquitur et securius; quaecumque dicit plus habent fiduciae quam curae* (*Epist.* 115.2). Here we see the Stoic theory being made to fit Seneca's own predilections. Emphasis on content justifies a neglect of form. The need to convince sanctions diffuseness of treatment.

The famous 'pointed' style, too, has its justification in Stoic theory. One of its virtues of style was συντομία or brevity.[32] This had been carried to great lengths by Cato[33] and can easily be viewed as a basis for the short, sharp sentences for which Seneca is noted. On only one point does he explicitly question the theory, and even then without completely overthrowing it. For the Stoics emotion clearly had no part to play in an orator's performance. Thus when it is suggested by the imaginary interlocutor at *De Ira* 2.17.1 that anger may on occasions improve an orator, he must reject this view. Yet he is clearly reluctant to deny the fact, which he must have experienced, that passion in the speaker appears to increase his impact on his audience. His way out is to say that the speaker will feign anger or any other appropriate emotion, but really remain quite unmoved. This is a not unusual example of the ambivalence in Seneca between theory and practice and the somewhat unsatisfactory way in which he resolved the conflict.

There was another form apart from the school dialogue which influenced Seneca. This was the diatribe.[34] It is hard to define the essential characteristics of this form. Its originators were the popular Cynic philosophers of the late fourth and third centuries B.C. Its first great practitioner was Bion the Borysthenite, and some of the flavour of his work may be found in the pages of Teles. Perhaps the defining feature was the popular nature of both material and style. The doctrines propounded were an amalgam of Cynicism and simple Stoicism. The simple life, avoidance of excess of all kinds, self-sufficiency through elimination of all but the most basic needs: these were the positive aspects. Over against these as targets for attack were luxury, greed, lust for power, and any other imagined good which lay outside our own control. These views could come easily from an orthodox Stoic. But he might not use such a hard-hitting style. One of its central features was the mixture of serious message and comic medium which the Greeks called σπουδογέλοιον, and which made it such an important influence on Roman satire. The rhetorical figures chosen were of the most vigorous kind: rhetorical question, exclamation, prosopopoeia. The arguments involved numerous comparisons and analogies with everyday life and copious examples from history or mythology.

The relevance of all this to Seneca must be obvious. The individual doctrines, techniques, and arguments can all be paralleled in him.[35] The total effect is, however, somewhat different. This is to be explained by the difference of audience aimed at. What might be effective in the hurly-burly of the Hellenistic market-place where the Cynic preachers held court would not do for the cultivated Roman auditorium or the study of the upper-class intellectual. So Seneca produced not diatribes, but dialogues, works in a more leisurely literary tradition. They did, none the less, share yet another common feature, the imaginary interlocutor. For the diatribist, as for Seneca, he is a kind of straight man, or sounding-board for the author's views. He has no independent existence of his own. His arguments can never be right. They are always rejected, without even a chance of modifying the speaker's stance. They serve only to enable him to develop his own positive point of view. Most important, perhaps, the interlocutor can supply the place of a logical connection in the argument. The author can change subjects completely without any carefully managed transition. The interlocutor simply introduces a new objection or question, and we are off on that.

To take one of many examples from Seneca: at *De Ira* 2.10 we come to the end of a long list of reasons for not becoming angry, based mainly on the consideration that what makes us angry is usually beneath the notice of the wise man; the world is full of sinners and he should view them as a doctor does his patients. Then: *utilis est, inquit, ira quia contemptum effugit, quia malos terret* (11.1). The subject is new and not directly related to the previous one. The inconsequentiality of the author is foisted upon the interlocutor and the lack of continuity partially concealed.

I hope I have now gone some part of the way with my defence. The literary and philosophical background against which we must see Seneca to a large extent determines and explains his methods of composition. Once these methods are accepted as valid for his situation much may become acceptable that would otherwise be rejected. Yet criticism is still possible within these terms. Repetition and inconsistency may reach a level that cannot be tolerated. We have given reasons for thinking that some of the accusations made against Seneca, though justified, may not represent crimes. Can we show that some of the charges cannot actually be held proved?

2

In this connection I think particularly of the criticisms of repetition. There is no doubt that he is far from averse to repeating the same argument more than once. What is less commonly recognized is that these are not always mere repetitions, but that the difference of context and the significance attached to the argument may do much to palliate the offence.

Let us take what appears to be a flagrant example of repetition.

No less than three[36] times in *De Ira* Seneca gives a fairly elaborate description of the physical appearance produced by anger in its subject. For some critics these repetitions (particularly the second pair) are intolerable, and can be used as evidence that the work has not come down to us in the form that the author intended. I am not convinced of this. In the first place, this is a *locus communis* extremely popular in the tradition of writings on anger.[37] It is one that is peculiarly adapted to Seneca's needs, providing as it does an admirable opportunity for rhetorical embellishment and vivid illustration of his philosophical message.

Second, and this is the more important point, it serves a different purpose on each of the occasions on which it is introduced. At the beginning of Book 1 it provides a striking and persuasive *exordium*. The ugliness and fury of anger, justifying the traditional equation of it with madness, is a powerful incentive to the study of anger with a view to its extirpation, which is the object of the work. Here it is the rhetorical possibilities of the theme that attract Seneca to it. Its purpose is to engage people's attention and convince them of the value of what Seneca is about to say. At 2.35 he is engaged upon a wholly different line of argument. He has reached the stage of considering different ways of curing anger. When it is first introduced at 2.35.3 the description of anger may appear to be on the same level as in 1.1, although the relationship of horrid outer aspect to horrid internal state of the soul is more completely worked out (2.35.4). At 2.36.1, however, we see the real reason for introducing the description here. It is related to a wholly concrete and practical cure recommended by Sextius,[38] that of having an angry man look in a mirror to restore him to his senses. The description thus takes its place naturally in a list of cures and serves a different purpose from that which it did in Book 1. In the opening chapters of Book 3 there are renewed general exhortations to fight against anger, and its description is again in place. He is aware that he is repeating himself, both in general: *atqui, ut in prioribus libris dixi, stat Aristoteles defensor irae . . .* (3.3.1); and over the description of anger in particular: *nulli certe adfectui peior est vultus, quem in prioribus libris descripsimus* (3.4.1). Here, however, it is used in a new way, as a stage in the anti-Aristotelian argument, and a very vital stage at that, since the ugly aspect of anger is treated as the one certain thing about it: *ut de ceteris dubium sit* (3.4.1).

To say all this is not necessarily to deny that the closeness of the correspondence between the passages may be excessive and produce a blemish in the work. It is to point out that Seneca, when he finds an argument rhetorically attractive, may quite consciously repeat it whenever it is appropriate to the matter in hand. Clearly one argument may be appropriate to more than one matter, and it is possible to argue that the same material set in a different context and fulfilling a different function does not constitute a straightforward case of repetition.

We must look at all alleged repetitions in Seneca with this in mind. Nor must we forget that this feature of his writings is especially susceptible of explanation by reference to the recitation and the nature of the ancient *volumen* or papyrus roll.[39] Neither form of publication makes it easy to refer back to earlier passages. In the case of the *recitatio* it is clearly impossible. In the case of the book-roll it is difficult and tedious, especially in the absence of all but the most rudimentary aids to the reader such as page numbers, paragraphing, and chapter-headings. Repetition is much more obvious to the researcher with his card-index than to the listener or ordinary reader.

I now move on to look at a complete work in this light. Many other features of Seneca's writing that I have mentioned will, of course, be apparent in the analysis, but I will direct my attention mainly to the question of repetitions. The *De Providentia* is short;[40] it has a single straightforward theme. If Seneca could not meet this challenge to his powers of composition there would be no answer to his critics. In fact we shall see that what appears at first sight disorganized and repetitive embodies a carefully organized dialectical progress.[41]

Chapter 1 constitutes the *exordium*. After stating the subject and his reason for writing (a request for information from a friend) Seneca at once goes into the long *praeteritio* of the argument from design which I have already mentioned.[42] This, although logically irrelevant, enhances the status given to Providence and creates a general good impression of its functioning. It is also connected with the assumption which Seneca can make that Lucilius does not doubt the existence of Providence (1.4). This presumption of agreement on the part of the judge[43] is a recommended feature of *exordia*. It is a part of the *captatio benevolentiae*. The aim of the work is not to prove to Lucilius something that he does not believe to be true, but to justify to him something that he already accepts but is worried about.

This introduction then closes with a preliminary outline of the answer which Seneca has for Lucilius. 'Why', he has been asked, 'do bad things happen to good men if the world is ruled by a beneficent Providence?' 'Because', he says, 'the gods love good men and expose them to misfortune to harden them.' In 1.5-6 he foreshadows most of the forms that this argument is going to take. Between the gods and good men there is *amicitia*, or rather *necessitudo* and *similitudo*. The good man is God's *discipulus*, *aemulator*, and *vera progenies*. God is the good man's *parens* and *sicut severi patres, durius educat* (1.5). The apparent paradox of evil befalling good men and good fortune coming to bad men is then explained by a comparison with our attitudes to our own children and our slaves' children: . . . *cogita filiorum nos modestia delectari, vernularum licentia; illos disciplina tristiori contineri, horum ali audaciam* (1.6). The same is true of God's attitude to good and bad men: *bonum virum in deliciis non habet; experitur, indurat, sibi illum parat* (1.6). Thus early in the work we see established two linked points on which almost all that follows is going to be based: (A) the gods care for good men as parents do for children; because (B) adversity is necessary to bring out the best in good men.

Chapter 2 contains further exploration of the problem posed by the apparent sufferings of good men. It is quite common for Seneca to include such a general discussion between the *exordium* and *divisio*.[44] It gives the reader a clearer picture of the points at issue and prepares the way for the more formal treatment that is to follow. Our two basic arguments occur again with slight variation or new illustration: (B) is illustrated by the example of wrestlers who seek out the strongest of opponents in training in order to increase their powers (2.3); (A) is varied through a contrast between fatherly and motherly love (2.5). A favourite *exemplum* closes the chapter (2.9-12): Cato unbowed before the blows of fortune. His suicide looks forward to the *peroratio* with its recommendation of suicide as the easy road to freedom from worldly ills (6.7-9).

Chapter 3 opens with the *propositio* of the work (*ostendam quam non sint quae videntur mala*) and the *divisio*, which indicates three main points to be demonstrated: (*a*) adversity is useful to the individual (3.2-4); (*b*) adversity is useful to the generality (5); and (*c*) the virtuous man cannot be unhappy (6).[45]

The proof of (*a*) begins with the analogy of painful medical treatment which is beneficial in the long run, and with the fact that some pleasures can be harmful, and even fatal. This brings us rapidly to our point (B) with a quotation from Demetrius, a Cynic contemporary of Seneca: *nihil, inquit, mihi videtur infelicius eo cui nihil umquam evenit adversi.*[46] *non licuit enim illi se experiri.* No matter how fortunate he has been: . . . *male tamen de illo dii iudicaverint* (3.3), and point (A) is alluded to. Fortune, like a gladiator who derives no satisfaction from victory over an inferior, seeks out worthy opponents: Mucius, Fabricius, Rutilius, Regulus, Socrates, Cato. *Magnum exemplum nisi mala fortuna non invenit* (3.4). The chapter closes with a more detailed examination of each of these examples in turn, pointing out how their sufferings were preferable to what the world considers good fortune.

From analogy and full-scale *exempla* in chapter 3 we move on in chapter 4 to direct arguments with appropriate illustrations. Adversity is the only means of discovering the great man: *magnus vir es, sed unde scio, si tibi fortuna non dat facultatem exhibendae virtutis?* (4.2). You cannot win a contest if you have no opponents. Without adversity you cannot even know yourself what you are capable of: *opus est enim ad notitiam sui experimento; quid quisque posset nisi temptando non didicit* (4.3). This is simply our point (B) in a new guise, and so it goes on throughout the chapter with a wealth of illustrative material. Two men may have performed the same feats in battle, but more glory accrues to him who returns wounded (4.4). The wealthy can never demonstrate their endurance of poverty (4.5). Just as a general chooses his best men for the most dangerous tasks, in the same way those who are chosen to suffer can say: *digni visi sumus deo in quibus experiretur quantum humana natura posset pati* (4.8).

This theme dominates the rest of the chapter, which concludes with a restatement of the first element of the *divisio* as it has now been established: *pro ipsis ergo bonis viris est, ut esse interriti possint, multum inter formidulosa versari et aequo animo ferre quae non sunt mala nisi male sustinenti* (4.16). We have had thus far a very striking series of repetitions of the three interlinked points of the gods' concern for good men (A), the value to good men of misfortune (B), and the corresponding dangers of unbroken good fortune.[47] The whole argument has been composed of *loci communes*, stock arguments, and examples available in the rhetorical handbooks or

FORM AND CONTENT IN THE 'MORAL ESSAYS'

from the popular tradition of the diatribe. They have not been peculiarly Stoic.

In chapter 5, where Seneca moves on to the second element of the *divisio*, he relates these themes to that of Providence and its workings considered in the strict Stoic sense. At this new stage in the argument the commonplaces play a smaller part and more technical, philosophical considerations are introduced. The chapter opens with an argument to the effect that the supposed goods and evils that befall men are neither good nor bad.[48] But the imaginary interlocutor is still worried about good men suffering and bad getting off scot-free. Seneca's reply is to quote the example of the brave man serving in the army, while the cowards idle at home, the Vestal virgins staying up all night to sacrifice while others less worthy sleep, the senate toiling all day while others play. The conclusion is: *labor optimos citat* (5.4).

Now, this is the same argument (B) as that which we have been noting all through, but its context makes it very different. Here it departs from the practical utility of adversity, which had been the earlier theme, and goes on to the higher plane of the moral value that the Stoics attached to it: *idem in hac magna re publica fit; boni viri laborant, impendunt, impenduntur, et volentes quidem* (5.4). Adversity is not simply a means of toughening yourself for a hard life; it affords the opportunity for that complete acquiescence with Fate which is the only and complete moral virtue. It is a necessary part of the world-order, without which good could not exist. Men who wish to be virtuous are 'willing' to suffer it: *non trahuntur [boni] a fortuna, sequuntur illam et aequant gradus. si scissent antecessissent* (5.4),[49] and in this desire to face whatever trouble fortune may bring lies the whole secret of the moral life. Thus the good man's misfortunes, and his consent to them, are an integral part of the whole world-order, the divine *Providentia* which Seneca is seeking to defend.

The remainder of the chapter elaborates these Stoic arguments in technical terms, but our old argument recurs. God, it is said, cannot change the material of the universe, he can only shape it to the degree that it permits. The sterner stuff that the good man must be made of will not encounter only quiet and peace: *Contra fortunam illi tenendus est cursus* . . . (5.9); *ignis aurum probat, miseria fortes viros; vides quam alte escendere debeat virtus; scies illi non per secura vadendum* (5.10). This last is then illustrated by the example

51

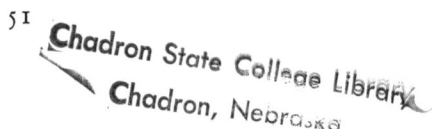

of the bold aspirations of Phaethon from Ovid's *Metamorphoses*,[50] the whole being summed up in the words: *humilis et inertis est tuta sectari; per alta virtus it* (5.11). The significant fact that emerges is that the same basic idea has been used, but in its new context it embodies a much more impressive truth for the Stoic. This is the result of the dialectical progress between 2–4 and 5. The first stage seeks to break down the objections to adversity by drawing attention to the general value of the effort which it induces; the second shows that this effort is in accordance with the general plan of the universe, which is identical with the divine will, acquiescence in which is the summit of human virtue.

These two stages employ first examples from ordinary living and then dialectical arguments, thus bringing the Stoic paradoxes into line with popular thinking on the subject; the final stage passes on to a still higher level where our realization of the facts as already demonstrated has led to a complete reversal of our values. All mere externals are realized to be worthless, and the life of internal virtue is recognized as the only thing that really matters. We are really past the need to emphasize the value of effort – it has already done its work – but even in chapter 6 there are some traces of the old arguments. This can be seen in the emphasis on God's genuine benevolence to good men (6.1, 3–5); in the idea that good men suffer to be an example to others (*nati sunt in exemplar*: 6.3); and finally in the loving care with which God has made the ultimate release from troubles (suicide) so simple. It is with this last thought that the work closes most effectively. In it, again, we can see the dialectical progress. At the end of chapter 2 Cato's suicide was a spectacle that afforded pleasure to the gods because it was so difficult physically and demanded such courage; here suicide is physically easy, it is on the mental side that it is seen as the ultimate acquiescence in Fate which crowns the good man's life.

So far we have dealt with only one complex of arguments that is frequently repeated; there are others, though not on quite such a large scale. I now consider one of the more prominent.

An important argument is that misfortunes only appear to be such. The forms in which this occurs illustrate very effectively the arrangement of the work which I have already described. At the opening of chapter 2 we read *nihil accidere bono viro mali potest; non miscentur contraria*. Nothing that happens can change the good man: *manet in statu et quicquid evenit in suum colorem trahit; est enim omnibus externis potentior* (2.1). This simply denies that anything that happens to the good man can be bad; if it happens to him it is not bad. We also have the additional point that these things are merely externals and so immaterial to the good man. Now, both these points are derived from Stoic dialectic, whereas the rest of the chapter is composed mainly of popular *exempla*. The popular counterparts of these arguments appear at 3.5ff., where each of the examples of noble adversity is concluded by asking whether the hero would have been better off in the enjoyment of some supposed pleasure. The implication is clear that the apparent misfortune is the real good, and the apparent good fortune, if not positively bad, is at least not to be preferred.

When we come to chapter 5 we should expect this point to be assimilated in some way to the great plan of the universe, and so it is, receiving here its most explicit formulation: *hoc est propositum deo quod sapienti viro ostendere haec quae vulgus appetit, quae reformidat, nec bona esse nec mala* (5.1). That is, they are indifferent, in the technical sense of being immaterial to the moral life, and God sets out to demonstrate this. The proof of this point is a logical one, based on the incompatibility of opposites which was mentioned in 2.1. A thing can be bad only if it happens only to those who deserve it; anything that happens to a good man cannot be bad; thus the misfortunes of good men that are the subject of complaint are not misfortunes at all. In the final chapter we encounter, as we would expect, the highest expression of this argument, where it demonstrates the complete psychological revolution in the good man. God does not allow the good man to suffer misfortune: *omnia mala ab illis removit, scelera et flagitia,* etc. . . . *ipsos tuetur ac vindicat*: *numquid hoc quoque aliquis a deo exigit ut bonorum virorum etiam sarcinas servet? remittunt ipsi hanc deo curam*: *externa contemnunt* (6.1).

Thus the true ills of mankind have been finally identified and the good man definitively relieved of them. They are mere externals and need not trouble him. The good man can live free of all fear for his moral safety, however much he may appear to suffer; it is the others who must fear. God can say: '*quid habetis quod de me queri possitis, vos, quibus recta placuerunt? aliis bona falsa circumdedi et animos inanes velut longo fallacique somnio lusi. auro illos et argento et ebore adornavi; intus boni nihil est*' (6.3). This whole passage illustrates perfectly the way in which all the arguments in the work lead up to the final state of perfect comprehension of and acquiescence in the divine law of the universe. This is the mark of the good man, and his real bulwark against what the world calls misfortunes. Again the same argument has been utilized in different ways according to its place in the whole work.

It remains a matter of taste and judgment whether this harping on a few familiar arguments is acceptable or not. What can, I hope, now be asserted is that the repetitions are not mere repetitions. They are coloured by a carefully planned development of the contexts in which they occur. At each stage new layers of meaning become visible and a new profundity is discovered in the apparently hackneyed slogans. Seneca's enthusiastic championing of Providence may cut little ice with the philosophical sceptic, but it may have had a powerful effect on a reader already prejudiced in its favour like Lucilius. Measured against that yardstick the repetitions are a good deal less reprehensible.

3

I now wish to consider another work, looking at it from all angles rather than concentrating on a single one. Let us turn to *De Ira* 1. Although it is the first of three books which deal with this topic so beloved of the Hellenistic philosophers,[51] it can be considered as a separate entity for our purposes.[52] Its interest is that it has a structure determined by the philosophical subject-matter, but not without rhetorical shaping. Moreover, careful planning and apparent formlessness run side by side in a way which is characteristic of Seneca.

Exegisti a me, Novate, ut scriberem quemadmodum posset ira leniri (1.1). This opening sentence tells us two important things. The work is written in the form of a response to a question about a moral problem. Seneca is here acting as a practical moral guide and counsellor to his brother. As such, we have seen, he is more likely to heap precept upon precept than to develop a continuous logical argument. Second, the work is concerned with the mitigation (*leniri*) of anger. It belongs to the therapeutic branch of the study of the emotions rather than the theoretical. Book 1, however, contains no account of how to cure. It concentrates on impressing upon the reader the foulness of anger and on rejecting firmly any supposed justifications of it.

Chapter 1 opens an admirable *exordium*, arresting our attention with its depiction first of the mental frenzy of the victim (1.2), and then of its physical manifestations (1.3–4), reinforced by a comparison with the frenzy of wild beasts (1.5–6). It is the most obviously visible of all violent emotions (1.7). In chapter 2 the *exordium* continues with a description of anger in terms of another aspect: its results, both on individuals (2.1–2) and groups (2.3).

At this point there is a lacuna in the text. Its contents can be partly supplied by reference to Lactantius, *De Ira Dei* 17.13, but even without that help we could see from internal evidence that the theme begun in 2.3 must have been concluded, thus bringing the *exordium* to a close, and then been followed by the statement of various definitions of anger and their discussion, which occupies 2.4–3.3.[53]

Here we encounter a passage which was earlier cited as an example of Senecan inconsistency. Now that we see it in context it will offer an interesting example of his concentration upon the argument in hand to the exclusion of what has gone before. In chapter 1 he wanted a vivid illustration of the way in which anger cannot be concealed but must show itself openly. What better example than wild beasts? *Non vides ut omnium animalium, simul ad nocendum*[54] *insurrexerunt, praecurrant notae* . . . ? (1.5); *nullum est animal tam horrendum tam perniciosumque natura ut non appareat in illo, simul ira invasit, novae feritatis accessio* (1.6). At 3.3ff., however, he is defending his own and Aristotle's definitions of anger, both of which involved repayment for injury suffered. Against this the point can be made that animals get angry without having suffered injury or seeking revenge. How is he to cope with this? A good philosophical argument lies to hand. Animals have no faculty of reason, but only impulses. Anger, however, can exist only where its enemy reason has a place. Therefore animals cannot get angry. Only men can. Thus the objection to the definitions falls to the ground.

No Roman orator[55] would have been horrified by this slight inconsistency with chapter 1. You selected the argument that supported you at a given moment and ignored everything else. The whole introductory section hangs together well and is consistently signposted. There is no need to imagine a conflation of several versions or a gap of some years between the composition of one chapter and another in order to account for this lapse.[56]

The theoretical discussion moves on from the definition of anger to the difference between *ira* and *iracundia* (4.1) and an account of the various species of anger (4.2–3). This concludes the introductory material, which has consisted of *exordium* followed by preliminary remarks on terminology.

Seneca now neatly sums up what has gone before and provides a *divisio* of material for the rest of the book: *quid esset ira quaesitum est, an in ullum aliud animal quam in hominem caderet, quo ab iracundia distaret, quot eius species essent;*[57] *nunc quaeramus an ira secundum naturam sit et an utilis atque ex aliqua parte retinenda* (5.1). This twofold division is faithfully followed, though in two parts of very unequal length.

We find the first aspect dealt with in chapters 5 and 6, with its beginning and end clearly indicated: *an secundum naturam sit manifestum erit si hominem inspexerimus* (5.2); ... *ergo non est naturalis ira* (6.5). The second aspect is then taken up: *numquid, quamvis non sit naturalis ira, adsumenda est quia utilis saepe fuit?* (7.1). The discussion of this continues in a somewhat disorganized manner to the end of chapter 19. There the plan announced in the *divisio* is complete and we might expect the book to end with, perhaps, a *peroratio*. Two chapters follow, admittedly in a slightly more elevated tone than some of the earlier material, but in fact introducing a completely new type of argument: *ne illud quidem iudicandum est aliquid iram ad magnitudinem animi conferre* (20.1); *nihil ergo in ira ... magnum, nihil nobile est* (21.1). Is this addition to his preconceived plan simply a piece of carelessness on Seneca's part, or does it make some sense?

The original *divisio* is made by Seneca because he wishes to refute the views on anger of Aristotle and the Peripatetics who were its most notorious defenders. They claimed that anger was both natural (or 'necessary') and useful. What, then, more natural than that Seneca should devote himself to the two topics of *naturale* and *utile*? But we have seen that he was fond of the rhetorical analysis in terms of *utile* and *honestum*. It looks here as if he has almost subconsciously carried on from the section on *utile* to one on *honestum*, which would, anyway, make an elevated and impressive conclusion to the book as demanded by the conventions of the *peroratio*. The point made in these two chapters was not, so far as we know, made much of in Peripatetic writing on the subject. There certainly seems to be no parallel between the content of *magnitudo animi* here and the Aristotelian concept of μεγαλοψυχία as elaborated at *EN* 1123a34ff.[58] What we have, rather, is a conflation of two separate classifications of topics, one philosophical and one rhetorical, thanks to their having certain common terms. At first sight it can be expressed thus:

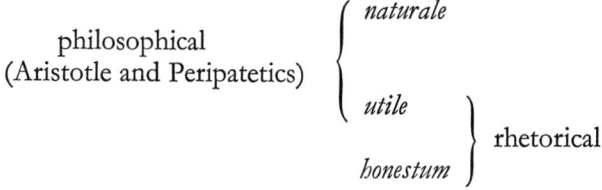

But there may have been rhetorical justification for all three categories. *Partes suadendi quidam putaverunt honestum, utile, necessarium,* Quintilian[59] tells us, only to reject the last classification. I have mentioned already that natural and necessary go together in philosophical contexts,[60] and we thus have Seneca providing what amounts to a *'dissuasoria'*. Anger is not natural (i.e. necessary), useful, or good. It can be argued that a really systematic writer would have told us what he was doing, but for an audience more attuned to the classifications of rhetoric than we are there would have been little problem.

The general shape of the book is clear. What is the state of the composition within that framework? There are some doublets and a certain diffuseness of argument. These are of interest as providing further examples of what I consider to be Seneca's habits of composition. For instance: *quid ergo? non aliquando castigatio necessaria est? quidni? sed haec sine ira, cum ratione; non enim nocet sed medetur specie nocendi* (6.1) is very similar to *corrigendus est itaque qui peccat et admonitione et vi, et molliter et aspere, meliorque tam sibi quam aliis faciendus non sine castigatione, sed sine ira; quis enim cui medetur irascitur?* (15.1). The frequency with which the conventional analogy between physical and mental health and healing is used by Seneca has already been mentioned. What we should note is that, while the point made is the same in each passage, the context of argument in which it is placed is completely different. At the beginning of chapter 6 the interlocutor is objecting to the picture of human nature as entirely benevolent painted in 5.2–3. The whole argument is concerned to show that anger is unnatural, and this is why it must be controlled by reason and not be permitted to inflict punishment for its own sake, just as remedies are applied without passion in physical medicine. At chapter 15 it is the question whether anger is useful that is under discussion. Punishment must be cool and dispassionate, not because such behaviour is most natural to man since it is in accordance with his divine reason which determines his true nature, but because it is most likely to be successful in curing the patient. Even if reform is impossible and execution is prescribed, anger must still be absent from the motivation: *quid enim est cur oderim eum cui tum maxime prosum cum illum sibi eripio?* (15.2)

This difference of context applies also to the arguments that develop out of this analogy at 6.2ff. and 16.1ff. These concern the way in which the ruler or judge will resort to progressively more drastic measures as the degree of wrongdoing increases, just as the doctor does according to the degree of illness. The idea is the same in each case, but the argument which it supports is different.

If we turn to the section dealing with the non-utility of anger we shall find that it is extremely diffuse and repetitive. The topics dealt with can be put briefly thus:

A (7–11) Arguments against the proposition that anger is useful and so should be retained in moderation; based mainly on the opposition and incompatibility of reason and emotion.

B (12–16) Arguments against the proposition that anger at wrongdoing is inevitable and a vital factor in bringing about just punishment.

C (17–19) Reason is in every way superior to anger, and the only proper guide in the punishment of wrongdoers.

There is a sense in which C to some extent combines the central ideas of A and B, but this is more obvious in summary than on reading. The argument moves abruptly from point to point, relying on the device of the imaginary interlocutor, who simply states some Peripatetic view or objection, or by direct appeal to Aristotle or Theophrastus in person.

The repetitiveness of these points can be illustrated by reference to the use of the Aristotelian argument that anger is a necessary ingredient of courage or valour in war. It recurs again and again throughout this section with little regard for its precise significance in the argument. Another example of this carelessness in construction is to be found at 13.1–2. Here, in the midst of much purely moralizing argumentation, we are suddenly faced with a piece of abstract school syllogizing quite unrelated to what lies on either side.[61] The point which it makes is quite effective in the context of Seneca's general argument, but it is somewhat incongruous and has not been worked into the position in the work which it occupies. The imaginary interlocutor has to be called in to save the day (13.3).

This rapid survey of Book 1 has displayed some of the main characteristics of the structure of the *Moral Essays*. The opening is well-organized and effective, engaging the reader's attention and getting preliminary technicalities out of the way. A clear-cut scheme of argument is then proposed and, on the level of major divisions of the work, pursued reasonably consistently with only a minor addition at the end. It is when faced with working out the detailed argument of one of the divisions at some length that Seneca's structural grip relaxes and the self-indulgence permitted by the device of the imaginary interlocutor takes over. Different points are made just as they occur to him or the same one crops up again and again. There are things to be said for and against the details of his handling of the subject, but an impartial reader is likely to feel the force of the vigorously expressed torrent of arguments with which he is faced. A cooler and more organized approach might have less impact.

4

The time has now come to abandon the apologetic mode and look at a single work from a positive angle. In the *De Constantia Sapientis* we find a complex meditation on the nature of the Stoic *sapiens*. Rhetorical categories and the use of recurrent themes give form and shape to Seneca's characteristic mass of material without imposing any straitjacket upon the discussion. It proceeds smoothly and naturally. The technique is highly accomplished, but held in check, observing the control he himself recommended in philosophical writing.[62]

The *exordium* of this work introduces us to the addressee but not to the actual subject. It consists of chapter 1, and if it were removed only the absence of the name of Serenus in 2.1 would tell us that the opening had been lost. But there is some point to it. The Stoic philosophy is praised as more manly and heroic than any other and at the same time claimed to be less demanding than is sometimes supposed. This is having the best of both worlds and forms a masterly *captatio benevolentiae*. Its imagery of the upward path to knowledge and wisdom is appropriate, too, in the context of a work whose aim is to enter upon and persevere in the way that leads to the detached and unassailable attitude of the *sapiens*.[63] The characterization of the Stoic way as *virilis* (1.1) is picked up and echoed in the emphatic use of *vir* towards the end of the work,[64] particularly at the very end where, in the all-pervasive military metaphor, Serenus is urged to occupy a hero's post in the battle of life.

The subject is introduced in chapter 2 by Seneca's recalling a conversation with Serenus about Cato. This technique of starting a discussion by reference to some conversation, event, or object is more familiar in the *Epistles*. Here it has some of the flavour of the older style of philosophical dialogue, since both sides of the conversation are reported. But by the end of the second paragraph the report has finished and we are being addressed by Seneca in his customary manner. What Cato provides is an interesting and concrete case history of the correct reaction of the *sapiens* under attack. This serves as a starting point for the discussion. We return to it every so often[65] and it thus helps to bind the work together and affords a repeated concrete example of the behaviour which is being recommended by theoretical argument. The basic doctrine to be expounded is twice stated as an answer to Serenus's solicitude for Cato: *nullam enim sapientem nec iniuriam accipere nec contumeliam posse* (2.2); *tutus est sapiens nec ulla affici aut iniuria aut contumelia potest* (2.4). The distinction between *iniuria* and *contumelia*[66] which forms the basis of the *divisio* is already apparent, and we are ready for the discussion proper to start.

Before the *divisio* is reached, however, we again find some additional material which serves to expand and clarify the points at issue. Chapters 3 and 4 state and rebut the two most obvious objections to Seneca's thesis: (*a*) that it is quite unreal, a mere piece of verbal trickery with no foundation in the facts of experience (3.1); and (*b*) that the wise man, whatever Seneca may say, is bound to be subject to injurious attacks (4.1). Some of the answers that are given to these criticisms foreshadow arguments that will appear later in the main body of the work.[67] Each of the chapters finishes with a reiteration of the invulnerability of the *sapiens* with the word *tutus* used, as at the end of chapter 2.[68] The points made here thus prepare the ground for what is to follow and emphasize the central feature of the nature of the *sapiens*. One might almost claim that they add up to a definition by description of that nature which secures him against any assault by *iniuria*. This enables us to see how similar these chapters are in function to those between the *exordium* and *divisio* of *De Ira* 1.

The *divisio*, for which the way has already been prepared, is quite straightforward: *dividamus, si tibi videtur, Serene, iniuriam a contumelia* (5.1). The detailed working out of this scheme is less simple. As we shall see, Seneca at first deals with the two subjects one after the other, but later oscillates between the two. I shall now attempt to chart this oscillation in such a way as to show its eventual coherence.

Iniuria is dealt with first, beginning at chapter 5.3[69] and going on to the end of chapter 9. This falls reasonably tidily into two sections,[70] each opening with a passage of syllogistic argument. After the first comes the highly rhetorical *exemplum* of Stilpo, complete with lengthy prosopopoeia. The speech put into his mouth consists largely of a list of apparently terrible sufferings set off against the heroic fortitude which disregards them. Seneca's comment on it, cast in a siege metaphor, concludes with a collection of points which we noticed in the introductory chapters: *illa [moenia], quae sapientem tuentur, et a flamma et ab incursu tuta sunt, nullum introitum praebent, excelsa, inexpugnabilia, diis aequa* (6.8). Security and divinity are again attributed to the *sapiens*. This section then ends with a double recurrence to the introduction.[71] The real existence of the Stoic wise man is once more asserted and Cato is cited as an actual example. The second passage of abstract reasoning is followed[72] by some miscellaneous arguments which include examples of apparent *iniuriae* which the *sapiens* escapes or turns to his advantage. There is almost a sense here of the utility of *sapientia*: *haec effugit sapiens, qui nescit nec in spem nec in metum vivere* (9.2); *adeo autem ad offensiones rerum hominumque non contrahitur ut ipsa illi iniuria usui sit* ... (9.3).

Chapter 10 opens with an announcement that the first part has been completed and the second is now beginning.[73] The basic argument is that, while *iniuria* may at least affect us physically, *contumelia* is entirely mental and thus more easily shrugged off. The main burden of this section is the listing of situations where we realize that the insult is really insignificant, and the assimilation of all cases to this class. Seneca begins, however, by defining and describing the nature of *contumelia* in terms of *humilitas animi*[74] which causes us to be affected by the imagined insult. With this is contrasted the *magnitudo* or *magnanimitas* of the *sapiens*.[75] What we may deduce from this is that Seneca is commending *sapientia* as great or noble and we are again reminded of the rhetorical category of *honestum*. The list of possible situations is brought to a halt by a question from the interlocutor, one which, as so often in such cases, ignores the logic of the previous argument. The question is whether the wise man will approach a door guarded by a surly doorkeeper. Seneca gives a detailed reply as to how to deal with this practical situation which may expose one to *contumelia* (14.2). It is at this point that the *divisio* is abandoned. This question and answer concerning an actual case of *contumelia* naturally provoke a similar exchange on an actual case of *iniuria*: being struck a blow (14.3). The answer reintroduces Cato and so connects with what has been said earlier, and leads to a general statement of the invulnerability of the wise man (14.4). The whole passage from 14.3 to 16.3 considers both *iniuria* and *contumelia* together. The reason is that it is concerned with this general total invulnerability which can be exemplified by either type indiscriminately.

Chapter 15 works round to a depiction of the heroic fortitude of the *sapiens*. The essential totality of his victory over Fortune is epigrammatically summed up: *vincit nos fortuna, nisi tota vincitur* (15.3). A digression follows which arises naturally from the uncompromising nature of this stand: *ne putes istam Stoicam esse duritiam, Epicurus . . . 'raro', inquit, 'sapienti fortuna intervenit'* (15.4).[76] We are at once reminded of Seneca's eagerness in the *exordium* to mitigate the popular view of Stoicism as a harsh and demanding discipline. He uses the Epicurean doctrine to provide an *a fortiori* argument in favour of the Stoic position: if even the devotees of the flesh disregard or at least devalue injuries, how much more must they be irrelevant to a Stoic. The difference between the schools is not totally obscured, but it is minimized: *non est quod putes magnum quo dissidemus* (16.3). An interesting feature

FORM AND CONTENT IN THE 'MORAL ESSAYS'

of the digression is that the *a fortiori* argument from the Epicurean position is used to show that resistance to injury is not *supra humanae naturae mensuram* (16.1). Even of the more extreme Stoic position it can be said: *nec enim est quod dicas hoc naturae repugnare* (16.1). It would seem to follow that Seneca is here saying that *constantia* is natural.

The end of the digression is not marked. In fact the transition is sufficiently subtle to repay careful study. It takes place in the middle of a sentence! We are told at the beginning of 16.3 that both schools recommend contempt for (*a*) *iniuriae* and (*b*) the mere shadows of these, which are *contumeliae*. The latter are then expanded upon in a relative clause, and it is *contumelia* which occupies the rest of the work up to the *peroratio*. A list of practical methods is given by which even the ordinary reasonable man can conquer it. Only a few things need be said about this passage, but we shall find in it features which recall earlier comments. First there is the disproportionately long and only partially relevant *exemplum* of Caligula (18). It clearly takes on a life of its own. Then at its conclusion we move with only a half-explicit notification from this example to be avoided to Socrates whose patience is to be praised – and, presumably, copied.[77] Finally at 19.2 we are told of the damage done to our public and private lives by becoming involved in insult and injury. This again implies the utility of *constantia*.

The work concludes with a *peroratio* which briefly sums up how to cope with the injuries and insults which are encountered in the world. It is based on the duality of the *sapiens* and the *affectator sapientiae*, the man who has not attained complete wisdom but is striving earnestly to that end. This duality makes a fitting conclusion to a work which has concerned itself both with the theoretical absolutes of the Stoic faith and with suggesting practical ways of coping with everyday human problems.

It should be clear by now that to look at the structure of this work simply in terms of the crude analysis of the *divisio* is wholly inadequate. That serves well enough in the central section, but a more complex interlacing of *iniuria* and *contumelia* is at work elsewhere. Other structural members are visible. Just as anger was not natural, useful, or good, so *constantia* is all these things.[78] Similarly the study of human psychopathology had both a theoretical and a practical therapeutic part.[79] The former is more apparent in the earlier parts of the work, the latter comes into its own towards the end. Recurrent themes and images play an important part in binding the work together and giving it unity: the references to Cato,[80] the emphatic use of *vir*[81] to characterize the good Stoic, the *magnitudo* or *firmitas animi* of the *sapiens*,[82] his divine nature,[83] and the all-pervasive metaphors of physical struggle and combat.[84] The result is a coherent work which makes its impact unobtrusively and without obvious contrivance.

5

In conclusion, I do not want to say any more about Seneca's methods of composition. I want instead to point to aspects of the work of three other writers which may help to illuminate the way in which we should approach Seneca. All three are generally valued much more highly than him as literary artists. I have no wish to quarrel with this evaluation. At the same time I do not regard my comparison as ludicrous. What I hope to offer is an opportunity to consider Seneca afresh in the light of some examples of ancient literary structuring which call for a considerable intellectual effort of appreciation on our part.

The first case is perhaps the simplest. I have referred to the interlacing of two or more themes in certain Senecan works. Something similar is to be found in the complex interweaving of the themes of philosophy and rhetoric in Plato's *Gorgias*.[85] There, too, the compartmentalization of arguments which some critics seem to want in Seneca is lacking. The poet Tibullus offers an even more elaborate example of these techniques. The repetition of themes, the return to themes apparently fully treated and abandoned, above all the subtlety and imperceptibility of the transitions,[86] all these have their parallels in Seneca. But his greatest similarity is perhaps with another poet. Whether in the *Ars Poetica* or the *Odes*, Horace delights in working with more than one structural scheme.[87] The reader can never relax, confident of what will come next. His attention is thus kept fixed upon the immediate context and the general structure appears only from time to time.

The habits of mind which these writers reveal must have been natural and acceptable to their readers, and these were the arbiters whom Seneca recognized. A writer could not flout the stylistic conventions of the time.[88] It is we now who must make the effort to appreciate what these conventions were. It is at our peril that we reject the testimony on Seneca of a near-contemporary who was a master of the writer's craft both in style and structure and who, unlike Caligula and Quintilian,[89] had no axe to grind: ... *oratio a Seneca composita multum cultus praeferret, ut fuit illi viro ingenium amoenum et temporis eius auribus accommodatum.*[90]

Notes

1. That is, the works contained in the three volumes of the Loeb edition which bear this title. These are the twelve books of *Dialogi*, *De Clementia* and *De Beneficiis*. The last I have mentioned only occasionally, since it is clearly not a unitary work in the same sense as the others and raises problems that go beyond the scope of this discussion. The most comprehensive treatment of my topic is to be found in E. Albertini, *La Composition dans les ouvrages philosophiques de Sénèque* (Paris, 1923). This contains a very full collection of material and some useful points are made, but there is little subtlety in the approach used. Much more sophisticated and penetrating is K. Abel, *Bauformen in Senecas Dialogen* (Heidelberg, 1967), which contains detailed analyses of the three *Consolationes*, *De Providentia* and *De Constantia Sapientis*.
2. Suet. *Cal.* 53.2.
3. Cf. W. Trillitzsch, *Seneca im Literarischen Urteil der Antike* (Amsterdam, 1971), pp. 101–3, and the literature cited there.
4. Cf. Suet., loc. cit. and Dio Cassius 59.19.7–8.
5. And even, perhaps, a certain mordant wit. Is it an accident that the three nouns used can all refer to some aspect of the theatre and the games: *commissio* = a celebration of games, *harena* = the theatre, *calx* = the finishing line? Seneca's rather priggish Puritanism was established at an early age (*Epist.* 108.22) and doubtless included the distaste for the games which he later expressed forcefully (*Epist.* 7.3–7; 95.33; *Brev. Vit.* 12.2; 13.6–7; *Clem.* 1.25.1). Was it therefore all the more insulting to describe his vaunted literary production in terms which would remind the listeners of the theatre?
6. E.g. *Ira* 1.1.5–6: the effects of anger are clearly visible in wild beasts; ibid. 3.3ff.: wild beasts, having no faculty of reason, cannot have emotions (e.g. anger) but merely impulses.
7. For an extreme example of such criticism cf. R. Pfennig, *De librorum quos scripsit Seneca de ira compositione et origine* (Diss. Greifswald, 1887).
8. *Epist.* 89,13.
9. This medical metaphor had been implicit in Greek language about the emotions from the earliest times (e.g. Hom. *Il.* 4.36; Aesch. *Pr.* 378). It was much used by Plato (e.g. *Gorg.* 477e7ff.) and is of great importance in Aristotle; cf. W. Jaeger, *JHS*, 77 (1957), pp. 54ff. But it was of most

10 E.g. *Epist.* 88, esp. 1–2, 23.
11 E.g. *Epist.* 117, esp. 20. Not that Seneca rigorously eliminates from his own work either liberal studies or syllogistic reasoning.
12 E.g. Epicur. *Fr.* 523 (Us.) = Epict. *Ench.* 2.20.6; Sen. *Brev. Vit.* 7.4; 18.3; Epict. *Ench.* 2.19.34. Cicero, too, uses the phrase in his philosophical works (e.g. *Fin.* 2.113), though with him it may be simply part of the orator's stock-in-trade. For the part played by quasi-religious belief in ancient philosophy cf. A. D. Nock, *Conversion* (Oxford, 1933), pp. 164–86.
13 The word *salus* (e.g. *Epist.* 28.9) is characteristic; cf. the Greek σώζεσθαι, Nock, op. cit., p. 180.
14 This is not quite true of *De Beneficiis*, although it does have a formal addressee.
15 On the theoretical basis of this aspect of Seneca's activity see A. Guillemin, *REL*, 30 (1952), pp. 202ff., 31 (1953), pp. 215ff., 32 (1954), pp. 250ff. For English readers S. Dill, *Roman Society from Nero to Marcus Aurelius* (London, 1905²), pp. 289–333 remains instructive.
16 For discussion of these and other types of argument used by Seneca cf. W. Trillitzsch, *Senecas Beweisführung* (Berlin, 1962).
17 For the Spanish family background see now M. Griffin, *JRS*, 62 (1972), pp. 1ff.; and on the literary debt to his father E. Rolland, *De l'Influence de Sénèque le père et des rhéteurs sur Sénèque le philosophe* (Ghent, 1906).
18 Cf. n. 4 above.
19 The lead in exploring this area has been taken by P. Grimal: on *Const. Sap.*, *REA*, 51 (1949), pp. 246ff. and the introduction to his commentary (Paris, 1953); on *Brev. Vit.*, *Studi in onore di Luigi Castiglioni* (Florence, 1960), pp. 407ff. and the introduction to his edition (Paris, 1959); on *Prov.*, *REA*, 52 (1950), pp. 238ff. While I would not accept all of the very precise analyses and classifications of parts of the works made by Grimal, he has made out an excellent case for saying that Seneca is certainly conscious of the traditional rhetorical forms and employs them in his works.
20 E.g. *Prov.* 3.1; *Const. Sap.* 5.1; *Clem.* 1.3.1; *Ot.* 2.1–2; *Tranq. An.* 6.1; *Ben.* 1.11.1.
21 Another example of *propositio*, namely *brevissimam esse occupatorum vitam*.
22 E.g. *Prov.* 3.1ff. (*utile*); 4.1 (*honestum*); *Const. Sap.* 9.3 (*utile*); *Clem.* 1.3.2 (both); *Ben.* 1.11.1 (*utilia*); 2.14.1 (*utilia*); 4.16.1 (both).
23 It is interesting that this work has defied Grimal's type of analysis; cf. my remarks *CQ*, n.s. 22 (1972), pp. 414f.
24 On what follows cf. H. MacL. Currie, *BICS* 13 (1966), pp. 76ff. We inevitably cover a good deal of the same ground and are in broad agreement about the forces shaping Seneca's literary form. It will be clear, however, that I attach rather more weight to formal organization

than Currie, who seems to limit it to *Cons. Helv.*, *Const. Sap.*, and *Cons. Marc.* (op. cit., p. 80). The *Consolationes*, of course, belong to a special tradition with its own formal rules and are thus not wholly typical of Seneca's production.

25 On this whole subject cf. S. F. Bonner, *Roman Declamation* (Liverpool, 1949), esp. pp. 51ff. Despite Seneca's criticisms of the worst excesses of the declamatory style (listed by Bonner, pp. 74f.) he could not escape its influence.

26 Yet even in this catalogue, where the transitions are reminiscent of some of Ovid's more desperate achievements in the *Metamorphoses*, a degree of formal shaping is used and made explicit: *et haec cogitanda sunt exempla quae vites, et illa ex contrario quae sequaris*...(22.1). Cf. Clement Al. *Paed.* 1.2.1.

27 Fro. *Ant.* 2, p. 68 (146N) = *S.V.F.* 2.27.

28 Cf. C. N. Smiley, *University of Wisconsin Studies in Language and Literature* 3 (1919), pp. 50ff.

29 Cf. e.g. *Epist.* 75.1.7.

30 Cf. *Epist.* 52.14.

31 Cf. *Epist.* 100.5.

32 Cf. Diog. Laert. 7.59.

33 Cf. Cic. *Parad.* 2.

34 The standard work is: A. Oltramare, *Les Origines de la diatribe romaine* (Lausanne, 1926). Specifically on Seneca, H. Weber, *De Senecae philosophi dicendi genere bioneo* (Diss. Marburg, 1895) is still relevant. Both works may exaggerate its influence a little in their enthusiasm for the diatribe but are still valuable collections of material.

35 Cf. e.g. his view on ostentatious learning (*Tranq. An.* 9.4–7), on excesses in eating (*Cons. Helv.* 10.8–9), and for σπουδογέλοιον the gentleman who was so affected that he required someone to tell him whether he was sitting down or not (*Brev. Vit.* 12.7). For lengthy lists cf. Oltramare, pp. 263ff.

36 1.1; 2.35; 3.4. For the question of the unity or otherwise of this work cf. n. 52 below.

37 Cf. e.g. Philodemus *Ir. fr.* 1; Cic. *Tusc.* 4.52; Plu. *Mor.* 455Eff. For the interest of Seneca and the Stoics in physiognomy and its use in Roman historical writing cf. E. C. Evans, *HSCP*, 46 (1935), pp. 43ff.

38 Seneca may have learned this from his master Sotion, a pupil of Sextius, either verbally (cf. *Epist.* 10817f.) or from his book on anger (cf. Stob. 3.14.10, etc.).

39 Cf. Albertini, op. cit. n. 1, pp. 315ff.

40 But not incomplete; cf. Abel, op. cit. n. 1, p. 171.

41 The phrase is Grimal's. It will be clear that in what follows I am deeply indebted to his article on this work (cf. n. 19). I reject some of his rhetorical classifications, but accept the central points of his analysis.

42 Cf. p. 43.

43 The work is represented by Seneca as a pleading: *causam deorum agam* (1.1).

44 Cf. my analyses of *Ira* 1 and *Const. Sap.* below.

45 The whole of chapter 6 deals with this theme, but, as I have already suggested, the concluding section on the possibility of suicide (6.7–9) can be considered a *peroratio*.
46 I take it, with most editors, that the quotation ends here and that the rest is comment by Seneca.
47 For this last cf. 2.5; 3.2, 5–13; 4.1, 6, 9–10.
48 That is, they are morally indifferent (ἀδιάφορον) in the technical Stoic sense.
49 Cf. the famous *ducunt volentem fata, nolentem trahunt* (*Epist.* 107.11, quoting Cleanthes; cf. *SVF* 1.527).
50 2.63ff., 79ff.
51 Works on anger exist by or are ascribed to Bion, Antipater, Posidonius, Philodemus, Sotion, Seneca, and Plutarch. There are many other doubtful ascriptions, and, of course, a vast number of treatises περὶ παθῶν.
52 Many have held the view that the *De Ira* as we have it cannot be a unitary composition. I do not share this belief and hope to explain why elsewhere. For a sensible review of the controversy with relevant bibliography cf. M. Coccia, *I problemi del De ira di Seneca alla luce dell' annalisi stilistica* (Rome, 1958), pp. 18ff.
53 Cf. *Aristotelis finitio non multum a nostra abest* (3.3); *quid esset ira satis explicitum est* (4.1); *quid esset ira quaesitum est* (5.1).
54 The desire to inflict damage is central to the ancient idea of anger.
55 Cf. e.g. the two flatly contradictory *loci de testibus* pronounced by Cicero at *Cael.* 21–2 and 54, or the contradictory tendency of his remarks about Roman translations of Greek drama at *Ac.* 1.10 and *Fin.* 1.4. In each case the view expressed is determined by the immediate argument that it is required to buttress.
56 This fantasy is Albertini's (pp. 251ff.).
57 The words up to this point summarize everything said from the lacuna to the end of chapter 4. This supports my contention that 1–2 are viewed separately as an *exordium*.
58 The two closest passages in Aristotle are *EN* 1109b17f., 1126b1f., where he describes people who get angry as sometimes earning praise for being ἀνδρώδεις, and thus suitable as rulers.
59 *Inst.* 3.8.22.
60 Cf. e.g. Arist. *EN* 1135b21. By 'necessary' in this context I mean 'an inescapable part of our nature'. The Peripatetics would have agreed that this was true of anger, the Stoics would not. This, too, is the kind of meaning (i.e. the inevitability of acting in a certain way) which Quintilian is concerned with. A different sense of *necessarius* is to be found at e.g. *Ira* 1.9.2 where it is associated with *utilis* and means 'required in order to achieve a given object'. This seems to be the sense of *necessaria* at 6.1 in the interlocutor's objection to Seneca's characterization of anger as unnatural, but there may be some ambiguity. The interlocutor's full argument would be: Punishment is a necessary part of human life. Punishment requires anger. Therefore anger is a necessary (i.e. natural) part of human life.

61 For a similar intrusion of technical Stoic argument into a general ethical discussion cf. *Vit. Beat.* 8.4–5.
62 Cf. *Epist.* 40, *passim*.
63 Cf. the travelling metaphor at the very end of the work: ... *hanc spem, dum ad verum pervenistis, alite in animis* ... (19.4).
64 15.4; 18.3; 19.3.
65 7.1; 14.3.
66 Cf. Grimal, *Commentaire*, ad 5.1.
67 E.g. the divine nature of the *sapiens* (3.3; 4.2); the value of suffering as a stimulus to and material for virtue (4.3.).
68 *Ut tam tutus sit ab iniuria quam illa quae rettuli* (3.5); ... *tuta securitas in hostium terra* (4.3); cf. *securitas autem proprium bonum sapientis est* (13.5).
69 *Iniuria propositum hoc habet aliquem malo afficere.*
70 5.3–7.1; 7.2–9.5.
71 7.1; cf. 2.2; 3.1ff.
72 9.2–5.
73 The distinction between arguments that are *propria* and those that are *communia* (10.1) does not seem to be of structural significance: cf. Grimal, *Commentaire*, ad loc.
74 10.2.
75 10.3; 11.1.
76 Cf. Epicur. *Sent.* 16. Seneca's technique of seeking support for Stoicism from Epicurus is, of course, familiar from the earlier *Epistles*.
77 Cf. n. 26.
78 This is hardly to be wondered at since anger is, in Seneca's terms, the wrong reaction to *iniuria*. Dealing with *iniuria* and avoiding anger thus come to virtually the same thing.
79 Cf. *quoniam quae de ira quaeruntur tractavimus, accedamus ad remedia eius* (*Ira* 2.18.1).
80 2.1–3; 7.1; 14.3.
81 15.4; 18.3; 19.3; cf. *virilem* (1.1).
82 6.2; 9.4; 11.1; 13.1; 14.3; 15.2–3.
83 3.3; 4.2; 6.8; 8.2–3.
84 4.1–3; 5.4–5; 6.8; 8.3; 9.1; 10.4; 16.2; 19.3–4, etc.
85 Cf. E. R. Dodds, *Plato, Gorgias* (Oxford, 1959), pp. 1–5.
86 Cf. e.g. the subtle interlacing of the themes of wealth/warfare as against poverty/*inertia* (= love) in 1.1, or the complete unobtrusiveness of the modulations from one theme to another at 1.3.33–5, 49–52, and 79–83.
87 Cf. C. O. Brink, *Horace on Poetry* (Cambridge, vol. 1 1963, vol. 2 1971), *passim*, but especially the masterly essay 'Poetic patterns in the "Ars Poetica" and the "Odes"' in vol. 2, pp. 445ff.
88 Cf. *Epist.* 114. 13.
89 Cf. *Inst.* 10.1.125–31, a fine example of praising with faint damns.
90 Tac. *Ann.* 13.3. In general see too B. Mortureux, *Recherches sur le 'De Clementia' de Sénèque*, Collection Latomus 128 (Brussels, 1973).

III

Letters to Lucilius

D. A. Russell

1

'Tu me', inquis, 'vitare turbam iubes, secedere et conscientia esse contentum? ubi illa praecepta vestra quae imperant in actu mori?' Quid? ego tibi videor inertiam suadere? In hoc me recondidi et fores clusi, ut prodesse pluribus possem. Nullus mihi per otium dies exit; partem noctium studiis vindico; non vaco somno sed succumbo, et oculos vigilia fatigatos cadentesque in opere detineo. Secessi non tantum ab hominibus sed a rebus, et in primis a meis rebus: posterorum negotium ago. Illis aliqua quae possint prodesse conscribo; salutares admonitiones, velut medicamentorum utilium compositiones, litteris mando, esse illas efficaces in meis ulceribus expertus, quae etiam si persanata non sunt, serpere desierunt. (8.1–2)

('Are you asking me', you say, 'to avoid the crowd, to retire and be content with my conscience? Where are the precepts of your school that enjoin death in activity?' Do you really think I am counselling inaction? I have hidden myself away and closed the doors for a purpose: to be of service to more people. Not a day of mine passes in idleness; I claim part of the night for study; I have no time for sleep, though I yield to it; I keep my eyes at work, weary as they are and dropping with wakefulness. I have retired not only from men, but from affairs, and especially from my own affairs: it is posterity's business I am doing. For them, I am writing down some things which may be helpful; I am committing to paper salutary admonitions, like prescriptions for useful medicines, having found them efficacious in my own ulcers – which, even if not fully healed, have at least stopped spreading.)

This passage sets the scene well. In the immediately preceding letter, Seneca had warned Lucilius of the moral dangers of the crowd, and especially of gladiatorial and animal shows.[1] In this, he speaks of the positive side of his *secessus*; a life of studying and writing philosophy is in fact more useful than a life of legal and political services to friends. He is turning his own experience to the good of others.

But what precisely are the *salutares admonitiones*? Are they something identifiable in his literary works? Seneca's period of retirement, like Cicero's, was a time of intense literary activity. It was indeed an anxious time, a *meditatio mortis*: the obsession with suicide in the letters and the ultimate outcome both make this plain. But it was also very productive: *De Otio*, *De Providentia* and *Quaestiones Naturales* date from this period, not to speak of the Letters themselves and the lost, perhaps never completed, work on *moralis philosophia*.[2] It might of course be this last to which he refers in our passage; but to judge from the topics excerpted, or hived off, from it in the Letters, it was a comprehensive theoretical work, not a collection of practical admonitions. We are surely meant to think rather of the Letters themselves; they are specimens of an activity of 'moral consultancy', real or imaginary, which Seneca wants us to regard as his substitute for the life of political action. The philosopher in fact offers a higher kind of *otium*, for which the rulers of this world provide the external conditions (73.1, 10):[3]

> Errare mihi videntur qui existimant philosophiae fideliter deditos contumaces esse ac refractarios, contemptores magistratuum aut regum eorumve per quos publica administrantur. Ex contrario enim nulli adversus illos gratiores sunt, nec inmerito; nullis enim plus praestant quam quibus frui tranquillo otio licet . . . Philosophia . . . confitebitur ergo multum se debere ei cuius administratione ac providentia contingit illi pingue otium et arbitrium sui temporis et imperturbata publicis occupationibus quies.

> (People are wrong, I think, who believe that those who are loyal to philosophy are contumacious and refractory, despisers of magistrates or princes or those who control public affairs. On the contrary, no class of persons is more grateful to these – and deservedly so; for philosophers offer most to those who

can enjoy peaceful leisure ... Philosophy ... will therefore confess that she owes much to the man through whose service and foresight she is allowed to enjoy rich leisure, the power to dispose of her own time, and peace undisturbed by public cares.)

Precise dating of the works of retirement is uncertain; but it seems probable that *Quaestiones Naturales* was finished in 63, and that the work on *moralis philosophia* succeeded it as the main endeavour. The Letters are the sort of thing that could be done concurrently; indeed, they refer to work on the ethical treatise (106.2; 108.1; 109.17).

If we look for dates in them, there are some to be found. Letter 91 takes the great fire of Lugdunum as an event lately in the news, and this points to late summer or autumn 64. There are also five passages (18.1; 23.1; 67.1; 86.16; 122.1) where there is some indication of the passage of the seasons.[4] The minimum period which would fit these data is about a year, from autumn 63 to late 64. This assumes that the tardy spring of 23.1 and the still tardy, but more advanced, spring of 67.1 belong to the same year. If we suppose that the letters are thought of as written almost daily, this is not unreasonable; 'spring' could easily cover seven or eight weeks. The alternative is to spread the timetable over two years, and begin in autumn 62. Dates thus arrived at are, of course, dramatic dates. It seems safe to assume that the correspondence is intended to look chronological. But to assume further that the letters were all written in this order, or that the absolute dates are dates of composition, is to go further than the evidence warrants.

The question of the relation of the Letters to real facts has been very much discussed. There are two lines of approach. One is from the expectations we can reasonably form from what we know of the theory and practice of epistolography. The other is from the evaluation of the internal evidence of the Letters. The most divergent views have been held. At one extreme, Hermann Peter took the collection as a set of moral discourses to the youth of Rome, dedicated to Lucilius, in the same sense in which the *Naturales Quaestiones* were dedicated to him.[5] At the other end of the scale, writers like Eugène Albertini[6] treated the whole correspondence as real, and explain difficulties by saying that some

Letters have been expurgated or suppressed. As usual, extremes are too simple.

On the question of form, Seneca himself has some professions to make (75.1):

> Minus tibi accuratas a me epistulas mitti quereris. Quis enim accurate loquitur nisi qui vult putide loqui? Qualis sermo meus esset si una desideremus aut ambularemus, inlaboratus et facilis, tales esse epistulas meas volo, quae nihil habent accersitum nec fictum.

> (You complain that the letters I send you are not careful enough. Who talks carefully unless he wishes to talk affectedly? I want my letters, which have no artificial or fictitious side to them, to be like what my conversation would be if we were sitting or walking together: easy and unlaboured.)

Here two concepts of what a literary letter should be like are made to conflict. Lucilius complains of lack of *cura*; he wants something more like Pliny's *epistulas si quas paulo curatius* (v. 1, *accuratius*) *scripsissem*.[7] Seneca's answer is that the letters should have the freedom of actual conversation. Now in the classic account of the theory of letter-writing in Demetrius (223ff.), we have in effect the same two attitudes. Artemon, the editor of Aristotle's letters, held that a letter was 'as it were one side of a dialogue' and should be written in the same manner. Demetrius corrects this: a letter needs more finish than a dialogue, because, instead of reproducing impromptu speech as the dialogue does, it is a written work, 'and in a manner of speaking is sent as a gift'. Seneca's view is bound up, as the context shows, with his insistence that *res* matter more than *verba*, and that the problem of philosophy is a matter not only of intellect (*ingenium*) but also of the soul (*animus*). His notion of what he is doing follows from this. He would therefore agree with part of Demetrius's prescription, and especially the doctrine (227) that a letter is an 'image of one's mind'. But he disagrees at least in practice with other parts. Demetrius excludes 'writing about sophisms and physics' from letter-writing; the longer letters in Seneca are a flagrant breach of this.

What does *nihil accersitum nec fictum* imply? It does not, I suspect, refer to style, like the rest of the sentence, but to content;

Seneca is saying that his letters contain only points of view that he believes in. We must read this, however, as we should read all such professions in ancient literature, as a pronouncement that helps to define the *persona*. It would be naïve to treat it as a straightforward statement of fact. And what about *inlaboratus et facilis*? This clearly does refer to style. In interpreting it, we have again to be on our guard. 'Unlaboured' is a relative term, and it would be wrong to imagine that Seneca is suggesting that his letters abandon the rules of formal prose. They certainly do not: the rhythms are regular,[8] the rhetorical devices familiar from his other works are there in force. The special characteristics of ordinary speech – lively imagery, short sentences, homely sayings – give a distinct flavour to the Letters, but they do not make them a radically different kind of book.

There is something of a paradox in the situation. Seneca's relative carelessness about literary form, which in so facile a writer is naturally more than a profession, has the consequence that he does not consistently study to be simple. The Letters often rise in tone to the high, emotional rhetoric of the treatises. This is part of their lack of *cura*. They are, of course, what Pliny calls *scholasticae litterae*.[9] In other words, they belong not so much to the tradition of the theorists, of Pliny himself, and of the trivial epistles of the Greek Second Sophistic, but to the philosophical line of Plato and Epicurus. But they are also much influenced by Cicero, whose unstudied day-by-day correspondence gave Atticus immortality. Seneca's claims are proud (21.4–5):

> Quis Idomenea nosset nisi Epicurus illum litteris suis incidisset? Omnes illos megistanas et satrapas et regem ipsum ex quo Idomenei titulus petebatur oblivio alta suppressit. Nomen Attici perire Ciceronis epistulae non sinunt. Nihil illi profuisset gener Agrippa et Tiberius progener et Drusus Caesar pronepos; inter tam magna nomina taceretur nisi sibi Cicero illum adplicuisset. . . . Quod Epicurus amico suo potuit promittere, hoc tibi promitto, Lucili: habebo apud posteros gratiam, possum mecum duratura nomina educere.

> (Who would have known Idomeneus, if Epicurus had not inscribed him in his letters? Deep oblivion drowns all the nabobs and magnates, even the king himself, from whom Idomeneus's title to fame was derived. Cicero's letters do not

let Atticus's name perish. That Agrippa was his son-in-law, Tiberius his grandson-in-law, and Drusus his great-grandson would have done him no good; he would have gone unmentioned among all those great names if Cicero had not attached him to himself. . . . What Epicurus was able to promise his friend, I promise you, Lucilius: I shall have influence with posterity, I am capable of raising up names to endure with me.)

Who was this Lucilius? How important is it that Seneca chose him? The Letters duly supply a fair amount of biographical detail. He was of equestrian status (44.2), had held posts in the imperial service in the Alps and in Illyria (31.9), and at the time reflected in the Letters was procurator in Sicily (45.1; 49.3; 79.1), nearing retirement but younger than Seneca (26.7). Of humble origin from Pompeii or the neighbourhood (49.1), he had made his way by his talents (19.3):

> In medium te protulit ingenii vigor, scriptorum elegantia, clarae et nobiles amicitiae.
>
> (The vigour of your intellect, the elegance of your writings, your noble and distinguished friendships, have brought you into the centre of the stage.)

Career and literary interests alike make him seem a reflection of Seneca himself; and this, we may well think, is the key fact that brings the correspondence to life. Marcus Aurelius wrote 'to himself'; Seneca writes to an *alter ego*. In any case, the role that Lucilius has to play in the Letters is distinct from what he played as addressee of the *Naturales Quaestiones* and *De Providentia*. He clearly is in some sense a character in the plot. His 'progress' under Seneca's guidance, his efforts to obey the peremptory *vindica te tibi* with which the first letter begins, are a central theme throughout.

It is important, however, not to exaggerate the 'plot'. It is indeed quite conspicuous; consider, for example, this sequence of letter-beginnings from the earlier part of the collection:

2.1 Bonam spem de te concipio.

4.1 Persevera ut coepisti.

19.1 (Epistulae tuae) iam non promittunt de te sed spondent.

20.1 Mea ... gloria erit, si te istinc ubi sine spe exeundi fluctuaris extraxero.

31.1 Agnosco Lucilium meum; incipit quem promiserat exhibere.

And the development from simple *praecepta* or 'useful thoughts' in the earlier letters to the lengthy and complex doctrinal discussions of the central and later part of the collection may plausibly be thought to reflect not only Seneca's reading and a tendency to handle the genre with growing freedom, but also Lucilius's progress in Stoic learning. All the same, we must not overlook the fact that short and simple letters occur in the later part also. For example, letters of support in testing situations are to be found throughout: comfort (of a kind) in legal troubles (24), consolation in illness (78) or in trouble with runaway slaves (107). Lucilius never rises superior to fortune; if he ever did, the correspondence would cease, as surely as C. S. Lewis's *Screwtape Letters* (an instructive contrast in many ways) ends with the failure of poor Wormwood.

It is, I hope, evident that the plot, such as it is, need not be real; in other words, it need not reflect actual progress or setbacks in Lucilius's character. Our appreciation of the work should not be much affected by a failure to resolve to everyone's satisfaction the question whether it in fact is real. There is not much to go on here; it is not easy to say what sort of material we should expect in a real correspondence that could not be counterfeited in an imaginary one. Allusions that seem both pointless and obscure would perhaps be an indication, though an unsure one. For example (42.5):

> Meministi, cum quendam adfirmares esse in tua potestate, dixisse me volaticum esse ac levem et te non pedem eius tenere sed pennam? Mentitus sum: pluma tenebatur, quam remisit et fugit. Scis quos postea tibi exhibuerit ludos, quam multa in caput suum casura temptaverit. Non videbat se per aliorum pericula in suum ruere; non cogitabat quam onerosa essent quae petebat, etiam si supervacua non essent.
>
> (Do you remember, when you declared that a certain person

was in your power, I said he was liable to fly away, unreliable; and it wasn't his foot you'd got hold of, it was his wing. I was wrong. He was held by a feather, and he let it go and got away. You know what a game he led you thereafter, all the attempts he made that were doomed ro recoil on his own head. He didn't see that he was rushing into his own peril through the perils of others; he did not consider how onerous were the things he sought, even if they were not superfluous.)

This sounds enigmatic; Seneca has been proved right in his pessimistic view of somebody's character about which Lucilius has been too credulous. No names, no details; we have to guess what we can. Now it seems to me important to realize that the enigma is not puzzling: we can understand the drift of the passage perfectly well without knowing any more. In this it differs from the enigmas that one finds, for example, in Cicero's private notes to Atticus. Let us consider the context. The letter begins with a similar riddle. Someone, unnamed, has convinced Lucilius that he is a *vir bonus*. Even in an everyday sense, not to speak of the Stoic sense, this cannot be true; and as a matter of fact, Seneca continues, the man only lacks opportunity to display his viciousness. The *volaticus* is a parallel case. He had not renounced worldly ambition, or made a proper judgment of *supervacua*. He is in fact not a treacherous business associate, as might appear at first sight, but a disappointing philosophical 'patient'. The conclusion shows this; for Seneca goes on, not to lecture Lucilius on credulity, but to preach a lesson on true and false values, picking up the word *supervacua*. The two unsatisfactory characters, whether they are real or imaginary, have done their job; the wrongs they have done Lucilius and his disappointment matter less than the lesson we learn from observing them, namely that their imperfections spring from false evaluations of things. The second part of the Letter hangs together with the first. There is nothing in the enigmas to suggest that they are part of a real, private communication.

This whole question of the reality of the correspondence is bound up with that of its arrangement. Here again, very diverse views have been held. Did Seneca write a letter every day or so, without much idea where tomorrow's material was coming from, and then publish them in the order in which they were written? Or did he plan the work as a whole, devise Book I as a general introduction, and place his material artfully to preserve both variety and continuity of interest?[10]

The book-divisions are significant. They are at least as old as Aulus Gellius, and may well be Seneca's own. The first three books (Letters 1–29) certainly form a separate whole. The letters in this series regularly have a postscript, in the shape of a 'thought for the day', often from Epicurus, which Seneca represents as a regular instalment that Lucilius expects him to pay.[11] Now, in 33.1, Seneca makes Lucilius complain that this practice of the *priores epistulae* is not still being continued. Letter 33 thus belongs to the new series, but is not the first of the series, since the implication is that Lucilius has already received letters in the new style.[12] Moreover, Book III ends with what looks like a transitional episode, in which Seneca appears to leave Lucilius for a more serious patient, Marcellinus (29.9):

> Dum me illi paro, tu interim, qui potes, qui intellegis unde quo evaseris et ex eo suspicaris quousque sis evasurus, compone mores tuos, attolle animum, adversus formidata consiste.

> (While I am getting ready for him, do you – who have the capacity, who understand where you have risen from and what points you have reached, and glimpse the heights to which you will yet rise – do you, I say, put your character in order, lift up your soul, stand firm against what you fear.)

It is tempting to think that Seneca meant this as an end of a phase.

It is clear also that there are groups of related letters in the rest of the corpus; but any reconstruction of the process of composition is bound to be hypothetical. This was a literary work of pretensions; design therefore plays a large part in its internal arrangement. But it was also a facile and rapid work, and its nature made it easy to expand and develop as the business went on. The probabilities seem to me to be these:

(*i*) Seneca conceived a series of letters to Lucilius on moral progress, *otium*, and philosophic life and death. Lucilius's personality helped to determine what the book was like; but it was not an actual correspondence. Books I–III at least belong to this initial impulse; the arrangement was deliberate, the epistolary form an essential.

(*ii*) Seneca found this a congenial medium. Not only reflections that could be based on incidents or occasions, but also consolations, discussions of technical philosophical points, and *Beiträge* of the *moralis philosophia* could be handled in this way. Grouping was still important; but there was no overall plot, and no end was envisaged.

(*iii*) Apart from Books I–III, we do not know in what groups the Letters were published, or indeed how much came out in Seneca's lifetime. But, given the scale and time available, it seems likely that the order in which we have them not only gives the relative dramatic dates but more or less reproduces the order of composition. We must of course allow for the possibility that Seneca kept some letters in the drawer and used them later; this might help to explain the reversion to earlier types and themes in the last few books.

In a word: the *Epistulae* are a work of art that claims immortality, but a work that was growing and developing throughout Seneca's last year or two of life. Most people think them his greatest achievement.

2

There are three immediately attractive features that go a long way towards explaining this popularity: the self-revelation, the vivid contemporary detail, and the literary criticism.

(*i*) The self-portrait that emerges is a fascinating one; the modern reader recognizes a fellow neurotic,[13] apparently prepared to disclose his most private history. We hear some revealing anecdotes of youth, and of Seneca's formidable father. At one stage, Seneca took a vegetarian diet; a mild aberration, but one that had dangers at the time, because of its association with foreign *superstitiones* to which Tiberius's administration was hostile (108.22):

> Patre itaque meo rogante, qui non calumniam timebat sed philosophiam oderat, ad pristinam consuetudinem redii; nec difficulter mihi ut inciperem melius cenare persuasit.
>
> (At the request of my father, who did not fear calumny but

did hate philosophy, I returned to my old habits; nor did he find it difficult to persuade me to begin to dine better.)

There is a lot here: admiration of his father's courage, recognition of his dislike of the son's lifelong enthusiasm; and an ironical glance at his own easily-overcome ideals.

A great deal of the autobiography in the Letters is concerned with illness; Seneca deserves a place with Aristides among the articulate hypochondriacs of the ancient world. Consoling Lucilius on an illness, he goes back to his own young days (78.1–2):

> Vexari te destillationibus crebris ac febriculis, quae longas destillationes et in consuetudinem adductas sequuntur, eo molestius mihi est quia expertus sum hoc genus valetudinis, quod inter initia contempsi – poterat adhuc adulescentia iniurias ferre et se adversus morbos contumaciter gerere – deinde succubui et eo perductus sum ut ipse destillarem, ad summam maciem deductus. Saepe impetum cepi abrumpendae vitae: patris me indulgentissimi senectus retinuit. Cogitavi enim non quam fortiter ego mori possem, sed quam ille fortiter desiderare non posset.

> (That you are troubled by frequent catarrhs and the little fevers that follow long and habitual catarrh is the more grievous news to me, because I have myself experienced this sort of ill-health. I despised it at first – my youth could still tolerate injuries and take a bold line with illness – but later I succumbed and reached the stage of dripping away altogether, reduced as I was to a state of great emaciation. I often formed the impulse to break life off short; but my indulgent father's great age held me back. I thought not of how capable I was of dying bravely, but of how incapable he was of bearing my my loss bravely.)

In the ill-health of old age, Seneca reasons in a similar way about his wife (104.3–5):

> Ille qui non uxorem, non amicum tanti putat ut diutius in vita commoretur, qui perseverabit mori, delicatus est. . . . summae humanitatis existimo, senectutem suam, cuius maximus fructus est securior sui tutela et vitae usus animosior,

attentius ⟨curare⟩, si scias alicui id tuorum esse dulce utile optabile. Habet praeterea in se non mediocre ista res gaudium et mercedem; quid enim iucundius quam uxori tam carum esse ut propter hoc tibi carior fias?

(A man who doesn't value a wife or a friend highly enough to stay alive, but who insists on dying, is self-indulgent. . . . It is, I believe, a mark of great humanity to cherish one's old age, whose greatest advantage is that one need not guard oneself so anxiously but can use life with more spirit, if you know it to be pleasant, useful and desirable for someone in your family. Moreover, there is a good deal of joy and reward in it; what is pleasanter than being so dear to your wife that you become thereby more dear to yourself?)

Seneca suffered from asthma, a recurrent rehearsal for death (54.1–2), and from fevers and fainting fits. He lived to a strict régime, and swam regularly in sea or river, or the notoriously chilly Aqua Virgo, till he was an elderly man (83.5). The daily round is a natural topic for a letter (83.3–4):

Hodiernus dies solidus est, nemo ex illo quicquam mihi eripuit; totus inter stratum lectionemque divisus est; minimum exercitationi corporis datum; et hoc nomine ago gratias senectuti: non magno mihi constat. Cum me movi, lassus sum; hic autem est exercitationis etiam fortissimis finis. Progymnastas meos quaeris? unus mihi sufficit Pharius, puer, ut scis, amabilis, sed mutabitur: iam aliquem teneriorem quaero. Hic quidem ait nos eandem crisin habere, quia utrique dentes cadunt. Sed iam vix illum adsequor currentem et intra paucissimos dies non potero: vide quid exercitatio cotidiana proficiat. Cito magnum intervallum fit inter duos in diversum euntes: eodem tempore ille ascendit, ego descendo, nec ignoras quanto ex his velocius alterum fiat.

(Today is a solid day; no one has stolen a scrap of it from me. It has been entirely spent between bed and reading, with a very small concession to physical exercise. This is a point I am grateful to old age for; it doesn't cost much. I feel tired as soon as I move, and tiredness is the end of exercise even for the strongest. You ask about my running-partners?

> Pharius is sufficient by himself; he's a lovable boy, as you know, but he will change; I'm already looking for a younger one. Pharius says that he and I are both at the same stage, we're both losing our teeth. But I can hardly keep up with him, and in a few days I shan't be able to: observe the effect of daily exercise! There soon comes to be a great gap between two people going in different directions: while he goes up, I go down; and you know how much quicker the latter process is!)

This is typical Seneca: the moral, the irony at his own expense, the obsession with age, the unembarrassed banter with the slave-boy.[14]

(*ii*) Description leading to reflection is a common formula in the Letters, and it accounts for some of the best of them. Letter 12 is a notable example. Seneca visits a villa he owns. The building he designed needs repair, the trees he planted are old and gnarled, his child *deliciae* is a toothless old man. It all shows him his old age: 'let us embrace it and love it'. Another trip to the country is the subject of Letter 104. Seneca is ill; the change of air and interest cures him (104.6):

> Ut primum gravitatem urbis excessi et illum odorem culinarum fumantium quae motae quidquid pestiferi vaporis sorbuerunt cum pulvere effundunt, protinus mutatam valetudinem sensi. Quantum deinde adiectum putas viribus postquam vineas attigi! in pascuum emissus cibum meum invasi.

> (As soon as I had left the heaviness of the city, the smell of smoking kitchens whose activity diffuses with the dust every particle of pestiferous vapour they have sucked in, I was immediately conscious of a change in my condition. How much do you think was then added to my strength when I got to a vine-yard?[15] I was put out to pasture, and I fell upon my food.)

One would think this proved the value of travel; on the contrary, the lesson that follows is the familiar one that the mind can be secure anywhere, it is not the place that matters.

There is a cluster of letters of this form in Books V and VI, and a good many more in Books VIII–IX. A whole series is connected with incidents observed while visiting Campania: the immorality of Baiae (51); Seneca's adventure by sea in crossing from Naples to Pozzuoli (53); Vatia's villa (55); the noises of the bath-house (56); the return to Naples through the tunnel (57). Close observation and vivid detail reveal a talent not often indulged. Seneca's real-life description of the public baths makes a splendid commentary on the scenes in Petronius where Trimalchio takes exercise before his dinner (56.1–2):[16]

> Propone nunc tibi omnia genera vocum quae in odium possunt aures adducere: cum fortiores exercentur et manus plumbo graves iactant, cum aut laborant aut laborantem imitantur, gemitus audio, quotiens retentum spiritum remiserunt, sibilas et acerbissimas respirationes; cum in aliquem inertem et hac plebeia unctione contentum incidi, audio crepitum inlisae manus umeris, quae prout plana pervenit aut concava, ita sonum mutat. Si vero pilicrepus supervenit et numerare coepit pilas, actum est. Adice nunc scordalum et furem deprensum et illum cui vox sua in balineo placet, adice nunc eos qui in piscinam cum ingenti inpulsae aquae sono saliunt. Praeter istos quorum, si nihil aliud, rectae voces sunt, alipilum cogita tenuem et stridulam vocem quo sit notabilior subinde exprimentem nec umquam tacentem nisi dum vellit alas et alium pro se clamare cogit.

> (Just imagine all the kinds of noises that can disgust the ear. When the more vigorous take exercise and toss their arms about with the lead weights, straining or pretending to strain, I hear them groan; when they let out a deep breath, I hear the hissing and the grating. When I happen on some lazy fellow, content with a man-in-the-street oiling, I hear the smack of hand on shoulder, which varies according to whether the descending palm is flat or cupped. And if the ball-player turns up and starts to count the balls, it's all over. Don't forget the brawler either, the thief caught in the act, and the man who likes his own voice in the bath. Don't forget the gentlemen who leap into the basin with a mighty splash. At least, all their voices are natural; but you have also to imagine the hair-plucker with the shrill falsetto that he constantly uses to attract attention, never silent except when he's plucking armpits and making somebody else howl instead.)

(*iii*) The Letters are also much concerned with literature. This was in accordance with the conventions of the genre; Cicero's and Pliny's letters often deal with such things. Moreover, Lucilius was himself a man of letters; Seneca quotes his poetry (24.21) and suggests Etna as a possible theme; Ovid, Virgil and Cornelius Severus had pointed the way rather than exhausted the subject (79.5–6: an important passage for our understanding of 'originality' in Latin literature). It is obvious that Seneca had a wide knowledge of earlier poetry, especially Lucretius and Virgil.[17]

It is obvious too that he is interested in language – in questions of usage or archaism for example – even though he recognizes that the work of the *grammaticus* is on a level below the philosopher's.[18] Nevertheless, the general philosophical theme of the correspondence determines the literary point of view also. Philosophy is a matter of *res, non verba* (40, 115); dignity and plainness are important; style is a reflection of character. Letter 114, a key document in our knowledge of first-century stylistic theory, is wholly moralistic in approach.[19] Affected style is a manifestation of *luxuria*, not only the extravagance of the *discinctus* Maecenas, but all the excesses of archaists and others who choose their words on principles not related to sense. Letter 115, the sequel, underlines the moral (115.1–2):

> Quaere quid scribas, non quemadmodum; et hoc ipsum non ut scribas sed ut sentias, ut illa quae senseris magis adplices tibi et velut signes. Cuiuscumque orationem videris sollicitam et politam, scito animum quoque non minus esse pusillis occupatum. Magnus ille remissius loquitur et securius; quaecumque dicit plus habent fiduciae quam curae. Nosti comptulos iuvenes, barba et coma nitidos, de capsula totos: nihil ab illis speraveris forte, nihil solidum . . . Non est ornamentum virile concinnitas.

> (Ask what to write, not how; and ask this, not in order to write, but in order to feel, so as to apply your sentiment more closely to yourself and as it were seal it. Anyone whose style you see to be anxious and polished, has a mind, you may be sure, occupied with little things. Your great man speaks in a more relaxed and carefree way. In all his words there is more confidence than care. You know those young

dandies with their beards and hair neat and glistening, all straight out of the band-box: you can't expect anything strong and solid from that quarter. . . . Neatness isn't a masculine adornment.)

Observe the key words: *securius, forte, virile*, on the positive side; *sollicitam, politam, concinnitas* on the negative.

These three features – the autobiography, the social description, the literary attitude – are thus all part of the grand design of representing the philosophic life in the personal style of a set of letters. At the same time, it is comparatively easy to isolate them, and it is very understandable if one finds these incidentals a great deal more attractive than what we may call the central propositions of the argument: the superiority of mind over body; the praise of philosophy as a guide of life; the proper valuation of 'indifferent' things, and especially death; the difference between joy and pleasure; the evils of *luxuria*; the pursuit of *humanitas*. These and some similar motifs are the threads out of which various patterns of precept, example and exhortation are woven. How this is done is best seen if we look at two or three letters in some detail.

3

I begin with Letter 24, one of the more elaborate ones in the first series.[20] The occasion is provided by Lucilius's anxiety about a lawsuit with which he is threatened by an enemy's *furor*. Instead of the expected advice to hope for the best and not face trouble till it comes (advice he had given in 13.4–5), Seneca judges that Lucilius is now ready for a more radical cure: think of the worst, and be prepared even for that. The threatened evil will be either *non magnum* or *non longum*, like pain (24.14), according to a celebrated Epicurean line of consolation.[21] *Exempla* of endurance are easy to find: Rutilius, Matellus, Socrates, Mucius bore exile, prison or death with fortitude (24.6):

'Decantatae', inquis, 'in omnibus scholis fabulae istae sunt; iam mihi, cum ad contemnendam mortem ventum fuerit, Catonem narrabis'. Quidni ego narrem . . . ?

('The stories', you say, 'are chanted in every rhetorical school; I've no doubt, when we get to Contempt for Death, you'll be telling the tale of Cato.' And why shouldn't I ?)

Seneca's use of the most overworked material he can find is thus deliberate; it is part of his presentation of the good life as traditional wisdom: there is nothing new to know; the crux lies in making the effort to act.

The point of the example of Cato is soon seen; it is to introduce the possibility of death as an escape from evil. So far from being something to fear, it does us the service of freeing us from fear of other things (24.12):

> Securus itaque inimici minas audi; et quamvis conscientia tibi tua fiduciam faciat, tamen, quia multa extra causam valent, et quod aequissimum est spera et ad id te quod est inimicissimum compara.

> (Hear therefore your enemy's threats without anxiety; and, however much your conscience gives you confidence, nevertheless, since many factors have weight apart from the case itself, hope for the most favourable outcome; but at the same time prepare yourself for the most unfavourable.)

It is not much comfort in a real situation to suggest suicide as the remedy for failure; and this reflection strengthens the impression that the story of the *iudicium* is not a real one. All the same, Seneca did after all take his own life a year or two later. His preoccupation with suicide throughout the letters is very striking; and he seems to have viewed it, even more than most Stoics, as a matter of free choice to end your life when you will.[22]

Further very commonplace thoughts follow. The essential step in facing a situation like this is to recognize the true values of things. We are all deceived by false appearances, as children are by masks. The masks must be stripped off. For example, the pain of torture seems terrible, and Seneca has the linguistic resources to bring it vividly before us (24.14):

> Singulis articulis singula machinamenta quibus extorqueantur aptata et mille alia instrumenta excarnificandi particulatim hominis . . .

> (Special instruments designed for the wrenching apart of particular joints, a thousand other tools for butchering a man bit by bit . . .)

The cries of the suffering are excruciating (24.14):

> gemitus et exclamationes et vocum inter lacerationem
> elisarum acerbitatem.

> (Groans, cries, the hoarseness of words forced out in the
> process of laceration.)

But the invalid or the girl having a baby tolerates as much.

All familiar talk: *saepe audisti, saepe dixisti*. The point is: have you taken it in? It is a common complaint against us that we are concerned with the words of philosophy, not its works. Now is the time to prove the charge false. Do not let your mind sink under anxiety, for that will impair its capacity for effort when the time comes to be up and doing. There are consolatory reflections to help: for example, the thought that even pleasures may lead to pain, dinners to indigestion, drink to paralysis and trembling, lust to degeneration of the joints. Whatever the misfortune, a ready remedy comes to mind (24.17):

> Pauper fiam: inter plures ero. Exul fiam: ibi me natum putabo
> quo mittar. Alligabor: quid enim? nunc solutus sum? ad hoc
> me natura grave corporis mei pondus adstrinxit. Moriar:
> hoc dicis: desinam aegrotare posse, desinam alligari posse,
> desinam mori posse.

> (I shall become poor; then I shall be with the majority. I
> shall become an exile; then I shall think myself a native of the
> place I am sent to. I shall be bound in chains: well? Am I
> free now? Nature has bound me to this grievous weight of my
> body. I shall die. You mean, I shall stop being liable to be ill,
> I shall stop being liable to be bound in chains, I shall stop
> being liable to die.)

Once again, Seneca harps deliberately on the most overworked themes. This strain continues, in the conventional form of a *praeteritio*: *Non sum tam ineptus ut Epicuream cantilenam hoc loco persequar* (I am not so foolish as to repeat the Epicurean refrain at this point). No one is silly enough to believe in Cerberus and ghostly skeletons.[23] Whatever happens after death, whether we survive without the body or are totally destroyed,[24] good and evil are alike taken from us. Lucilius's own poetry provides an appropriate text: *Mors non una venit, sed quae rapit ultima mors est* (We have more deaths than one; the last removes us). So the lesson is not only hackneyed; it is one Lucilius knows himself.

All the letters of this first series conclude with a 'thought for the day', regularly taken from Epicurus. Often they are not closely connected with the main subject. Here, however, there is a connection: Seneca draws on Epicurus for a warning against suicide for the wrong reasons: for boredom, not for contempt of life. *Vitae fastidium* may be the consequence of a sort of shallow philosophy, that makes us exclaim (24.26):

'Quousque eadem? nempe expergiscar dormiam, ⟨sitiam⟩[25] esuriam, algebo aestuabo: fit aliquando et huius rei nausia.'

('How long the same old round? I shall wake up and go to sleep, be thirsty and hungry, be cold and hot. One sometimes feels sick even of this.')

Like the rest of the letter, this *topos* is very much a commonplace. But it is vivid, and the mood of boredom and despair is well evoked. The whole letter is both coherent and moving: this is how the *vir fortis ac sapiens* should approach circumstances in which he may feel it right to end his days.

It may be useful to compare all this with a letter from the latter part of the corpus, Letter 110. This has no occasion like Lucilius's supposed lawsuit; Seneca begins instead by giving a new twist to the initial greeting: *Te saluto et iubeo habere mentem bonam*. This is to replace the customary wish for health by a wish for mental health.[26] But it is also to give a new sense to *mens bona*, Seneca's usual term for a wise and virtuous state of mind. For he goes on:

... hoc est propitios deos omnis, quos habet placatos et faventes quisquis sibi se propitiavit.

Anyone who has made peace with himself has the gods at peace with him too; and this is what it means to have *bona mens*.

Two theological problems now come to mind: the doctrine of the guardian spirit, *genius* or *daimon*, and the question whether the gods care for ordinary mortals. These are dismissed by a form of *praeteritio*: *sepone in praesentia* ... *postea videbimus*. But we should reassure ourselves: the wicked may appear to prosper, but the gods are really against them. What is important is to value our situation aright. Evil often issues in good and good in evil: *Scies plura mala contingere nobis quam accidere*. Seneca makes his point by contrasting the two verbs. Death is near (24.4)

> Prope est rerum omnium terminus, prope est, inquam, et illud unde felix eicitur et illud unde infelix emittitur.

(The end of all things is at hand, at hand, I say, is the point where the happy man is thrown out and the unhappy is let out.)

Here again, the point is verbal: it is explained by 24.8, where Cato *generosum . . . spiritum non emisit sed eiecit*. The wise man's exit is a forceful one. Our hopes and our fears prolong our joys and sorrows; we should measure everything in human terms and contract them.

But there is an easier consolation still. Our fears are vain. As Lucretius said,[27] we are frightened in the light of day as children are frightened in the dark; or rather, we are sillier than the children, because we are in darkness of our own making. Yet we have the means of making the light come: *sed lucescere, si velimus, potest* – but only in one way, by thoroughly soaking ourselves in knowledge of things human and divine. This of course is the standard Stoic definition of philosophy, and Seneca goes on to spell it out. It includes not only ethics, but physics, the study of the origin and destiny of the world. We have neglected this, and for what (110.9)?

> Ab hac divina contemplatione abductum animum in sordida et humilia pertraximus, ut avaritiae serviret, ut, relicto mundo terminisque eius et dominis cuncta versantibus, terram rimaretur et quaereret quid ex illa mali effoderet, non contentus oblatis.

(We have withdrawn our mind from this divine spectacle and dragged it down to a foul and lowly sphere, to be a slave to avarice, to abandon the universe, its bounds and its all-controlling masters, and to ferret about in the earth and see what trouble it can dig up, not content with what comes its way anyhow.)

The movement of this passage is interesting. The last three words contain the clue to what is coming: Seneca has passed from the positive view of philosophy as elevating the mind to a characteristic condemnation of avarice and luxury. God is not to blame for our troubles; all that is good for us is easily obtained, our addiction to pleasure and vainglory is entirely our own fault.

The answer? Once again, *nihil novi*: simply the capacity to distinguish the necessary from the superfluous. But Seneca wishes to go further; it is not enough for glory to despise wild boar or flamingos' tongues; a higher form of asceticism despises even ordinary bread. We detect a note of hysteria:

> Vis ciborum voluptatem contemnere? exitum specta.

> (Would you like to despise the pleasure of food? Look at what happens to it!)[28]

The letter ends with a report of a diatribe of the Stoic teacher Attalus. Witnessing a great procession, he is suddenly convinced of the vanity of riches. They pass like a show. True wealth is being content with little; if that little can be reduced to nothing, freedom is complete and human life can attain to divine felicity:

> Nihil desideres oportet si vis Iovem provocare nihil desiderantem.

> (Want nothing, if you wish to challenge Jupiter, who himself wants nothing.)

This is the loftiest possible expression of the philosopher's aim: to make himself like God.[29]

The resemblances between this letter and Letter 24 are, I think, fairly clear. The thought of suicide is common to both; so is the deliberate use of familiar ideas. The main difference lies in the reference to philosophy as a whole as a means of conversion. It is, I think, fair to see in this a stage in the plot; the long doctrinal letters of the central part of the corpus have deepened the concept of the philosophical life by the addition of an element of theoretical study. One might consider making a comparison with a much greater work, Plato's *Republic*: there, what follows the metaphysical theory of Books VI–VII is on a deeper level because of it.

The long central letters themselves deserve careful study: especially 65, on theories of causation;[30] 88, on the liberal arts as handmaids of philosophy; 92, on the sufficiency of virtue for happiness;[31] 94–5, on the necessity of both elements in ethics, the preceptive and the theoretical. I conclude with a brief word on Letter 90,[32] which deals with the services of philosophy to mankind, and has a particular claim to be read because of its fascinating evidence about ancient anthropological theory.[33]

It makes no concession at all to the epistolary form: no 'occasion', no personal touches. We go straight to the subject. It is the gift of philosophy to us that we live well, *quod bene vivimus*, and not simply exist. And philosophy itself comes from the gods; or rather, the capacity for it does, since if it were not dependent on effort, it would have lost its highest value. This last point is a key one in Seneca's mind; he returns to it later.

Philosophy has only one function: to discover the truth about 'things human and divine'; but she is accompanied by all the virtues (90.3):

> Haec docuit colere divina, humana diligere, et penes deos imperium esse, inter homines consortium. Quod aliquamdiu inviolatum mansit antequam societatem avaritia distraxit et paupertatis causa etiam iis quos fecit locupletissimos fuit.
>
> (She has taught us to worship god and love man, that rule belongs to the gods, that community exists among men. For a time this community remained undamaged, until avarice pulled the union apart and proved a cause of poverty even for those whom she made most wealthy.)

The historical statement, with which most of this letter is concerned, begins in this sentence; but does it begin with *mansit* or with *docuit*? Seneca has been speaking of philosophy as something achieved by effort. Yet in the Golden Age no effort was needed for the achievement of a life indistinguishable externally from that of the *sapiens*. The original *consortium* therefore was not the product of philosophy. Again: primitive men presumably worshipped the gods, but not because philosophy taught them to do so. If therefore we take the *docuit* sentence as general ('has taught' rather than 'taught'), and begin the history at 'quod . . .', a coherent argument appears, even though Seneca (as often) does not mark its stages very clearly.

But difficulties continue. Primitive man needed leaders; these were naturally the *optimi*, the morally best, since this is what corresponds in mankind to strength, or size in bulls or elephants. These leaders were identified by Posidonius, whom Seneca is following, with *sapientes*; Seneca assents. They are however only *sapientes* by analogy, since they do not owe their wisdom to the teaching of philosophy. Moreover, they protected, enriched and restrained their subjects: but why should they need to restrain in a society where, as we are told later (40), 'everyone cared for others as much as for himself'? There seems no way round this; and we must suppose that Seneca has assented to a statement of Posidonius which he should really have rejected. It would be a characteristic slip.

The next stage presents less of a problem. Vice crept in with avarice; kings degenerated into tyrants; laws became necessary. It is easy enough for Seneca to attribute this activity to *sapientes*, as Posidonius did. Zaleucus and Charondas learned to be legislators in the school of Pythagoras.

Hactenus Posidonio adsentior (7). Where Seneca takes issue is over the advance of technology. The material inventions that come with civilization cannot be the work of the *sapiens*, because they are in principle indistinguishable from the materials of luxury. There is no essential difference between inventing a hut and inventing a palace. We should compare the point in 110.12: plain bread is as dispensable as flamingos' tongues. This moral criticism gives Seneca ample opportunity to develop the favourite theme of *luxuria*. He also takes up a number of points in detail: building, weaving, pottery, the arch. Posidonius, though a great philosopher, has been misled by *dulcedo orationis*: yet another victim of the seduction of words.

What does the *sapiens* in fact do? He is, says Seneca, the craftsman of life, *artifex vitae*. In two parallel passages – proof of casual or else deliberately repetitive composition – Seneca enlarges on this. The first account (28–9) is the fuller. Philosophy investigates ethical questions; she distinguishes true evils from apparent, real greatness from empty form. She explains the nature of gods, of the *inferi*, or secondary divinities, *genii* or souls. These are her mysteries, through which she reveals the cosmos to the mind. She returns then to the first principles, to the *logos* that pervades the whole, and to the soul and its nature. Finally, she turns to truth and to logic: both in life and in language there are ambiguities to be resolved. The second passage (34ff.) – which, like the first, contrasts the real actions of the *sapiens* with some that Posidonius attributed to him – is simpler: the first function of the philosopher is to discover and reveal the truth about nature; the second is to teach mankind how to follow the universal law. Once again, he assigns things their true value, and will have us look to that true felicity that needs nothing outside itself.

Philosophy in this sense, says Seneca, cannot have existed in the Golden Age. Before *avaritia* and *luxuria* (36), mankind acted instinctively as the wise act. Theirs was a life of peace and simplicity (4.1):

> Arma cessabant incruentaeque humano sanguine manus odium omne in feras verterant. Illi quos aliquod nemus densum a sole protexerat, qui adversus saevitiam hiemis aut imbris vili receptaculo tuti sub fronde vivebant, placidas transigebant sine suspirio noctes. Sollicitudo nos in nostra purpura versat et acerrimis excitat stimulis: at quam mollem somnum illis dura tellus dabat!

> (Arms were stilled; hands unstained with human blood had turned all their hostility against the beasts. Protected from the sun by some thick wood, living safe under the leaves in their cheap refuge from the savagery of storm or rain, they passed nights of tranquillity without a sigh. Anxiety troubles us in our purple, and goads us with the sharpest spur; what soft sleep the hard ground gave them!)

In much of this letter, Seneca, as elsewhere, appears diffuse, unsubtle, incoherent in his moral vehemence. But a more or less consistent position appears. Philosophy alone gives happiness; it does more than reproduce the bliss of the Golden Age, because it offers not innocent ignorance but virtue born of struggle. It is because his achievement is his own that the *sapiens* towers above primitive innocence. We should recall that he also, in a sense, towers above God, because God is free of fear by nature's doing, but the *sapiens* by his own (53.11).

It is perhaps appropriate to end in this exalted strain. There are many good reasons for valuing the Letters: for their realism of scene and language, for their psychological revelations, for their brilliant technique. But we shall not read them right if we do not also take the main theme seriously. With all the paradoxes and exaggerations, this is Seneca's last word; the manner of his death gives it weight.

Notes

Editions. As well as the editions of F. Haase, O. Hense, and F. Préchac (Budé), which form part of complete Senecas, note: A. Beltrami (1949, ed. 2), and L. D. Reynolds (OCT, 1965). The selection most used in English schools and universities (W. C. Summers, 1910) contains much valuable information and is a good choice.

General interpretation. Besides works cited below, see especially C. Martha, *Les Moralistes sous l'empire romain,* 1865; and the articles of A. M. Guillemin in *REL* 30, 31 and 32 (1952–4).

1 Cf. e.g. 7.3; 70.20; 80.2; 95.33.
2 Cf. M. Lausberg, *Untersuchungen zu Senecas Fragmenten,* 1970, pp. 168ff.
3 Seneca goes on to quote Virgil, *Ecl.* 1.6: 'O Meliboee, deus nobis haec otia fecit . . .' Note both the use of Virgil and the attitude to Nero's Principate.
4 We may compare the fictional use of changing seasons in Longus: 1.9; 1.23; 2.1; 3.12; 4.1.
5 *Der Brief in der römischen Literatur,* 1901, pp. 225ff.
6 *La Composition dans les ouvrages philosophiques de Sénèque,* 1923, pp. 136ff.
7 *Epist.* 1.1: A. N. Sherwin-White, *Commentary,* 1966, pp. 2ff.
8 E.g. in the passage from 8.1 quoted at the beginning of this essay, note the many instances of the commonest *clausulae*: vĭtārĕ tūrbām iŭbēs; ēssĕ cōntēntūm; impĕrānt ĭn āctū mŏrī; ēt fŏrēs clūsī; plūrĭbūs pōssēm; ab hŏmĭnĭbūs sĕd ā rēbūs; ā mĕīs rēbūs; persānātă̆ non sūnt; dēsĭĕrūnt.
9 *Epist.* 9.2.3.
10 Two recent and important books develop this approach: H. Cançik, *Untersuchungen zu Senecas epistulae morales,* 1967; G. Maurach, *Der Bau von Senecas epistulae morales,* 1970.
11 Financial metaphors are common coin in the Letters. It was a field of activity that was often in Seneca's mind: e.g. 21.11; 25.3; 26.5; 36.5; 73.9; 81.3; 81.17; 118.1; 119.1. See D. Steyns, *Métaphores et comparaisons de Sénèque le philosophe,* Ghent, 1906, pp. 99f.
12 *Contra:* Maurach, op. cit., pp. 128–9.
13 A preliminary sketch of an interpretation of this side, E. P. Barker in *OCD*[1], p. 828 (not reprinted in ed. 2).
14 The intimacy and sentiment contrast neatly with the urbane scene-setting of Dio Chrysostom *Orat.* 52.1 (in D. A. Russell and M. Winterbottom, *Ancient Literary Criticism,* 1972, p. 504). Several speeches of Dio recall Senecan letters in their scale, scope and use of an 'occasion' to introduce reflection.
15 Viticulture was a passion of Seneca's, and a profitable one: see 112.2 and the evidence of Columella (3.3.3) and Pliny (*NH* 14.51) on the wonderful yield of the vineyard of the 'Nomentanum'.
16 Petronius 26ff.
17 Note especially 21.5; 86.15; 108.24ff.
18 On the relationship between the *artes liberales* and philosophy, see the important Letter 88, with the commentary of A. Stückelberger, 1965.
19 See A. D. Leeman, *Orationis Ratio,* 1963, pp. 271–83.
20 See I. Hadot, *Seneca und die griechisch-römische Tradition der Seelenleitung,* 1969, pp. 126ff.
21 E.g. *Kuriai Doxai* 15.

LETTERS TO LUCILIUS

22 So J. M. Rist, *Stoic Philosophy*, 1969, pp. 246ff.
23 Cf. Lucretius 3.976; Cicero *Tusc. Disp.* 1.10.
24 Cf. 36.9–10; 71.16; 93.9–10.
25 The supplement is conjectural; editors also print ⟨edam⟩ or ⟨satiabor⟩.
26 Cf. 15.1; H. Koskenniemi, *Studien zur Idee und Phraseologie des griechischen Briefes*, 1956, p. 131, n. 1.
27 For Seneca's use of the poets in this way, see W. Trillitzsch, *Senecas Beweisführung*, 1962, pp. 83–95. The image of the mask is also Lucretian, and from the same context: 3.58.
28 Reflections on luxury of eating: 78.22; 95.15; 119.13–14; *Nat. Quaest.*, 3.17–18; 4.13.
29 Cf. 9.16; 53.12; 73.12.
30 Commentary by G. Scarpat, Brescia, 1970 (ed. 2).
31 K. Reinhardt in *RE* s.v. 'Poseidonios', pp. 757ff.
32 Commentary by S. Blankert, Amsterdam, 1940.
33 On this, see (e.g.) A. O. Lovejoy-G. Boas, *Primitivism and Related Ideas in Antiquity*, Baltimore, 1935; W. Spoerri, *Späthellenistische Berichte über Welt, Kultur und Götter*, Basel, 1959; T. Cole, *Democritus and the Source of Greek Anthropology*, 1967.

IV

The Tragedies

C. D. N. Costa

Senecam nullo Graecorum maiestate inferiorem existimo, cultu vero ac nitore etiam Euripide maiorem (J. C. Scaliger, 1561)

[Seneca's whole writings] penned with a peerless sublimity and loftinesse of style are so far from countenauncing vice, that I doubt whether there bee any among all the Catalogue of Heathen wryters, that with more grauity of Philosophical sentences, more waightynes of sappy words, or greater authority of sound matter beateth down sinne, loose lyfe, dissolute dealinge, and unbrydled sensuality: or that more sensibly, pithily, and bytingly layeth doune the guedon of filthy lust, cloaked dissimulation and odious treachery: which is the dryft, whereunto he leueleth the whole yssue of ech one of his Tragedies. (Thomas Newton, 1581)

In the plays of Seneca, the drama is all in the word, and the word has no further reality behind it. His characters all seem to speak with the same voice, and at the top of it; they recite in turn. (T. S. Eliot, 1927)

The tragedies . . . suggest the clever immaturity of a youngish man. Though false standards of taste and their peculiar survival-position gave them an undue influence on the early moulding of modern tragedy in England and elsewhere, it is now less by their own merits than as a clue to the author's character that they interest us. (E. P. Barker, 1949)

These criticisms give some idea of the change of attitude towards Seneca's tragedies during the last four hundred years. The veneration in which they were held by translators and imitators in the sixteenth and seventeenth centuries was succeeded by dislike, contempt and neglect, and it is only in comparatively recent years that the plays are being evaluated on their own terms, and judged in relation to the educational training which produced them. Aspects of their influence on English literature are examined elsewhere in this volume: this essay will confine itself to the tragedies themselves, and try to arrive at some conclusions on Seneca's purpose in writing them, by considering first some dominant literary influences which gave them birth and then their characteristic stylistic features.

So far as we know the plays attributed to Seneca – the only surviving complete Latin tragedies – represent virtually his whole poetic output, for most of the epigrams that passed under his name are very probably spurious. The titles are: *Hercules Furens, Troades, Phoenissae, Medea, Phaedra* (or *Hippolytus*), *Oedipus, Agamemnon, Thyestes, Hercules Oetaeus, Octavia*.[1] The *Octavia* has a scarcity interest as the only extant Latin historical play, *fabula praetexta*, but on good grounds (partly of metre) it is nowadays usually held to be not by Seneca. Of the others, the *Hercules Oetaeus* is in all likelihood not entirely his, and the *Phoenissae* is fragmentary.

It is worth mentioning that earlier scholars postulated multiple authorship of the plays: in the introductions to their editions Lipsius (1588) and Daniel Heinsius (1611) argued seriously for four or five different authors of the corpus. Furthermore, many early editions of the *opera omnia* of 'Seneca the philosopher' exclude the tragedies, a practice which survived at least until the Didot edition of 1844. This can nowadays be regarded as a curious quirk of scholarship; there is no good reason to doubt that most of the plays were written by the Younger Seneca. They cannot be dated with any certainty,[2] but it is not improbable that their composition diverted many an empty hour during the long years of Seneca's exile in Corsica, 41–9.

Greek tragedy supplied the themes of these plays, as the titles indicate, though the treatment and approach are vastly different, and often little but the framework of the legend survives its metamorphosis in Seneca's hands. Euripides lurks dimly behind the *Hercules Furens, Troades, Medea* and *Phaedra*; Sophocles behind *Phoenissae, Oedipus* and *Hercules Oetaeus*; Aeschylus's play is a notional exemplar for the *Agamemnon*. No Greek *Thyestes* survives, but

Sophocles and Euripides wrote plays with that title, as did earlier Latin tragedians. Formal comparisons between Seneca and the Greek writers are to a large extent misconceived and unrewarding. He was engaged in a quite different exercise, and while we can show that he has used a speech in the original here, or adapted a scene there, we have to be cautious about generalizing and putting forward a theory about Seneca's use of his sources.

Even more uncertain is Seneca's relation to earlier Latin tragedy. Only fragments survive of the large output of the old tragedians, and we have, therefore, to be cautious in drawing inferences, but it seems that in its heyday in the third and second centuries B.C. Latin tragedy, however freely it used its sources, was comparable in treatment, as it was in theme, with Greek tragedy.[3] If so, Seneca was, apart from the language he wrote in, as distant in the essentials of his art from Ennius, Pacuvius and Accius, as he was from Aeschylus, Sophocles and Euripides. He retained the chorus, as his Latin predecessors apparently did,[4] and therewith the framework of episodes divided by moralizing choral lyrics. He used the stock figures of the messenger and the nurse, and gave them their characteristic functions. The messenger reports horrific news of events off-stage, like the death of Hippolytus in the *Phaedra*, and the destruction of Creusa and Creon in the *Medea*; the nurse is the conventional loyal confidante to Medea, Phaedra and Deianira, and Seneca thus helped to steer her onwards into French and English literature. But apart from these and a few other formal elements, like the use of the iambic trimeter in dialogue, Seneca's plays stand on their own. He took from the Greeks what he needed in plot-outline and the basis of the leading characters, and he may have taken something too from earlier Latin plays; but the distinctive stamp and features of his plays derive from his own time.

Few people nowadays deny that at least one accurate descriptive label for the tragedies is 'rhetorical' or 'declamatory', but behind this apparent unanimity lies a wide range of reactions to them, from the favourable through the bored to the frankly hostile. Let us for the moment avoid value judgments and try to assess objectively what is meant by this description. Rhetoric, the technique of persuasion, had to a greater or less degree been a characteristic of Latin literature from its beginnings, and as a formal educational training it dated at least from Cicero's boyhood.

Attendance at a school of rhetoric was the third stage in a boy's education after successively passing through the hands of a *litterator* and a *grammaticus*. The point to grasp is that this phase of training under a professional declaimer, *rhetor*, had by the time of Seneca's youth become extremely important and influential, and the young man's performance at a rhetorical school could make or mar his professional life, whether forensic or literary. In fact, as the political conditions of the early Empire discouraged the development of real forensic talents, it was literature which mainly benefited, and suffered, from the education in rhetoric.

The teaching techniques and exercises of the declaimers are fortunately well documented for us, largely through the labours of Seneca's own father. His interest in rhetoric, his industry, and his astonishing memory have left us collections of school exercises, *Suasoriae* and *Controversiae*, which tell us in the clearest terms what went on. This is invaluable to us, for even a brief look at the schools helps to explain the nature of Seneca's tragedies. To put it shortly, *suasoriae* were speeches composed to be put into the mouths of historical characters facing a crisis and deliberating what to do, e.g. 'Cicero deliberates whether he should beg Antony to spare his life' (*Suas.* vi); *controversiae* were debating speeches concerning a legal or moral issue. An invented situation was offered to the students of rhetoric, often of a quite extraordinarily contrived and far-fetched nature, and the object of the exercise was to arrive at a conclusion through a maze of arguments and counter-arguments which matched in their intricacy the situation under discussion. Typical examples of the problems offered are:

> A girl is captured by pirates and sold to a pander, who makes her a prostitute. She asks money from those who come to her, and when a soldier refuses to pay and offers her violence she kills him. She is tried and acquitted, and returns to her own people, where she seeks the priesthood (for which chastity is a necessary qualification). (*Contr.* i.2)

> The penalty for rape is either death or marriage to the wronged girl. In one night, a man rapes two girls: one demands his death, the other, marriage. (*Contr.* i.5)

> A father refuses to ransom his son who has been captured by

pirates. As a condition of freedom, the son is forced to swear to marry the chief's daughter. He returns home and marries her, and when he subsequently refuses to divorce her and marry another woman on his father's orders, his father disinherits him. (*Contr.* i.6)

It is not hard to imagine the kind of talents fostered by such dialectical brain-teasers. Skill and inventiveness in language were mainly evoked, and the subtlety of the argument mattered more than the rights or wrongs of the case. There was a premium on all the tricks and flourishes of rhetoric for which the Latin language is in any case a highly suitable vehicle: elaborately structured antithesis, epigram, every kind of striking linguistic effect, and, more than all, that favourite handmaid of persuasion, the *sententia*, a terse thought crisply expressed. Almost every page of the Elder Seneca's collection reveals examples of this dialectic ingenuity, and almost every page of his son's prose works and tragedies shows the fashionable rhetorical tricks informing a literary style. It is in any case unreal to distinguish the rhetorical from the literary in much first-century Latin literature; but in Seneca, as in his nephew Lucan, the symbiosis is nearly complete.[5]

Thus Seneca had, as it were, a domestic interest in rhetoric inherited from his father, in addition to the routine training he underwent himself; and his natural and very considerable gifts as a writer found a congenial outlet in the current declamatory style. When he turned to the writing of tragedies, the results formed one of the most curious and interesting byways of Latin literature. It should not be necessary nowadays to labour the point that they were not written for performance, if by that we mean a full-dress stage production. With a few notable exceptions, the writing of tragedy had declined steeply by the Neronian age, and the evidence we have suggests that the production of complete plays was giving place to the presentation of single scenes as the material for a solo recital. So, in Tacitus's *Dialogus* (referring to A.D. 74–5) we are told that Curiatius Maternus had recently recited (*recitaverat*) his tragedy *Cato*, and under Nero he won fame *recitatione tragoediarum*.[6] The picture is uncertain, but at any rate, the characteristic features of Seneca's tragedies are best explained on the assumption that they were not meant for production.

We need not take seriously the old arguments that the horror and bloodshed were unactable (e.g. Thyestes's feast in the *Thyestes*, the mutilated body of Hippolytus in the *Phaedra*): the Elizabethans successfully managed a great deal in that line, and the public were used to such sights in the arena of Neronian Rome. More cogent reasons can be found in the structure of the plays: the fragmentation of the dramatic action and the dominance of the individual scene; uncertainty about entrances and exits, so that we often do not know exactly who is present during a scene; and, perhaps most important, the careful and circumstantial descriptions by characters of the actions or personal appearances of others which would obviously be visible to the audience of a staged play. Examples of this are: the murder by Hercules of his wife and children (*Hercules Furens* 1001ff.) – one can cheat by supposing that he goes off stage to do it, but there is no indication of this in the text; the sacrifice in *Oedipus* 302ff. (there is some excuse here in that Manto is reporting it to the blind Tiresias); the frenzied Medea rushing about, flushed, shouting, weeping – the nurse details all the signs of strong emotion (*Med.* 380ff.); Thyestes eating his horrible meal (*Thy.* 909ff.).

If we accept, then, that we are dealing with a special kind of declamatory drama, we can make sense of and appreciate features of these plays which have offended critics who expected of them what they were never intended to offer. Their style, founded as we have seen on the training of the schools, is epigrammatic, 'pointed', and crisply antithetic. The plots usually advance, if they can be said to advance, through a succession of debating scenes or set-piece monologues. In the arguments between characters, the techniques of stichomythia (dialogue in alternating lines) and antilabe (division of a line between two speakers) are often used, where one speaker caps a point made by another, often by repeating or varying the phraseology of the other. So Medea and the nurse argue (*Med.* 159–63):

>   *M.* fortuna fortes metuit, ignavos premit.
>   *N.* tunc est probanda, si locum virtus habet.
>   *M.* numquam potest non esse virtuti locus.
>   *N.* spes nulla rebus monstrat afflictis viam.
>   *M.* qui nil potest sperare, desperet nihil.

(*M.* Fortune fears the brave and crushes the cowardly.

N. Only then should courage be proved if there is a place for it.
M. Never can there be no place for courage.
N. No hope points out a course for our shattered fortunes.
M. Let him despair of nothing who can hope for nothing.)

Pyrrhus and Agamemnon debate whether to slay Polyxena (*Tro.* 327–36):

P. est regis alti spiritum regi dare.
A. cur dextra regi spiritum eripuit tua?
P. mortem misericors saepe pro vita dabit.
A. et nunc misericors virginem busto petis?
P. iamne immolari virgines credis nefas?
A. praeferre patriam liberis regem decet.
P. lex nulla capto parcit aut poenam impedit.
A. quod non vetat lex, hoc vetat fieri pudor.
P. quodcumque libuit facere victori licet.
A. minimum decet libere cui multum licet.

(P. It is the act of a great king to grant life to a king.
A. Why did your hand take life from a king?
P. Often will one in pity give death instead of life.
A. And now in pity you seek a maiden for the tomb?
P. What? Now you think it wrong that maidens be sacrificed?
A. It is right for a king to put his country before his children.
P. No law spares a captive or prevents punishment.
A. What the law does not forbid, shame forbids.
P. A victor can do whatever he likes.
A. Who can do much should like to do least.)

This kind of cut-and-thrust dialectic was very dear to Seneca, and loses much in the English translation, with its lack of inflection and its more inflexible word-order.

The set speeches are of various kinds, the most characteristic being the 'To be or not to be' variety, or dramatized *suasoria* (Hamlet's soliloquy, incidentally, is a lineal descendant of the Roman *suasoria*), as in *Medea* 893ff. (should she kill her children?); and the speech of self-defence: *Hercules Furens* 399ff. (Lycus defends his usurping of Thebes, raising and demolishing imaginary objections); *Medea* 236ff. (Medea recalls the moral dilemma she had faced at Colchis between obeying her father and rescuing the Argonauts). The importance of the set speech, whether a soliloquy or in dialogue, leads in turn to the dominance of the single scene as a virtually self-contained unit in the play. This point can be well illustrated from the *Medea*, where the plot consists essentially of a progression of debates between Medea and, successively, the nurse, Creon and Jason. One can very similarly analyse other plays, e.g. the *Troades* and *Phaedra*, where the major scenes explore a tension between a harshly contrasted pair of attitudes, and the reader forgets the wider aspects of the total play in concentrating on the polarity before him. This would be a structural fault in an acted play, where one expects a homogeneous whole with, in Aristotelian terms, a beginning, a middle and an end. But this is not what Seneca is doing.

It must also be admitted that many soliloquies and dialogues are marred by an obvious reliance on contrived rhetorical techniques, which take command over the natural sentiments of the speaker. There is a cold intellectuality in Andromache's soliloquy which reflects the debating schools rather than the anguished decision she has to make, whether to give up her son to death or to allow her husband's tomb to be desecrated (*Tro.* 642ff.):

> quid agimus? animum distrahit geminus timor:
> hinc natus, illinc coniugis sacri cinis.
> pars utra vincet? testor immites deos,
> deosque veros coniugis manes mei:
> non aliud, Hector, in meo nato mihi
> placere quam te. vivat, ut possit tuos
> referre vultus. – prorutus tumulo cinis
> mergetur? ossa fluctibus spargi sinam
> disiecta vastis? potius hic mortem oppetat. –
> poteris nefandae deditum mater neci
> videre? poteris celsa per fastigia
> missum rotari? potero, perpetiar, feram,
> dum non meus post fata victoris manu
> iactetur Hector. – hic suam poenam potest
> sentire, at illum fata iam in tuto locant. –

> quid fluctuaris? statue, quem poenae extrahas.
> ingrata, dubitas? Hector est illinc tuus –
> erras: utrimque est Hector; hic sensus potens,
> forsan futurus ultor extincti patris –
> utrique parci non potest: quidnam facis?
> serva e duobus, anime, quem Danai timent.

(What am I to do? A double fear tears my soul apart: on this side my son, on that my sacred husband's ashes. Which side will conquer? I swear by the pitiless gods, and that true god, my husband's ghost: nothing else, Hector, is dear to me in my son than yourself. Let him live, to recall your features. – Are your ashes to be cast from their tomb and sunk in the sea? Shall I allow your bones to be scattered wide over the mighty waves? Rather let Astyanax meet his death. – Can you his mother watch him handed over to an unholy death? Can you see him thrown hurtling over the lofty roof-tops? I can, I will steel myself to do it, endure it, so long as my Hector is not scattered after his death by the conqueror's hand. – But Astyanax can feel punishment, while Hector is now in the haven of death. – Why hesitate? Decide whom you are to save from vengeance. Ungrateful one, can you still doubt? Your Hector is on that side – no, Hector is on both sides; but his son can still feel pain, and may one day avenge his dead father. I cannot save both: what to do? Of the two, my soul, save the one whom the Greeks fear.)

To even the most casual reader, the most memorable literary feature of the tragedies must be the ubiquitous *sententiae*. These pithy, balanced epigrams had in the inflections and flexible word-order of Latin a most admirable vehicle, and the 'Silver' writers enjoyed them enormously. No one showed a more refined skill than Seneca in composing them in both prose and verse, and (like Juvenal) he owes his popularity as a source of adages to the neatness of his *sententiae*. A few examples from the three best plays will illustrate:

> optanda mors est sine metu mortis mori. (*Tro.* 869)
> qui nil potest sperare, desperet nihil. (*Med.* 163)
> tibi innocens sit quisquis est pro te nocens. (*Med.* 503 – the balanced symmetry of this line is particularly notable)

quod non potest vult posse qui nimium potest. (*Phae.* 215)
pars sanitatis velle sanari fuit. (*Phae.* 249)
curae leves locuntur, ingentes stupent. (*Phae.* 607)
mori volenti desse mors numquam potest. (*Phae.* 878)

Here again, the flavour of declamation tends to distance the thoughts from reality and human feeling, and Seneca seems to abandon the exploration of mankind's behaviour in favour of formulating its more unoriginal thoughts. But as expressions of the axiomatic they are unbeatable, and it is fair to Seneca to see this as a conscious part of his purpose.

The tragedies have not many passages of great lyrical charm, but Seneca does occasionally evoke a scene of natural beauty, as at *Phaedra* 9ff.:

> hac, hac alii qua nemus alta
> texitur alno, qua prata iacent,
> qua rorifera mulcens aura
> Zephyrus vernas evocat herbas . . .

(Here, here let others go, where the grove is interwoven with tall alders, where lie the meadows, where the West Wind, soothing with his dewy breeze, brings forth the springtime growth . . .)

So, too, from the attractive *aubade* in the *Hercules Furens* (139ff.):

> pastor gelida cana pruina
> grege dimisso pabula carpit;
> ludit prato liber aperto
> nondum rupta fronte iuvencus,
> vacuae reparant ubera matres;
> errat cursu levis incerto
> molli petulans haedus in herba.
>   pendet summo stridula ramo
> pinnasque novo tradere soli
> gestit querulos inter nidos
> Thracia paelex, turbaque circa
> confusa sonat murmure mixto
> testata diem.

> carbasa ventis credit dubius
> navita vitae, laxos aura
> complente sinus. hic exesis
> pendens scopulis aut deceptos
> instruit hamos aut suspensus
> spectat pressa praemia dextra:
> sentit tremulum linea piscem.

(The shepherd, putting out his flock, pastures them on the ground white with hoar frost. The bullock still with hornless brow sports freely in the open meadow, while the cows at leisure fill again their udders. On the soft grass the saucy kid wanders, skipping aimlessly about. The shrill nightingale perches on the top of a tree among her plaintive nestlings, longing to spread her wings to the early morning sun, and all around confused sounds of the bird-throng's mingled voices announce the dawn. The sailor hazarding his life entrusts his sails to the winds, as the breeze swells the loose canvas folds. A fisherman perching on weather-beaten rocks prepares again his cheated hooks, or, gripping tightly, excitedly watches for his prize, as the line feels the quivering fish.)

The chorus in Seneca fulfils much the same function as the Euripidean chorus. It moralizes in more or less general terms on a theme drawn from the action (e.g. the irresistible anger of a wronged wife, *Medea* 579ff.; the beauty of Hippolytus, suggesting the theme of beauty as an ambiguous blessing, *Phaedra* 741ff.), and in this way puts the characters and their world in perspective against a wider background of history or mythology. Thus, the chorus gives Seneca scope for his absorbing interest in geography (often muddled) and mythology; and one of the more tiresome features of the lyrics is his fondness for extensive catalogues of peoples and places. In addition, the chorus serves the practical purpose of filling up time in the action while something happens off-stage, and it sometimes enters the action, for example in order to interrogate a new arrival (*Med.* 881ff.). At least once it plays a much more organic role, when it forms the wedding procession and sings the epithalamium for Jason's marriage to Creusa at *Medea* 56ff. This lyric in the *Medea*, as well as being an interesting example of a minor literary genre, shows that Seneca in retaining the dramatic chorus is not simply paying lip-service to an outworn convention; though elsewhere in the plays the chorus is generally the 'ideal' listener and commentator familiar to us from Euripides.

In one important respect, however, Seneca's choruses depart from the Greek practice: though the metres (mainly anapaestic, sapphic, glyconic, and asclepiadic) are Greek, there is no attempt at responsion, and in fact only one strophic chorus (*Med.* 579ff.). Partly for this reason it is a fair charge against Seneca that in many places his lyrics are metrically boring, as the same unvaried metre is hammered out for too long; and to our ears there does seem to be an insensitivity here which is hard to explain. However, at least in the *Medea* – which is, in general, one of the more carefully written plays – he has made a real attempt at metrical variety. The *Medea* also illustrates clearly a point which has long been noticed: Seneca's strong debt to Horace in many of his lyrics: e.g. *Medea* 301ff. and Horace *C.* i.3, on the folly of the first navigator.[7]

Another interesting chorus is the long dithyramb to Bacchus in the *Oedipus* (403ff.), in which the learned Senecan treatment of myth is given a successful buoyancy for a hundred lines by the vigorous metrical variety. The closing lines, describing the wedding of Bacchus and Ariadne, are (488–508):

> Naxos Aegaeo redimita ponto
> tradidit thalamis virginem relictam,
> meliore pensans damnum marito.
> pumice ex sicco fluxit
> Nyctelius latex;
> garruli gramen secuere rivi,
> conbibit dulces humus alta sucos
> niveique lactis candidos fontes
> et mixta odoro Lesbia cum thymo.
> ducitur magno nova nupta caelo:
> sollemne Phoebus carmen
> infusus humero capillis
> cantat et geminus Cupido
> concutit taedas;
> telum deposuit Iuppiter igneum
> oditque Baccho veniente fulmen.
> lucida dum current annosi sidera mundi,

> Oceanus clausum dum fluctibus ambiet orbem
> Lunaque dimissos dum plena recolliget ignes,
> dum matutinos praedicet Lucifer ortus
> altaque caeruleum dum Nerea nesciet Arctos,
> candida formosi venerabimur ora Lyaei.

(Naxos, surrounded by the Aegean Sea, gave him to wed the deserted maiden, requiting her loss with a better husband. Wine flowed from the dry rock; babbling streams criss-crossed the meadows; the earth drank deeply of sweet juices – both springs of snow-white milk and wine mingled with fragrant thyme. The new bride was brought to the high heavens; with his hair flowing over his shoulders Phoebus sang a festive song, and twin Cupids flourished the bridal torches; Jupiter put aside his fiery weapon, hating the thunderbolt when Bacchus came. As long as the bright stars run their courses; as long as the ocean flows round the earth and bounds it with his waters; as long as the full moon regains the brightness she lost at waning; as long as the morning star foretells the rise of day and the lofty Bear shall never know the blue sea; so long shall we worship the radiant face of fair Bacchus.)

The *Hercules Oetaeus* is an oddity in that it has two choruses, but its authorship is suspected on many grounds, and Seneca may have been only partly responsible for this shapeless play of nearly two thousand lines, the longest surviving classical drama.

If we look for an answer to the question why Seneca wrote these rather unusual plays, we may first clear the ground of unlikely suggestions. The tragedies were not written as spectacles for reasons outlined above. It is most unlikely that they were written, as Miss B. Marti once suggested, to be a formal programme of Stoic teaching. This theory supposed that the order of the plays in the Etruscus manuscript was canonical, and that they were intended to give in dramatic verse form a kind of teaching comparable to that of the prose Letters.[8] There are certainly many passages reflecting Stoic doctrine (as there are also Epicurean sentiments), and the leading Stoic writer of his day would have a predictable interest in Hercules, the great Stoic hero-saviour. (He is the central figure in one genuine and one questionable play, and there are several other references to him, e.g. the extended list of his deeds at *Agamemnon* 808–66.) But it needs a good deal of special pleading to infer Stoic teaching from all the plays, though it may well have been a conscious, if minor, ingredient in some.

One mistake is to look for a uniform purpose behind the plays, and to regard them as a planned collection. Another possible mistake is to assume too august a motive in Seneca's mind. It is less forced and more straightforward to see in the tragedies an attempt at a new form of literary drama. Seneca was perhaps the greatest stylist of his generation, and whereas the Letters and the treatises were written with the philosopher's pen, the plays were the *tour de force* of an experimenting littérateur. He was steeped in Greek drama, and chose the old tales as his framework. Contemporary conditions discouraged staged plays, and his training in rhetoric steered him towards arguments embroidered in language rather than characters evolving in action. The declaimers moved in a world of type-figures (the tyrant, the loyal, misunderstood son, the wronged wife), and a feature of the tragedies is the metamorphosis of some leading figures of legend into these types. So, for example, Lycus in the *Hercules Furens* and Creon in the *Medea* are clearly stock *tyranni*. By generalizing and exaggerating characteristics Seneca could set up starker contrasts and intensify the clash of wills and arguments.

Perhaps from the same motive he sometimes simplifies a received plot, as in the *Medea*. In this play he is largely indebted to Euripides's version (though Ovid's *Medea* was no doubt a contributing influence), but he has cut out the Aegeus scene altogether and reduced the number of confrontations between Medea and Jason. The nurse has a bigger role than in Euripides, so that she can play a more equal part in her verbal tussles with Medea. Furthermore, as Medea dominates the play with her own statements of her claims and rights, a further balance is ensured by making the chorus hostile to her, whereas in Euripides it was sympathetic to her.

The *Medea* is a particularly good example of Seneca's treatment of a traditional plot, but similar points could be made about the other plays where parallels are possible with an exemplar. The conclusion seems to be that Seneca the dramatist wanted most of all to explore the tensions and struggles of human beings, usually in hopeless or nearly hopeless situations, as typified and highlighted by the characters of legend. Of course most playwrights are doing something like this, but Seneca concentrates on the formulation of the arguments by which passionate individuals in conflict justify themselves, particularly ringing the changes on the anguish of hatred, love or despair. It was with some justification that Regenbogen saw the words from the *Hercules Oetaeus* 252–3 *et formas dolor/errat per omnes* as a Senecan motto.⁹ In doing this, as a child of his time he used all the resources of declamation of which he was undisputed master. This approach tends, of course, to superficiality: the psychology of the plays is generally unsubtle, and the well-springs of human conduct are scarcely revealed. But even a self-conscious debating speech or a reflective monologue can tell us something about men and women, however they may be tricked out with endless rhetorical questions and self-apostrophes. Seneca's characters, like Chekhov's, spend much of their time exposing their souls to us; but in Seneca it is not the revelation but the technique of exposure which is paramount.

It would be a very biased apologist who denied that there is much in these works that is banal, unlovely and boring. No one defends the piling up of horror at the climaxes of the *Thyestes* and *Phaedra*. It is hard not to take as a grotesquely sick joke lines like Atreus' remark to Thyestes, who has just unknowingly eaten his sons, *hic esse natos crede in amplexu patris* (*Thy.* 976); or the words of the blinded Oedipus, feeling his way over the stage on which Jocasta lies dead, *i profuge vade – siste, ne in matrem incidas* (*Oed.* 1051). But the plays should not be remembered only for lines like these, and I append some passages which give an idea of the range of descriptive and reflective poetry (mainly in the choruses) which Seneca was capable of writing. (See also the passages quoted on pp. 197ff.)

It is fair to claim for the plays a judgment which regards what they aim to be and not what the critic thinks they should have been. As exercises in declamatory drama they are not simply the only surviving Latin tragedies but unique in European literature. Seneca is often accused of having an unoriginal mind: his plays, at least, are an original creation.

The grove where Atreus sacrificed Thyestes's sons (*Thy.* 650–6; 665–79):

> arcana in imo regio secessu iacet,
> alta vetustum valle compescens nemus,
> penetrale regni, nulla qua laetos solet
> praebere ramos arbor aut ferro coli,
> sed taxus et cupressus et nigra ilice
> obscura nutat silva, quam supra eminens
> despectat alte quercus et vincit nemus . . .
> fons stat sub umbra tristis et nigra piger
> haeret palude: talis est dirae Stygis
> deformis unda quae facit caelo fidem.
> hinc nocte caeca gemere ferales deos
> fama est, catenis lucus excussis sonat
> ululantque manes. quidquid audire est metus
> illic videtur: errat antiquis vetus
> emissa bustis turba et insultant loco
> maiora notis monstra; quin tota solet
> micare silva flamma, et excelsae trabes
> ardent sine igne. saepe latratu nemus
> trino remugit, saepe simulacris domus
> attonita magnis. nec dies sedat metum:
> nox propria luco est, et superstitio inferum
> in luce media regnat.

(In a remote retreat there lies a secret place, enclosing in a deep vale an ancient grove, the inner sanctum of the kingdom, where no tree extends cheerful branches or suffers the pruning-knife. Only the yew, the cypress and woods of dark ilex wave their gloomy leaves, and above them all, tallest in the grove, a lofty oak looks down. . . . In the gloom a melancholy spring emerges, oozing along its black and miry course, like the ugly stream of fearful Styx by which the gods swear their oaths. They say that late at night the gods of death groan in this place; the grove echoes with the clanking of chains, and there is a shrieking of ghosts. All that is fearful simply to hear of is there actually seen: a crowd of the ancient dead leave their old tombs and prowl around, while monstrous forms, greater than any known before, leap about the place. More than that, all through the wood there is always the gleam of fire, and lofty trees glow though no flames are seen. Often the grove echoes with a triple barking; often the dwelling is terrified by great phantom shapes. Nor does daylight soothe the fear: night is the grove's natural condition, and a dread awe of the underworld reigns even at midday.)

In praise of a quiet life (*Thy.* 391–403):

>stet quicumque volet potens
>aulae culmine lubrico:
>me dulcis saturet quies;
>obscuro positus loco
>leni perfruar otio,
>nullis nota Quiritibus
>aetas per tacitum fluat.
>sic cum transierint mei
>nullo cum strepitu dies,
>plebeius moriar senex.
>illi mors gravis incubat
>qui, notus nimis omnibus,
>ignotus moritur sibi.

(Let whoever wishes stand on the slippery height of royal power; let me have my fill of sweet repose. In a humble place let me enjoy untroubled calm, while unknown to my fellow-townsmen let my life's course go quietly on. So, when my days without uproar have passed by, let me die, an old man of lowly rank. On him death lies heavy who, too well known to all others, dies unknown to himself.)

The captive Trojan women reflect on death (*Tro.* 371–408):

>verum est an timidos fabula decipit
>umbras corporibus vivere conditis,
>cum coniunx oculis imposuit manum
>supremusque dies solibus obstitit
>et tristis cineres urna coercuit?
>non prodest animam tradere funeri,
>sed restat miseris vivere longius?
>an toti morimur nullaque pars manet
>nostri, cum profugo spiritus halitu

immixtus nebulis cessit in aera
et nudum tetigit subdita fax latus?
quidquid sol oriens, quidquid et occidens
novit, caeruleis Oceanus fretis
quidquid bis veniens et fugiens lavat,
aetas Pegaseo corripiet gradu.
quo bis sena volant sidera turbine,
quo cursu properat volvere saecula
astrorum dominus, quo properat modo
obliquis Hecate currere flexibus:
hoc omnes petimus fata nec amplius,
iuratos superis qui tetigit lacus,
usquam est. ut calidis fumus ab ignibus
vanescit, spatium per breve sordidus,
ut nubes, gravidas quas modo vidimus,
arctoi Boreae dissicit impetus:
sic hic, quo regimur, spiritus effluet.
post mortem nihil est ipsaque mors nihil,
velocis spatii meta novissima.
spem ponant avidi, solliciti metum:
tempus nos avidum devorat et chaos.
mors individua est, noxia corpori
nec parcens animae: Taenara et aspero
regnum sub domino limen et obsidens
custos non facili Cerberus ostio
rumores vacui verbaque inania
et par sollicito fabula somnio.
quaeris quo iaceas post obitum loco?
quo non nata iacent.

(Is it true, or does a myth cheat our timid hearts, that souls
live on though bodies have been buried, when the wife has
closed her husband's eyes, the last day has shut out the sun, and
our ashes fill the mournful urn? Is there no good in giving up
the soul to death, but some wretched existence then still
remains? Or do we wholly die and nothing of us remains, when
with the last breath the spirit has passed into the air and
mingled with the clouds, and the funeral torch has touched the
naked corpse? Everything the rising sun, everything the
setting sun knows, everything the ocean washes with his blue

waters and his double ebb and flow, time will consume
with the swiftness of Pegasus. Swiftly as the whirling rush of
the Zodiac signs, swiftly as the lord of the stars sends the ages
rolling onward, swiftly as the moon hastens on her slanting
curve, so do we all make for our dooms, and he no more
exists who has once reached the waters which give the gods
their oath. As smoke from blazing fires passes away and is foul
for but a moment, as clouds which just now seemed heavy
are scattered by the onset of northern Boreas, so this breath of
life which rules us will waft away. There is nothing after
death and death itself is nothing – the final goal of a swift life's
course. Let the greedy abandon their hopes and the anxious
their fears: greedy time and chaos swallow us up. Death is
indivisible: it cannot spare the soul while it destroys the body.
Taenarus and the harsh lord's realm and Cerberus, guarding
the threshold not easy to pass, are idle stories and empty
words, a tale worthless as a feverish dream. Do you ask where
you will lie after death? Where lie all those unborn.)

On immutable fate (*Oed.* 980–94):

> fatis agimur: cedite fatis.
> non sollicitae possunt curae
> mutare rati stamina fusi.
> quidquid patimur mortale genus,
> quidquid facimus venit ex alto,
> servatque suae decreta colus
> Lachesis nulla revoluta manu.
> omnia secto tramite vadunt
> primusque dies dedit extremum:
> non illa deo vertisse licet
> quae nexa suis currunt causis.
> it cuique ratus prece non ulla
> mobilis ordo: multis ipsum
> metuisse nocet, multi ad fatum
> venere suum dum fata timent.

(We are driven by fate: yield to fate. Anxious cares cannot
change the threads on the unalterable spindle. Whatever we
mortals endure, whatever we do, comes from above, and
Lachesis keeps firm the decrees of her distaff which no hand

can reverse. All things travel on an established path, and our first day has determined our last. God cannot alter those things which, linked to their causes, move swiftly onward. For each man the fixed pattern of his life goes on and no prayer can change it. To be afraid is in itself harmful to many, for many have come to their doom through their fear of it.)

Notes

1 The best edition of the tragedies to date is that of G. C. Giardina, Bologna, 1966. An edition by O. Zwierlein is in preparation for the Oxford Classical Texts series.
2 Though many attempts have been made, using various criteria, e.g. O. Herzog in *RhM*, 77 (1928), pp. 51ff.
3 But for important differences between Latin and Greek tragedy, see H. D. Jocelyn, *The Tragedies of Ennius* (Cambridge, 1967), pp. 23ff.
4 See ibid., pp. 18ff., 30ff.
5 For the whole subject of rhetoric in Roman education and its influence on Seneca see the excellent book of S. F. Bonner, *Roman Declamation* (Liverpool, 1949). He remarks (p. 167): 'There is scarcely an aspect of declamatory rhetoric which could not be illustrated from his plays.'
6 Tacitus *Dial.* 2 and 11. See too the sensible remarks of E. F. Watling in the introduction to his *Seneca: Four Tragedies and Octavia* (Harmondsworth, 1966), p. 21, on the unreal distinction between 'performance' and 'recitation' by two or more persons.
7 For the influence of Horace, see I. Spika, 'De imitatione Horatiana in Senecae canticis choris' (Jahresb. 1889–90, Staatsgymn. Wien II, Vienna, 1890), pp. 3ff.
8 See B. Marti in *TAPA*, 76 (1945), pp. 216ff, and *REL*, 27 (1949), pp. 189ff. The theory is criticized by N. T. Pratt in *TAPA*, 79 (1948), pp. 1ff.
9 O. Regenbogen, *Schmerz und Tod in den Tragödien Senecas* (Vortr. Bibl. Warburg, 1927–8, Leipzig-Berlin, 1930), p. 193.

V

Seneca's Philosophical Influence

G. M. Ross

In this chapter, my purpose is to give a general survey of Seneca's philosophical influence from his own time to the present. I shall, however, concentrate on the first twelve centuries A.D., since the relevant material is sufficiently limited for a more or less complete account to be practicable, and such completeness is necessary for establishing my largely negative thesis, that Seneca's ancient and early medieval influence was much less than has often been claimed. As for the remaining period, I say enough to give an overall picture of the fluctuations in his popularity; but anything more than a cursory account, particularly of the sixteenth and seventeenth centuries, when his influence was at its height, would require at least a chapter on its own.

It may be felt that my approach is too negative, especially in the sections dealing with antiquity; but if anything I would say it is not negative enough. On the whole I accept as genuine influence any instance in which Seneca's views are explicitly approved, even though more is really needed to establish that knowledge of them had any formative effect. But in the absence of detailed information about the genesis of an individual's philosophical beliefs, this is normally the best evidence available. I am much more sceptical about the value of parallels, whether of thought or of expression. In the first case, there is rarely any way of telling whether we have to do with specifically Senecan influence, and it is often a matter of conjecture whether even Stoic influence is at work. In the second case, there is no clear criterion for establishing how many parallels there must be, or how close, before we can safely conclude not only that there is borrowing, but also that it is from Seneca and not from some common source or intermediary; and then it still needs to be shown, as before, that there is a transfer of ideas as well as of words. The most prudent methodological principle to adopt is that where there is insufficient positive evidence of influence, it should be assumed, at least provisionally, that there is no influence.

1 Seneca in pagan antiquity

Seneca is for us one of the best known of ancient philosophers. It can therefore come as a surprise that he had no influence on the subsequent history of pagan philosophy as a technical discipline. He was completely ignored not only by the adherents of rival philosophical systems, but even by the other surviving representatives of his own school, Epictetus (*c.* 50–138) and Marcus Aurelius (121–80), despite close similarities in the versions of Stoicism all three were propounding.[1] Having seen why this should be so, we shall be in a better position to understand what influence Seneca did have, and why.

The principal reason for Seneca's failure to leave any impression on the mainstream of philosophical thought is that this was not his purpose. His ambition was not to produce new developments in philosophy (in fact he was highly critical of those who became too involved in the technicalities of the subject), but to propound and defend the Stoic view of life in a way that would appeal to the layman, indulging only in as much metaphysics as was necessary to provide a framework for the practical aspects of Stoicism. So, since he was little more than a popularizer of views that earlier Stoics had argued for more thoroughly, it is only natural that later philosophers should turn to them rather than to him for formulations of the Stoic position. Besides, we should not forget that Seneca's prominence in modern accounts of Stoicism is due largely to the accident that his are the earliest Stoic writings to have survived in any more than a fragmentary state.

Seneca's philosophical superficiality is closely connected with another factor tending to limit his influence on later philosophers, namely the fact that during his lifetime philosophy was largely in the province of amateurs. In most periods, major philosophers have had their influence virtually guaranteed by their role as teachers or scholars within an established institution whose intellectual traditions they could modify.[2] But the disestablishment of philosophy which was a feature of Seneca's time not only cut off this avenue of influence, but also encouraged an eclectic spirit which makes it almost impossible to trace clear lines of influence at all. In addition to these factors, Seneca was unlikely to appeal to later philosophers both because Stoicism began to suffer a decline within a few decades of his death, so that by the third century philosophy was almost exclusively Platonic; and also because he wrote in Latin, whereas virtually every subsequent pagan philosopher, whatever his nationality, wrote in Greek. Nevertheless, even taking all these mitigating circumstances into account, we can only conclude from their silence that later philosophers regarded Seneca as at best second-rate.

While it is certain that Seneca had no significant influence on professional philosophers, the position is very different with regard to the popular philosophy of his day. During the latter part of the first century, the culture of the Roman Empire was to a striking extent pervaded by Stoic ideas and values. It is impossible to judge how far this state of affairs was due specifically to Seneca's work, since there were innumerable other Stoic writers, teachers and preachers in the early imperial period. There is, however, a strong presumption that his contribution was a significant one, both because of the effectiveness of his literary style, and because of the moral authority he must have had as a respected statesman. But more positive evidence is hard to come by, and the assertion that he helped to form the general climate of contemporary thought would be a mere guess were it not for a number of explicit testimonies to his reputation. Seneca's fellow-countryman and contemporary, Columella, writes (*De re rust.* III.3.3): *Seneca, vir excellentis ingenii atque doctrinae* . . . ; and in *Nat. Hist.* XIV.5.51 Pliny the Elder (23/4–79) refers to him as *princeps tum eruditorum ac potentia*. Quintilian (b. *c.* 30/35) says he was almost the only author read by the younger generation (*Inst. Orat.* X.1.125): *tum autem solus hic fere in manibus adulescentium fuit*; and later makes the very fair point that Seneca excelled as a moralist rather than as a philosopher (ibid. 129):

> In philosophia parum diligens, egregius tamen vitiorum insectator fuit. Multae in eo claraeque sententiae, multa etiam morum gratia legenda.

Seneca's protégé Martial (*c*. 40–*c*. 104) calls him *fecundus* in *Ep*., VII.45.1, but this could just be out of flattery for his patron.³ Far more important is the evidence provided by Tacitus (b. *c*. 56), who says (*Ann*. 12.8) that Agrippina recalled Seneca from exile because of his popularity and scholarly reputation: *laetum in publicum rata ob claritudinem studiorum eius*; and in *Ann*. 13.3 that Seneca's polished and pleasant style was in fashion when he wrote the speech Nero delivered at Claudius's funeral: *quamquam oratio a Seneca composita multum cultus praeferret, ut fuit illi viro ingenium amoenum et temporis eius auribus accommodatum*. Again, he asserts that the dissertation Seneca wrote while dying was too well known for him to need to repeat it (*Ann*. 15.63): *quae in vulgus edita eius verbis invertere supersedeo*.⁴

Even hostile historians admit his reputation: Suetonius (b. *c*. 69) refers to him as *tum maxime placentem* (*Cal*. 53.2); and Dio Cassius, writing in the third century, says (59.19.7): 'Lucius Annaeus Seneca, who surpassed all the Romans of his day in wisdom, and many others besides . . .' Finally, a more indirect piece of evidence for general familiarity with Seneca's work is given by the convincing theory that Petronius was satirizing Seneca's literary style and Stoic attitudes in the *Satyricon*;⁵ and, as Bourgery says, 'On ne parodie que les auteurs en renom.'⁶

The only remaining basis for assessing Seneca's influence on his contemporaries is by finding traces of it in the literature of the time. But the evidence here is almost bound to be inconclusive, since virtually nothing that survives deals with the same sort of topics, so as to be capable of revealing either clear Senecan influence, or the lack of it. The most obvious candidate is Plutarch (before 50 to after 120) in his *Moralia* and *Quaest. Nat*.; but all we find (in *Mor*. VI.461F) is one *bon mot* attributed to Seneca (though not derived from his writings), and a few tenuous parallels between Plutarch's and Seneca's *Quaest. Nat*.⁷ However, since Plutarch was both Greek and an opponent of Stoicism, his virtual ignoring of Seneca gives us no basis for concluding that the latter was generally unknown or despised at the time. As might be expected, Pliny the Elder occasionally uses Seneca as a source of information about scientific matters: in *Nat. Hist*. I he claims to have used him for Book VI (on geography), Book IX (on aquatic animals) and Book XXXVI (on stones), though he refers to him explicitly only in VI.21.60, IX.78.167 and XIV.5.51.

But this gives no evidence either way about the extent of Seneca's influence as a philosopher or moralist.

As for the poetry of the period, the dependence on Seneca of the anonymous tragedy *Octavia* is beyond question: it both imitates his style, and shows his character in a favourable light.[8] But elsewhere the position is less clear. It is generally agreed that Seneca left a profound impression on his Stoic nephew Lucan (39-65): for instance, Bourgery writes: 'Un surtout a lu avidement les ouvrages du grand philosophe et s'en est profondément impregné, c'est Lucain.'[9] However, most of the parallels that have been found with Seneca's works are with the *Naturales Quaestiones* and the *Agamemnon*;[10] that Seneca influenced him specifically in his Stoicism seems to be an assumption (though a perfectly reasonable one) based on the similarity in their attitudes and their personal relationship, rather than on any direct evidence from Lucan's verse. It is equally generally agreed that Seneca had no influence *on* the other extant Stoic poet of the time, Persius (34-62),[11] a judgment based mainly on a single statement in the *Vita Persi*: *sero cognovit et Senecam, sed non ut caperetur eius ingenio*.[12] But this is too vague to warrant the inference that he was totally unimpressed by Seneca's philosophy, particularly since Persius moved in the same circles as his friend Lucan, and presumably underwent similar influences. In neither case do we have enough information to judge how far their general Stoic orientation was due to Seneca.[13] For the rest, direct Senecan influence is either tenuous, as in the case of Juvenal[14] and Martial,[15] or not proved to be present at all, as with Statius,[16] Phaedrus[17] and the author of *Aetna*.[18]

Despite the near absence of direct Senecan influence in the extant literature, the evidence adduced earlier allows us to infer with reasonable certainty that he did make a significant impression on the thought of his time. However, such influence as he had seems not to have been of long duration. Aulus Gellius (*c.* 130–*c.* 180) attests that he still had admirers in the mid-second century (*Noct. Att.*, XII.2.1); but of any other than stylistic influence on extant writers there is not a hint. Indeed, it is not until the end of the fourth century that there is again any evidence even of his being read, and then not in such a way that his thoughts left any significant impression. Among the grammarians, Donatus quotes him once, and Diomedes and Servius twice each;[19] and it is possible that Ammianus Marcellinus (c. 330–95) used his *Naturales Quaestiones*, and Claudian (d. c. 404) the *De Ira*.[20] Early in the fifth century, Macrobius borrows two long passages from the *Epistles* without acknowledgment,[21] and there are a number of other parallels close enough to indicate dependence.[22] About the same time, Rutilius Namatianus may have borrowed, directly or indirectly, from the *De Superstitione*.[23] But even if other such incidental quotations or parallels could be found, this still would not alter the general picture, that from the second century Seneca's works fell into almost total obscurity in the pagan world. Considering the reputation he once had, this rapid decline is remarkable, and it cannot be fully explained by the factors which led to his being ignored by professional philosophers. But there are at least two good reasons why he ceased to have any influence even as a popular moralist.

The first of these is that the attitude of historians towards Seneca soon became predominantly hostile; and once he was no longer generally respected for the way he had conducted his own life, it is hardly surprising that he should fall into disfavour as a moral authority. While Tacitus is himself very careful to be fair to him,[24] it is clear from his account that Seneca's reputation had already been attacked from both sides: by those who regarded him as disloyal to Nero, and by those who regarded him as hypocritical in conniving at his atrocities. What little is said by Suetonius is broadly unfavourable,[25] and by the third century he is no longer just a hypocrite, but in Dio Cassius he has become the τυραννοδιδάσκαλος, the extortioner and adulterer who taught Nero all his vices.[26]

The second reason is that his literary style soon fell out of fashion. This mattered more than it would now, not just because people dislike reading books in a style which they find indigestible, but because education was then largely in the hands of grammarians and rhetoricians, who generally believed that a thought had to be properly expressed in order to be valuable, and feared that Seneca's manner of writing would have a corrupting influence on their pupils. Even during his own lifetime his style did not meet with universal approval: Caligula, for instance, referred to his speeches as *harena sine calce*.[27] Quintilian's opinion (*Inst. Orat.*, x.1.125–31), though on the whole unfavourable, seems to have been that his style was just acceptable in a master such as Seneca himself, but that it was a dangerous model for the less talented (ibid. 126–7): 'They admired rather than imitated him and fell as far short of him as he had of the ancients. It would be hoped they could equal or at least approach him. But he was liked only for his vices, which everyone tried to copy: so they were slandering him by boasting of their Senecan style.'

By the second century the only two extant writers to comment on his style are scathing in their condemnation (though we must not forget Gellius's report that he still had his admirers). Fronto (*c.* 100–*c.* 166), in his letter *De orationibus* to his pupil Marcus Aurelius,[28] admits any good at all in Seneca only with the greatest of reluctance: 'There are certainly some acute and weighty sayings in his books. But little pieces of silver are sometimes found in sewers; and is that a reason for us to undertake the cleaning of the sewers?' Similarly Gellius, who devotes a whole chapter of the *Noct. Att.* to a criticism of Seneca's style (XII.2: *Quod Annaeus Seneca iudicans de Q. Ennio deque M. Tullio levi futtilique iudicio fuit*), concludes by quoting one Senecan dictum which he admires, and saying (ibid. 14): 'Is that not well said? Certainly; but good sayings do not help the character of the young, so much as bad ones harm it – the more so if the bad are in the majority, and some of these occur not as inconclusive arguments on trivial and simple questions, but as considered conclusions on crucial ones.' Considering the depths to which Seneca's reputation both as a man and as a writer had sunk, it is hardly surprising that his philosophical work soon ceased to make any significant impact on the pagan world.

2 Seneca in Christian antiquity

It is generally believed that Seneca had a greater influence among Christians than among pagans. If this is true, it is a surprising phenomenon, since the reasons accounting for his decline in the pagan world would apply equally in the Christian world, together with the added disadvantage that he was a pagan. It is partly to account for this, and partly to explain real or alleged similarities between Seneca's thought and Christianity, that some scholars have put forward the theory that Seneca was actually converted to Christianity, or at least that he was directly influenced by it.[29] But it would take me too far afield to go into the vexed question of whether or not it is likely that Seneca had any direct contacts with Christians (e.g. St Paul), and if so, what effect they may have had on him. Besides, the whole discussion becomes pointless if it is accepted that his attitudes are too remote from Christianity for it to be credible that he underwent its influence.[30]

A more moderate and far more popular theory is that, during antiquity and the Middle Ages, Christians naïvely believed that Seneca had been converted to Christianity, though we now know this to be a sheer myth. But, as Momigliano has shown,[31] this theory is equally without historical foundation: there is no clear evidence of anyone having believed in Seneca's Christianity before the fourteenth century.[32] Moreover, even if it were true, it would hardly constitute a satisfactory explanation of Seneca's supposed influence on Christian writers. In an age when theologians were all too sensitive to the subtlest traces of heresy in the writings of men known to have been devout practising Christians all their lives, it is fantastic to suppose that these same theologians should have laid themselves open to Seneca's influence simply on the ground that he had been converted shortly before his death. While they might rejoice that a great pagan philosopher whose writings showed traces of a Christian spirit had finally found salvation, they could hardly have regarded those writings as in any way an expression of orthodoxy. At best he could be regarded as an authority in ethics, an area relatively independent of the niceties of dogma; but here only the most die-hard opponents of pagan learning would consider his non-Christianity a serious obstacle; and they are the very people least likely to accept any rumours of his having been converted.

It is true that Christian admirers of pagan wisdom have often been on the defensive about their attitude; but their justifications have invariably, and quite rightly, been *general*: e.g. by simply admitting that man can attain partial wisdom on his own without any special revelation; by claiming that the Greek philosophers learned from the Jews; or by supposing a direct divine revelation bestowed on a few privileged pagans, in the same way as on the Hebrew prophets.[33] The theory of Seneca's conversion, as a particular case, would be relevant only for a Christian who considered him the *only* wise pagan. But everyone who admired him had an even greater admiration for other pagan philosophers, such as Plato or Cicero, who could not possibly have been converted, and were never considered Christians.[34]

When we come to assess the actual extent of Seneca's influence in Christian antiquity, it appears broadly comparable to the impression he made on the pagan world: that is, more through the general climate of thought he helped to promote than through the direct impact of his writings. In its earliest years, Christianity had a philosophy only in the most limited sense; but there were many reasons why Christians should soon begin to develop and systematize it: for pure intellectual satisfaction, to define and justify orthodoxy in opposition to heresies, and above all to give Christianity the intellectual respectability it needed to make headway among cultured pagans.

It was almost inevitable that the first manifestations of Christian philosophy should have a heavily Stoic flavour,[35] not so much because of any similarities between Christianity and Stoicism,[36] but because Stoicism was the dominant philosophy during the formative years of Christian thought. This dominance consisted not just in its popularity as a system distinct from others (though this was important, since it meant that Stoic writings were easily available, and that many early Christians were taught philosophy by Stoics), but in the fact that Stoic ideas had penetrated every type of philosophy and become the common heritage of all who philosophized. Stoic conceptions had become embedded in language, in general moral attitudes, and in the human and natural sciences, all of which had important repercussions on the unconscious presuppositions of early Christian thought. (To take just one example, Christian teaching about the soul and its relation to God and the universe was heavily dependent on the current orthodoxy of psychology, which was largely Stoic in orientation.)

It would, however, be misleading to refer to any of the early Fathers as Stoics, even in the sense in which Augustine is called a Platonist, or Aquinas an Aristotelian. One reason for this is that although much of their philosophy did indeed have many general characteristics also found in Stoicism, these were often not exclusively Stoic, but also to be found in other philosophical systems, or implicit in biblical Christianity or Judaism. For example, there are strong tendencies towards materialistic monism in the early Fathers; but while these were undoubtedly reinforced by the prevailing Stoicism, their origin can clearly be seen within the Judaeo-Christian tradition itself (e.g. in the doctrine of the resurrection of the body); again, the empiricist epistemology which they often assumed is as much a characteristic of the Aristotelian and Epicurean as of the Stoic tradition.[37] But a more important reason is that, in so far as such ideas had become common property, they were no longer regarded as specifically Stoic, if explicitly recognized at all. Consequently the early Fathers were on the whole no more favourably disposed towards what they saw as the essence of Stoicism as a distinct philosophical system than they were to, say, Platonism.

Nevertheless, the unconscious Stoic influence on the Christian philosophy of the first two centuries was very considerable, and made it importantly different from the Christian philosophy that was the product of the predominantly Platonic era that followed. I shall shortly be arguing that the *direct* influence of Seneca's writings on early Christianity was minimal; but if it is accepted that he played an important part in bringing about this general Stoic climate of thought in the first place, then it follows that his *indirect* influence on early Christian thought was highly significant.

The evidence for direct Senecan influence on Christians is less meagre than in the case of pagan writers, but its importance has generally been exaggerated. It is certainly true that there are more admiring references to and quotations from Seneca among Christians; but they are still few in comparison with the respect paid to other non-Christian writers. Nor can we even conclude that Seneca was more popular within Christianity than outside it, since most of the surviving literature of the period is Christian, and a much larger proportion of it concerned with religious, philosophical and moral questions – almost the only areas in which we could expect to find anything directly inspired by Seneca's writings. Once this is allowed for, his influence would seem not to be significantly different in the two cases; and this should warn us not to read too much into the occasional admiring references, or possible parallels with his writings.

Although we should be prepared to find Christianity most responsive to Seneca's thought in its Stoic period, the earliest writers had only a limited interest in pagan literature, and there are no traces of any direct Senecan influence till the end of the second century, by which time Stoicism was already giving way to Platonism. Parallels with Seneca have been found in the two greatest Christian thinkers of the time, Clement of Alexandria (c. 150 to after 210) and his pupil Origen (c. 185/6–254/5),[38] but these are not sufficiently convincing to prove direct influence. Nor should we expect much, since they were among the first to produce a predominantly Platonic Christianity,[39] and both wrote in Greek.

For the same reasons it would be surprising to find Senecan influence in writers even more remote from the world of Roman Stoicism, such as the illustrious group of Eastern theologians consisting of Gregory of Nazianzus, Basil, and Gregory of Nyssa (all born c. 329), and the parallels claimed by Stelzenberger do not carry conviction.[40] But some interest in Seneca is definitely found in Africa, where the culture was Latin rather than Greek, and where the Platonization of Christianity was delayed (perhaps because of strong opposition to the gnostic heresies, which were seen as emanating from Platonism).[41] The first Christian to mention Seneca explicitly was Tertullian of Carthage (c. 160–c. 240), but his indebtedness to him has been much exaggerated. In *De anima*, xx.1, he introduces a quotation from Seneca with the words: *Sicut et Seneca saepe noster* . . . ; and this has led some into supposing that he regarded him as almost a Christian.[42] Now, it is true that Christian writers regularly used *noster* to mean *Christianus*, and it is quite natural to take the vaguer *saepe noster* as meaning that Seneca often wrote things in conformity with Christian truth. But before drawing any conclusions, we should balance this with what he says in *De praesc. haer.*, VII: 'What then has Athens to do with Jerusalem? Or the Academy with the Church? Or heretics with Christians? Our teaching is from the Porch of Solomon . . .'; i.e. *not* 'from the Porch of Zeno'. As he makes clear in *De an.*, II.1–5, his opinion is that pagans do sometimes accidentally hit upon the truth, and when they do so it is justifiable to use their authority to convince others. But his recognizing this of Seneca does not imply any special admiration of him or his philosophy.[43] And although Tertullian's writings do show strong traces of Stoicism, these are far more likely to have come from the general Stoic climate of thought, and from writers like Soranus, Musonius and Posidonius,[44] than from Seneca, whom he hardly ever mentions, and only on this one occasion with unambiguous approval.[45]

On the basis of a number of parallels found by Burger, it is also generally assumed that Minucius Felix (early third century) was heavily dependent on Seneca;[46] but none of these parallels are sufficiently close to prove a direct acquaintance with Seneca's writings, and if there are any genuine echoes of Seneca, it is quite possible that they were mediated by the handbooks used in the rhetorical training which Minucius had undergone.[47] Even more remote are the parallels with Seneca in Cyprian (c. 200–58)[48] and Novatian (mid-third century).[49]

Of all the Fathers, the most favourable to Seneca was undoubtedly Lactantius (c. 240–c. 320). He quotes him no less than twenty-two times, nearly always with approval,[50] and compliments him on a number of occasions, calling him *homo acutus* (*Inst.*, 1.7.13), and *omnium Stoicorum acutissimus* (II.8.23). Elsewhere he goes into greater detail: 'Anyone who wants to know all [about justice] should obtain the books of Seneca, who described public morals and vices very accurately and censured them with great vehemence.'[51] Again in VI.24.14: 'He could have been a true worshipper of God if someone had shown him how – provided, of course, he rejected Zeno and his teacher Sotion, and obtained a guide in true wisdom.' But though this last comment in particular is friendly, if somewhat patronizing, it is no more than he believed of most other major pagan philosophers: 'Our teaching is that no sect was so off the mark or any philosopher so worthless that he did not perceive something of the truth'.[52] Of these there are some, notably Cicero, for whom he had a far greater admiration;[53] and there is little evidence of any specifically Senecan influence outside the passages where he explicitly quotes him.[54]

After Lactantius, apart from a critical reference in Ausonius (d. c. 395),[55] Seneca seems to have made no impact till the very end of the fourth century, unless we accept as genuine the possible echoes in Bachiarius's *Letter of Consolation* (c. 385)[56] and in St Ambrose (c. 339–97).[57] This does not, however, mean that he was not read: Augustine implies that some of his books were part of the staple literary diet of the time, when he complains that his Manichean teacher Faustus had read little else (*Conf.*, v.6). It was also around this time that someone forged a correspondence between Seneca and St Paul, a text which has done more than anything else to stimulate the theory that Seneca was, or was believed to be, a Christian, even though it says nothing of the sort itself.[58] It had a wide circulation in the Middle Ages, and was often included in manuscripts of genuine Senecan works; but as I have said it was not actually used as an argument for his conversion till the Renaissance. Information from it was already incorporated by ps.-Linus (perhaps between the fourth and seventh centuries) in his reworking of the apocryphal *Passio Pauli*; but again there is no suggestion of Seneca's having become a Christian.[59]

At the end of the fourth century, Seneca is once more referred to by important Christian thinkers. Jerome (*c.* 348–420) has sometimes been held to have considered him a Christian on account of his entry in *De viris illustribus*, xii:

> Lucius Annaeus Seneca Cordubensis, Sotionis stoici discipulus et patruus Lucani poetae, continentissimae vitae fuit, quem non ponerem in catalogo sanctorum, nisi me epistolae illae provocarent, quae leguntur a plurimis, Pauli ad Senecam et Senecae ad Paulum. In quibus, cum esset Neronis magister et illius temporis potentissimus, optare se dicit eius loci apud suos, cuius sit Paulus apud Christianos. Hic ante biennium quam Petrus et Paulus martyrio coronarentur, a Nerone interfectus est.

> (Lucius Annaeus Seneca of Corduba, pupil of Sotion the Stoic and uncle of Lucan the poet, lived very temperately; but I would not have included him in the catalogue of saints if it were not for those letters between him and Paul which are read by many. In these, though he was Nero's teacher and the most powerful man of his day, he said he wished he had the same position among his people as Paul had among the Christians. He was killed by Nero two years before Peter and Paul were crowned with martyrdom.)

But the catalogue was not a list exclusively of Christians, canonized or otherwise, but of writers connected with the Church (for instance it also included the Jews Philo, Josephus and Justus, and a number of heretics); and Jerome not only avoids saying that Seneca was a Christian, but is hesitant about including him at all. From the way he talks of the apocryphal correspondence (*quae leguntur a plurimis*), it seems unlikely that he had seen it himself; and the one 'quotation' is not the most suggestive of Seneca's Christianity,[60] and not at all close to the original (*Ep. ad Paulum*, XII): *Nam qui meus, tuus apud te locus, qui tuus, velim ut meus.*[61]

Besides, if Jerome really thought him a Christian, or even simply inspired by St Paul, we should surely expect to find signs of special interest or admiration in the rest of his writings. But of these there are very few. He claimed to depend on Seneca among others for his knowledge of Greek philosophy (*Adv. Rufinum*, III.39): 'I have spoken of their doctrines not from their own books, but on the basis of what I could learn from Cicero, Brutus and Seneca'; but there is nothing in his writings to substantiate this. Again, in *Adv. Iovinianum*, 1.49, he refers to Seneca as *noster*: *Scripserunt Aristoteles et Plutarchus et noster Seneca de matrimonio libros* ('Aristotle, Plutarch, and our Seneca wrote books about marriage'); but this could mean almost anything: that his moral attitudes were in accordance with the Christian spirit; or simply that he, as opposed to Aristotle and Plutarch, also wrote in Latin.[62] He does lean heavily on Seneca's lost *De Matrimonio* in his discussion of virginity in *Adv. Iovinianum*, 1.41-9; but apart from this, there are only two or three passages which show any certain traces of Senecan influence.[63] In so far as he was prepared to lay himself open to pagan influence at all (a question that caused him much agonized heart-searching), it was to Cicero that he turned.[64]

The case with Augustine (354-430) is similar. Though some scholars have claimed that he owed a considerable debt to Seneca, this claim does not bear examination.[65] He mentions the apocryphal correspondence, probably relying on what Jerome had said: 'Seneca, who lived in the days of the apostles, and of whom certain letters to Paul the apostle are read. . . .'[66] But this does not seem to have affected his judgment of him in any way. Apart from one or two acknowledged quotations and the occasional striking parallel,[67] the only significant use he makes of Seneca is in *Civ.*, VI.10-11, where he quotes extensively from Seneca's lost *De Superstitione*. But even while commending what Seneca wrote, he criticized him for hypocrisy in not practising what he preached (ibid. 10): 'He did not show the same freedom [from superstition] in his life as he did in his writings'; and even for not writing what he really believed (ibid. 11): 'Of the Christians, already strongly anti-Jewish, he dared say nothing, so as not to offend the traditions of his country by praising them, and possibly his own feelings by criticizing them.' It would be an exaggeration to say, with Reynolds,[68] that he was one of Seneca's most hostile critics; but whatever Augustine may have meant by the suggestion that Seneca might have been more favourable to Christianity than he was prepared to admit publicly, there is no evidence of significant Senecan influence on his writings.

In the declining years of ancient Christian culture Seneca was still remembered, but his writings made little impression. Boethius (c. 480–524) exempted him from his general condemnation of the Stoics,[69] and quoted his lost *De Forma Mundi* as an authority for the theory of the earth's sphericity,[70] but significant Senecan influence on the *Philosophiae consolatio* is conspicuous by its absence, considering the subject-matter and approach of the work.[71] Apart from two references to Seneca's past glory in the verse of St Sidonius Apollinaris (c. 430–c. 479),[72] and an unfavourable mention in Honorius Scholasticus (sixth century),[73] the only remaining evidence for the survival of Seneca's memory comes from Spain. There are borrowings from him in the poets Prudentius (b. 348)[74] and Merobaudes (mid-fifth century);[75] and Isidore (Bishop of Seville, 602–36) uses the *Naturales Quaestiones* in his *Etymologies*.[76]

But by far the most significant of Seneca's debtors was St Martin of Braga (d. 580), who dedicated to King Miro a short treatise on the cardinal virtues (the *Formula honestae vitae*), which was taken almost entirely from Seneca, probably from the lost *De Officiis*. This was one of the most widely read works of the Middle Ages (over six hundred manuscripts are still extant), and it was normally attributed directly to Seneca. (In most manuscripts the dedication is missing, and it is called either *De quattuor virtutibus cardinalibus*, or, when copied alongside the apocryphal correspondence with St Paul, *Liber de copia verborum*, on the supposition that it was the work of that title referred to by Seneca in *Ep. ad Paulum*, IX.) Martin also wrote a *De Ira*, closely based on Seneca's work of the same name.[77]

Slightly different from Martin's reworkings of Seneca, though no less important, were a number of collections of short excerpts from the Senecan corpus, both genuine and spurious, which were to have a marked effect on his influence throughout the Middle

Ages, though these others have much obscurer origins. The most important was the *Liber de moribus*, a collection of one hundred and forty-five sentences, many of which may well stem from lost works by Seneca. It presumably already existed in the sixth century, since numbers 35–6 were quoted under Seneca's name at the second Council of Tours in A.D. 567.[78] Later, some of the sentences were used to supplement an alphabetical collection of quotations from the mimes of Publilius Syrus, and the whole became known as the *Senecae proverbia* or *Senecae sententiae*. Other such compilations were the *De Paupertate* (derived from the *Epistles*), the *De Remediis Fortuitorum* (probably an epitome of a genuine work), and the *Monita Senecae*.[79]

The existence of these excerpts makes it difficult to estimate the extent to which Seneca's works were known at first hand during the Middle Ages; and when judging of his influence even in antiquity, we should bear in mind the possibility that quotations and echoes derive from similar compilations, perhaps used as educational textbooks.[80] This might also help towards at least a partial explanation of the odd fact that nearly all quotations from Seneca by Christian writers, and all the extensive ones, are from lost works of whose authenticity we have no independent evidence (Lactantius from the *Exhortationes* and the *De Immatura Morte*, Jerome from the *De Matrimonio*, Augustine from the *De Superstitione*, and Martin from the *De Officiis*).[81] But whatever the explanation, it completely destroys the theory that it was Christian admiration for Seneca that guaranteed the survival of his works: not only is this admiration extremely limited, as I hope I have shown, but the only works the Christians obviously did admire are precisely those which have been allowed to disappear.

3 Seneca in the Middle Ages

During the seventh and eighth centuries, classical learning was confined mainly to Ireland and Britain. But though the scholars of the period had quite a wide knowledge of the literature, Seneca remained in almost total obscurity. The lines by Columbanus (543–615):

> Differentibus vitam
> Mors incerta subripit[82]

seem to reflect the ps.-Senecan *De Moribus*, 10: *Multos vitam differentes mors incerta praevenit*; and Aldhelm (*c.* 639–709) quotes as grammatical examples two lines from the *Agamemnon* (. . . *ut Lucius Annaeus Seneca in sexto volumine* . . .) in his book on metres.[83] But that appears to be all. He fared only slightly better during the Carolingian Renaissance of the ninth century, despite the much increased scholarly activity. Alcuin (735–804) sent Charlemagne a copy of the apocryphal correspondence with St Paul,[84] and twice quoted the *De Moribus* in his *Epistles*;[85] Hrabanus Maurus (776/84–856) copied Cassiodorus' reference to Seneca's lost *De Forma Mundi* in his *De Clericorum Institutione*, III.xxv; and Modoin of Autun (d. 840/3) mentioned Seneca's fate in his poem to the exiled Theodulf.[86]

The first medieval writer to show any knowledge of Seneca's genuine philosophical works was Paschasius Radbertus of Corbie (d. 860), who made an unfavourable contrast between Seneca's definition of hope (*Epist.* 10.2: *Spes incerti boni nomen est*) and Christian faith;[87] and about the same time Walahfrid Strabo (*c.* 796–849) copied out an extract from *Epistle* 120, and once mentioned Seneca in his writings.[88] Sedulius Scotus (mid-ninth century) made a collection of ps.-Senecan proverbs,[89] and Eugenius Vulgarius (*fl. c.* 900) had an intimate knowledge of the *Tragedies*.[90] Apart from these, the only other references to Seneca are in the ninth-century chronicler Freculphus, who gives an account of him almost identical to that given by Jerome;[91] and Hucbald of St Amand (840–930), who bequeathed eighteen books to his monastery, including Seneca's *De Morte Claudii* and the ps.-Senecan *Proverbia*.[92]

In the cultural recession that followed the Carolingian Renaissance, Seneca was again almost completely forgotten. In the tenth century, Ratherius of Lüttich (b. *c.* 887) gives Seneca as one of his many precedents for the use of the epistolary form,[93] but he quotes only ps.-Senecan sentences (about ten times, usually attributing them to Seneca himself).[94] Liutprand of Cremona (*c.* 922–*c.* 972) knew his *Tragedies*; and Gerbert of Rheims (*c.* 950–1003), later Pope Sylvester II, may have quoted part of *Epistle* 9.8 in a letter.[95] For most of the eleventh century the situation is much the same. Apart from a single quotation from the *Tragedies* by Papias,[96] the only significant Senecan influence is mediated by the pseudepigrapha, when Otloh of St Emmeran

(c. 1010–70) incorporated some ps.-Senecan sentences in his collection of proverbs. But he expresses his admiration for the pagan philosopher at the beginning of his prologue: 'I recently read the alphabetical collection of so-called *Proverbs of Seneca*, and my first reaction was one of astonishment that any pagan could have as much sense as is found in some of those sayings. Then I felt impelled to undertake a similar project, collecting proverbs suitable for the edification of the faithful from secular, sacred and even our own literature.'[97]

So far, Seneca's medieval influence, philosophical or otherwise, has been in effect non-existent – in marked contrast with that of Cicero, the classical poets and even some of the Greek philosophers. But from the end of the eleventh century he begins to come into view again. Desiderius, Abbot of Monte Cassino (1058–87), had ordered the copying of a Senecan manuscript, probably the *Codex Ambrosianus* of the *Dialogues*,[98] and one of his monks, Guaiferius of Salerno (*fl. c.* 1075), made extensive, though unacknowledged, use of them in his *Vita S. Lucii papae et martyris*, and to a lesser extent in his *Vita Secundi*. As Reynolds says, the opening of the *Vita Lucii* 'is in fact nothing but a brilliant Senecan pastiche, largely composed of elements derived from one body of Seneca's work, the Ambrosian dialogues'.[99] The influence of Seneca on Guaiferius's work as a whole may still be small, but it is of a quite different order from anything we have seen since Martin of Braga (and also the first appearance of the *Dialogues* since Martin epitomized the *De Ira*). Respect is paid to Seneca in a completely different way by the eleventh-century author of an anonymous poem on Paul and Seneca. Though he denies that Seneca was actually converted, he comes closer to formulating the theory of his Christianity than anyone before him, or than anyone else till the fourteenth century:[100]

> Quidam philosophus, de nomine Seneca dictus,
> Conpunctus verbis [i.e. Pauli] fit mox per cuncta fidelis . . .
> Qui, licet indignus fuerit baptismate Christi,
> Scriptis mirandus vitaque fuit venerandus.
> Hunc mentis voto, lector, complectere toto:
> Est ut divinus quare per cuncta sequendus.

> (A certain philosopher called Seneca was soon shamed by Paul's words into accepting the faith in its entirety. . . . Though he

was unworthy of Christian baptism, he should be admired for his writings and revered for his way of life. Honour him, reader, without reservation: he is almost divine and should therefore be followed in everything.)

It has been suggested[101] that Anselm of Canterbury (1033–1109) might have derived from Seneca the definition of God which he uses in his ontological argument for God's existence in *Proslogion* II. (The argument runs roughly as follows: Our conception of God is of a being than which none greater can be conceived. But a being which exists in reality is greater than one which exists only in the mind. Therefore God's non-existence is inconceivable, since to conceive God existing only in the mind is to conceive a lesser being than one which exists in reality also.) If so, Seneca would have the distinction of having contributed to one of the most important single pieces of philosophizing in the whole of the early medieval period. No one would deny Anselm's originality in the argument itself, and it has long been noted that there are similarities between his definition of God: *aliquid quo nihil maius cogitari possit*, and various formulations in Augustine. However, none of these include the crucial word *maius*, but use instead terms such as *melius*, *superius*, etc. The suggestion is that Anselm derived his definition from Seneca's *Naturales Quaestiones* I. *pref.* 13:

Quid est deus? Mens universi. Quid est deus? Quod vides totum et quod non vides totum. Sic demum magnitudo illi sua redditur, qua nihil maius cogitari potest, si solus est omnia, si opus suum et extra et intra tenet.

(What is God? The mind of the universe. What is God? What you do and do not see the whole of. So his greatness (size) comes to that than which nothing greater (larger) can be conceived, if he alone is everything, and contains his creation both outside and within himself.)

But while it is always possible that Anselm used the *Naturales Quaestiones*, it seems highly unlikely, since no one else had yet used them since antiquity, and Anselm was unusually suspicious of the pagan classics. Besides, it is clear from the context that Seneca intends *maius* merely in the sense of 'larger', whereas

Anselm, for the ontological argument to work, must mean 'greater' or 'more perfect'.[102]

The twelfth century saw a cultural renaissance, marked not just by an increase in intellectual activity, but by a strongly humanistic outlook; though this was soon to be swamped by the rise of scholasticism, till it rose again with renewed vigour in the Renaissance proper.[103] Although it was not till the end of the thirteenth century that the Ambrosian dialogues and Letters 89–125 became generally known,[104] Seneca shared in the new respect for classical literature, and during the twelfth century his popularity rivalled even that of Cicero.[105] At the forefront of the movement was the school of Chartres, and it is remarkable that, despite its generally Platonic outlook,[106] some of its leading figures show traces of Senecan influence not merely in the sphere of morality, but in metaphysics. For instance, Thierry of Chartres (mid-twelfth century), in his *Opusculum de opere sex dierum*, leaned heavily on Seneca's *Epistle* 65 in his discussion of cause;[107] and Gilbert of Poitiers (1076–1154) in his *De sex principiis* based his account of forms on Seneca's distinction between the Platonic idea and the Aristotelian form in *Epistle* 58.[108] In the same school, William of Conches (1080–1154) made use of the meteorological sections of the *Naturales Quaestiones* in his *Dragmaticon philosophiae*.[109]

In the sphere of ethics, few twelfth-century writers failed to quote Seneca, and in at least one case his influence seems to have gone deeper than that of a mere supplier of quotable *dicta*. Peter Abelard (1072–1142), the most outstanding philosopher of his age, though explicitly quoting him only about a dozen times, goes out of his way to show his admiration for him:[110]

Seneca maximus ille paupertatis et continentiae sectator, et summus inter universos philosophos morum aedificator.

maximus ille morum philosophus.

insignis ille tam eloquentia quam moribus Seneca.

nobilis quoque gentilis Seneca.

More significantly, he appears to have found in him an ideal to live up to, and a real moral guide in such questions as the extent to which asceticism should be carried, and that of his relationship with Héloïse.[111] Exceptional in a different way was William of Malmesbury (*c.* 1095–1143), who, in his *Polyhistor*, used Seneca's writings in a truly humanistic spirit: as much for the stories in them as for their moral *sententiae*.[112]

More typical was John of Salisbury (1110–80), who frequently quotes him as a moral authority (about thirty times in the *Policraticus*, and about thirteen in the *Metalogicon*),[113] but without undergoing deep Senecan influence. He is clearly an admirer of Seneca, whom he singles out as a famous pagan philosopher: *Testantur enim, ut de nostris taceam, Seneca et multi alii clari inter philosophos*.[114] But it is difficult to extract a consistent picture from his more detailed judgments of him, since they all come as comments on Quintilian's assessment, which is itself far from unambiguous.[115] In *Pol.* VIII.xiii John quotes Quintilian in full, but though he 'leaves it to the judgment of wiser men whether his opinion was right', his subsequent interpretation of Quintilian certainly puts Seneca in a very good light. And in the *Metalogicon* he is consciously more favourable to Seneca than he understood Quintilian to have been (*ut pace Quintiliani loquar*), when he writes:[116]

> For he is loud in the praise of virtue and ethics; and his aphoristic style is succinct, yet decorative; so he cannot fail to please those who love either virtue or eloquence.... Among the pagans no ethical writer is to be found (or at least hardly any) whose words or sayings can be more appropriately used on any question.

Another admirer of Seneca was Godfrey of St Victor (d. 1194), who wrote in his *Fons philosophiae*:[117]

> Nostris ut temporibus proprius accedam
> Quid tibi de Senece documentis edam?
> Seneca Lucilio commendavit quedam
> Que vix evangelio postponenda credam.

(To come nearer our own times, what shall I tell you of Seneca's writings? I would rate some of his advice to Lucilius almost as highly as the Gospels.)

Alan of Lille (*c.* 1125–1203) said of him in his *Anticlaudianus*:[118]

> More suo Seneca mores ratione monetat,
> Optimus excultor morum mentisque colonus.
>
> (In his own way Seneca devises moral principles, that supreme propagator of morality and cultivator of the mind.)

Extensive use, whether acknowledged or not, was also made of Seneca's works by such writers as William of St Thierry, Petrus Cantor and Giraldus Cambrensis, to name but a few.[119]

A different form of influence, and one which in the long term was perhaps more significant, was the extent to which Senecan sayings were included in moral *florilegia*. Since these were used in elementary education, they help to account for Seneca's being so widely known even among non-philosophers in the later Middle Ages and the Renaissance. Prominent among them were the highly influential *Moralium dogma philosophorum*, perhaps by William of Conches,[120] the *Florilegium Gallicum*,[121] and the *Florilegium morale Oxoniense*.[122]

If we ask why it should be that Seneca suddenly enjoyed such a vogue, the answer ought to be simple: that the twelfth century was a humanistic age in which scholars appreciated the classical writers, of whom Seneca was one of the most important, and were sufficiently broadminded to believe that worldly wisdom was not the exclusive possession of Christians. In the case of other classical authors who underwent a similar upsurge of popularity, such as Suetonius, Sallust, Lucan and Ovid,[123] nothing more would need to be said. But with Seneca the position is, as always, complicated by the presence of the apocryphal correspondence with St Paul. At least two writers, while never suggesting that Seneca was a Christian, do praise him in the context of the correspondence. First, it is when quoting *Epp. ad Paulum* I and VII that Peter Abelard calls him respectively *insignis ille tam eloquentia quam moribus Seneca*,[124] and *Seneca quoque inter universos philosophos, tam moralis doctrinae quam vitae gratiam adeptus*.[125] But this does not show that he admired him *because of* the correspondence. In the first case his purpose is to summon up as much authority as possible for Paul's greatness; and in the second, to find what pagan support he can for the Christian doctrines of the Trinity and of the Holy Ghost (and the only

'Senecan' reference to the *spiritus sanctus* is in *Ep. ad Paulum* VII). There is no reason to suppose that his general attitude to Seneca would have been any different if the correspondence had never existed.

More to the point is John of Salisbury's use of the correspondence in *Pol.* VIII.xiii as an argument for respecting Seneca: 'I consider mad those who, on whatever authority, refuse to respect one who is agreed to have earned the friendship of the Apostle, and was put in the catalogue of saints by the most learned Father Jerome'. But again this proves little. If there was any question of the propriety of using pagan authorities, it would be natural for humanists like John to use all possible arguments in their defence, even if this justification for using Seneca in particular could not be generalized to cover the pagans he admired even more. When we consider the extent of the general use made of other pagan authorities, many of whom were far further removed from the Christian spirit than was Seneca, it would be strange if Seneca's influence owed anything to the forged correspondence. Indeed, one twelfth-century writer, Philip of Harvengt, goes as far as to suggest that Paul was influenced by Seneca rather than the other way round.[126]

But the use of pagan writers in general, and Seneca in particular, was a controversial question in the twelfth century. For instance, Laurence of Durham (d. 1154) wrote a poem deprecating his earlier devotion to the classics, including the lines:[127]

> Proh dolor! Imberbi mihi plus instare Platoni
> Quam Moysi, Senecae quam Iosuae cor erat.

(Oh dear! Oh dear! When I was young Plato was closer to my heart than Moses, and Seneca than Joshua.)

More significantly, Walter of St Victor (d. after 1180), perhaps with his colleague Godfrey in mind,[128] produced a scathing attack on Seneca's doctrines and character in his *Contra quatuor labyrinthos Franciae*, Book IV, especially in chapter ii (*De blande et ideo mortifera Senece doctrina*):[129]

> E contra iste vir omni femina mollior cum peteretur ad mortem confugit ad balneas, ibique tamquam puerulus aquis delibutis et tepefactis ac si in mollissimis plumis se sepelivit usque ad

collum; deinde utriusque brachii venis molliter tactis in summa luxuria effeminatum animum ac si dormiendo evomuit; miro scilicet ingenio ipsam mortem mortisque dolorem vertit sibi in magnam voluptatem. Iste igitur non quidem fratricida sed peior suicida; stoicus professione, epicurus morte; putasne cum Nerone et Socrate et Catone suicidis receptus sit in celo? Crede mihi; melius illi erat si natus non fuisset homo, malletque semper luxuriari in balneo.

(Now, by contrast, consider that man, softer than any woman, how he behaved when his death was demanded. He resorted to his bath, and there, like a little boy, he buried himself to the neck in the warm, scented water as if it were the softest down; then with a delicate touch to the veins of each arm, he spewed out his effeminate soul in the height of luxury as if he were going to sleep. Yes, by a stroke of genius he had turned death itself and the agony of death into a great voluptuous experience. So that man was no fratricide – worse, he was a suicide; a Stoic by profession, an Epicurean in death. Do you think he, along with those other suicides, Nero, Socrates and Cato, has gained a place in paradise? Believe me, it were better for the man that he had never been born, or had preferred to continue luxuriating in his bath for ever.)

But Walter's case against Seneca does not rest on such rhetoric alone, magnificent though it is, and he goes on to produce some serious arguments: Seneca's philosophy as revealed in his writings and his behaviour is fundamentally opposed to Christianity; we should not be too impressed by what Jerome said, since his catalogue of saints was not a list of orthodox Christians; and as for the correspondence with St Paul, the fact that Seneca did not even die like a Christian, even when he had nothing to lose by it, proves that he deliberately rejected the Christian message. Thus we see that even when the authenticity of the correspondence was accepted, almost any conclusion could be drawn from it about Seneca's relations with Christianity or the value of his philosophy; and hence that it is unlikely to have been in any way responsible for his popularity among twelfth-century humanists.

But the revival of interest in Seneca was short-lived, and for the rest of the Middle Ages the only philosopher of note to pay any attention to him was Roger Bacon (*c.* 1219–94), who had a profound admiration for him, and often quoted him, especially in his *Moralis philosophia* (*Opus maius*, VII).[130] In the dedication of this work to Pope Clement IV, he not only expresses his own attitude to Seneca, but gives an indication of the general disrespect into which his writings had fallen: 'But the philosophical books of Aristotle, Avicenna, Seneca, Cicero and others can only be obtained at great expense. . . . Of some not a single copy is to be found in the higher schools, or anywhere else. . . . As for Seneca's books, which I have excerpted for your Holiness, I could not find any till the time you commissioned my work, though I searched diligently for more than twenty years. . . . Very few people know anything about such books, and they are inexperienced in them.'[131]

He complains of the neglect of Cicero, Pliny and Seneca again in his *Compendium theologiae*: 'I am especially concerned that the reader should search for books worthy of their authors, since they contain the beauty and dignity of wisdom, and at the present time are completely overlooked by teachers as much as by the mass of students.'[132] If he meant that Seneca in particular was completely neglected, this would be an exaggeration, since the great encyclopaedist Vincent of Beauvais (d. *c.* 1264) quoted him extensively in his *Speculum maius*,[133] and Albertanus of Brescia in his *florilegium*, *Liber consolationis et consilii* (1246);[134] and there are also scattered quotations and references in other writers. All the same, it is quite true that Seneca was generally out of favour, especially among professional philosophers. The reason for this is not far to seek: by this time the philosophical scene had become dominated by the interests and methods of Aristotelian scholasticism, embodying a conception of philosophy to which the writings of Seneca were diametrically opposed. Until other types of philosophy emerged to rival scholasticism, Seneca's influence was bound to remain peripheral.

4 Seneca since the Renaissance

Although Seneca was for a while disdained by professional philosophers, his influence still continued to be felt in non-philosophical literature, whether through the reading of his actual works, or of the partly Senecan moral *florilegia* so widely used in elementary education. For instance Dante (1265–1321) quotes him a few times (though far less than many other ancient authors),[135] and puts the 'moral Seneca' (i.e. the philosopher as opposed to the tragedian, the two still being considered distinct) in the privileged first circle of hell (*Inferno* IV.138). Chaucer (*c.* 1340–1400), who says of him 'For of moralitee he was the flour',[136] names Seneca more often than any other classical author save Ovid, though most of his borrowings are from the ps.-Senecan corpus or indirect (e.g. via Albertanus and John of Wales).[137] An even greater admiration for Seneca as a moralist was shown by the French poet Eustache Deschamps (*c.* 1346–*c.* 1406), who, incidentally, called Chaucer a 'Sénèque en mœurs'.[138] In some places his influence was felt at a more popular level: for instance he is quoted in a number of Provençal poems ('Seneca que fon hom sabens . . .'),[139] and in Spain he was represented in puppet theatres at least till the beginning of the eighteenth century.[140] Indeed he was always popular among Spanish writers, probably because they felt a special sympathy for their greatest fellow-countryman of antiquity.[141] But of Seneca's subsequent influence on non-philosophical literature I shall say no more, since it has been extensively covered by others, and is not directly relevant to my present purpose.[142]

Scholasticism, which was strongly antipathetic to Seneca, remained the orthodox philosophy of most universities and religious houses till well into the seventeenth century. But although its supremacy severely limited Seneca's philosophical influence in the thirteenth and early fourteenth centuries, he began to come back into favour with the rise of Renaissance humanism in the middle of the fourteenth. In conscious reaction against the abstractions and technicalities of the scholastics, the early humanists strove to develop a realistic and comprehensible philosophy of life, based as far as was consistent with Christian belief on a better appreciation of the wisdom of the ancients. Moreover, they were convinced that wisdom and eloquence went hand in hand, so that valuable truths were not to be found in the barbarous Latin of the scholastics, but in the impeccable language of the ancient Roman philosophers and their imitators.[143] For both these reasons it was natural that the humanists should have a greater admiration for Cicero or Seneca than for the Aristotle of scholastic philosophy.

The greatest of the early humanists, Petrarch (1304–74), seems to have owed more to Seneca than to any other ancient philosopher. Not only did he quote him more often than any other classical writer except Virgil, and model his style on him, but he found in him the source of the many Stoic elements in his philosophy of life, and an ally in his hostility to scholastic dialectic.[144] Typical is this passage from his *De sui ipsius et multorum ignorantia* (1367): 'Wanting peace and leisure, I willingly forgo the title of scholar, remembering Seneca's "Such praise costs much time, and annoyance for those who must listen. Scholarly man! Let us be content with the more rustic title: good man!" I stand by your advice, greatest of moral teachers; I am content with the more rustic title, as you call it, though I would say it is the better, the holier, and therefore also the more noble.'[145] One of the most influential of Petrarch's Latin works was his *De remediis utriusque fortunae* (1366), a moral treatise which was derived largely from Seneca, and which may have played an important role in sustaining interest in Stoicism during the following century.[146] But he was not blind to Seneca's faults, and his *Letter to Seneca* (1348) in *Le familiari* is devoted to a gentle criticism of the latter's conduct in life: 'Though you are worthy of great respect and unrivalled, if we are to believe Plutarch, as a moral teacher, I hope you will not take it amiss if I ask you to recognize where you went wrong in life.'[147] In his later years he developed an increasing fondness for Cicero, and as a result he tended to underestimate his earlier debt to Seneca.

The Calabrian monk Barlaam (*c*. 1290–*c*. 1348), who taught Petrarch the rudiments of Greek, had already used Seneca as his main source in his short exposition of Stoic ethics, *Ethica secundum Stoicos*;[148] and Petrarch's disciple Coluccio Salutati (1331–1406) had hardly less an admiration for Seneca than for Cicero.[149] Indeed there was sufficient interest in him for a chair in Senecan studies to be established at the University of Piacenza in 1389.[150] It is also in this century that we first find a clear formulation of the theory that he had been converted to Christianity, in Giovanni Colonna's *De viris illustribus* (*c*. 1332); this was elaborated on by Boccaccio (1313–75), who argued that the story in Tacitus's *Annals* (15.64) that Seneca, on dying, gave a libation to Jupiter Liberator, really meant that he offered it to Jesus Christ.[151] But these were only incidental speculations: there was no suggestion that the theory gave any special justification for submitting to Seneca's influence, and there is no evidence that Petrarch, the most Senecan of fourteenth-century humanists, had so much as heard of it.

Given the character and context of early humanism, there is nothing surprising about Seneca's popularity in the second half of the fourteenth century; more strange is the extent to which he was ignored in the fifteenth. His works were still copied, and frequently printed from 1475 onwards, and a few translations into the vernacular were made;[152] but apart from the occasional quotation or reference, Seneca appears to have been without any significant influence for the whole of the century.[153] As a philosopher he was cast into the shade by a new enthusiasm for Greek philosophy (especially Neoplatonism), and as a stylist by Cicero, whose writings rapidly became the exclusive standard of correct Latinity. It was not until the sixteenth century that he gradually came back into favour.

In the earlier part of his career, Erasmus (1469–1536) was a great admirer of Seneca.[154] He himself relates that he preferred him to Cicero in his adolescence,[155] and in 1515 he published an edition of Seneca's works, in the preface to which he wrote: 'There is nothing holier than his precepts; and he encourages virtue with such zeal that it is obvious he practised what he preached. He alone summons the spirit to the sublime, promotes contempt for the mundane, brings about hatred of baseness, and inspires love of virtue; in short, anyone who reads him with a desire for improvement will be left a better man.'[156] He then proceeds to defend him against the unfavourable judgments of Caligula, Quintilian and Gellius; and though he does allow minor criticisms of his style, he adds: 'But what author was ever absolutely perfect? He is so full of moral purity that even if he had been totally incapable of self-expression, he should still be read by all who seek to live well; but he is also so eloquent that even in that age of eloquence he is regarded as one of the masters of eloquence, and Quintilian is in danger of seeming jealous of Seneca.'

In the following year Erasmus recommended Seneca as suitable reading for the young, after parts of the Bible and Plutarch.[157] But during the next dozen years his attitude to Seneca underwent a radical change. In 1528 he published his dialogue *Ciceronianus*,[158] which was an attack on the extreme advocates of Ciceronian style; but so far from setting up Seneca as an alternative model, he barely even mentions him. Again, in his *De pueris instituendis* of 1529 he explicitly states that Seneca is unsuitable for elementary education.[159] In the same year he published a completely new edition of Seneca's works; but in this he was motivated not so much by a love of Seneca, as by his sense of shame at the shortcomings of the 1515 edition.[160] In his preface he gives detailed arguments against the authenticity of the correspondence with St Paul (an opinion which he had merely stated in the earlier preface), and goes out of his way to point out the divergencies between Seneca's teaching and Christianity:[161]

> In fact I think it is better that Seneca's books should be read as if written by a man ignorant of our religion. For if you read him as a pagan, he wrote like a Christian; if as a Christian, he wrote like a pagan. Though many of his sayings can rouse us to a desire for virtue, they will have a sting in the tail if we remember they came from a pagan. For some of the sayings or deeds of the pagans are to be strongly condemned by the standards of Christian philosophy ... So as far as morals are concerned, Seneca will be read with greater profit, if he is read as a pagan, which he was. For what he said in a Christian spirit will be more effective, and the opposite will be less harmful. Besides, he diverges most from Christian philosophy when he deals with the questions which are most important to us.

He also attacks his style, and even accuses him of insincerity:[162]

> Even the very respect for which Seneca is mainly praised is open to criticism. He attacks people's ways freely and sharply, but not always seasonably, sometimes immoderately, and on occasion with too much affectation; consequently he thus verges on scurrility. The way he describes some vices, while criticizing them, he seems to regret rather than hate them, and encourage rather than denounce them. For some are such that merely to have portrayed them is to teach or incite.

Perhaps the clearest indication of Erasmus's mature opinion of Seneca is given by the fact that in the final version of his *Adagia* (1533) – precisely the sort of work in which we should expect to find the greatest Senecan influence – Seneca occupies only twenty-first place in frequency of quotations among classical authors.[163]

Seneca had a more positive influence on some of Erasmus's contemporaries: the humanist Guillaume Budé (1467-1540) drew arguments from the *De Tranquillitate Animi* in his *De contemptu rerum fortuitarum* of 1520,[164] and the leading reformer Huldreich Zwingli (1484-1531) developed a broadly pantheistic philosophy derived largely from Seneca's Stoicism. In his *Sermonis de providentia Dei anamnema* (1530) he referred to him as *ille animorum unicus ex gentibus agricola*, and claimed that he and Socrates were more worthy of salvation than the Pope and his princes.[165] More problematic is the question of Seneca's influence on Calvin (1509-64).[166] His first work, written shortly before his conversion to the Reformation, was a commentary on Seneca's *De Clementia* (1532), and in the preface to this he is louder in his praise even than Erasmus had been in 1515:

> If I understand anything at all, he was a man of exceptional erudition and outstanding eloquence. For what realm of experience was not open to that happy genius? He had a perfect grasp of the mysteries of natural philosophy; and in ethics he was supreme and had no rival. . . . His style is pure and clear, typical of his age. . . . All that needs to be said is that our Seneca is a second Cicero, a pillar both of the philosophy and of the eloquence of Rome.

But in the commentary itself, he is very careful to point out Seneca's divergencies from Christian doctrine, and in his other writings he hardly ever mentions him. It is quite possible that his close study of Seneca at a critical period in his intellectual development had some influence on the direction it took, particularly on his predestinarianism; but he was very careful to distinguish between his own theory of predestination, and the fatalism of the Stoics.[167]

During the latter part of the sixteenth century, Stoicism in a more or less Christianized form achieved a popularity such as it had not enjoyed since the first century A.D. But Seneca no longer held the position of the only extant representative of the school (that is, discounting the Stoic elements in Cicero's writings). Epictetus had become known in the West in the previous century, and he now found a number of champions. In 1554, Thomas Kirchmaier (1511–63) published an annotated translation of the *Enchiridion*, in the preface to which he commended it as an introduction to Christianity.[168] Guillaume Du Vair (1556–1621), who also made a translation of the *Enchiridion*, went even further, and published a number of books, notably *La Philosophie morale des stoïques* (1585), in which he expounded a barely Christianized version of Epictetus's ethics.[169] Marcus Aurelius was less influential, since his *Meditations* were not published till 1558; but he too had his advocates. One of these was Thomas Gataker (1574–1645), who far preferred him and Epictetus to Seneca:[170]

> I give Seneca first place for chronological reasons, though I consider him inferior to both the others in dignity and true worth. He does indeed have many excellent, useful, bold, sublime, penetrating and subtle things to say, and he is well worth a careful, if critical, reading by students of Theology as well as of the humanities. But he is variable and often inconsistent – I don't just mean his hypocritical life, for which Dio Cassius attacked him..., but in his writings themselves.

However, despite this new competition, Seneca's popularity continued to grow unchecked, and by the end of the century there existed what can reasonably be described as a cult of Seneca. Two men in particular helped to bring this about. The French humanist Marc-Antoine Muret (1526–85), who was to publish an improved edition of Seneca's works in the last year of his life, rejected the slavish imitation of Cicero, and set up Seneca's style as an alternative model of eloquence. He succeeded in initiating an anti-Ciceronian movement, which rapidly became a powerful force in literary theory and practice; and although not all its adherents were strict imitators of Seneca,[171] the general admiration of his eloquence did much to enhance his reputation for wisdom.

More concerned with propagating Seneca's ideas was Montaigne (1533–92), whose *Essais*, particularly the earlier ones, were full of borrowings from him. On account of this he was deservedly called 'a French Seneca' by one of his contemporaries.[172] Montaigne himself admits: 'The only really solid books I have had to do with are Plutarch and Seneca, from whom I draw like the Danaides, continuously filling and emptying my vessel. Some of the results I put down on this paper; my own contribution is negligible.'[173] In a later essay he is revealingly frank about his reasons for liking Seneca:[174]

> As for my other lesson (which combines a little more profit with pleasure), that of learning to organize my moods and circumstances, the books I find useful are Plutarch ... and Seneca. They are both singularly suited to my temperament in that the knowledge I seek in them is treated in disconnected pieces, which do not require lengthy study (of which I am incapable), as are Plutarch's *Moralia* and Seneca's *Epistles*, the best and most profitable part of his writings.... These authors agree in most true and useful opinions.... Their teaching is from the cream of philosophy, and presented in a simple and relevant manner.

Montaigne was clearly conscious of one of the most important factors governing the fluctuations in Seneca's influence, that he was not a philosopher's philosopher. But despite his admiration for Seneca, the philosophical system to which Montaigne adhered was not Stoicism, but Pyrrhonian scepticism.[175]

An even greater admirer of Seneca, and closer to Stoicism, was Montaigne's friend and disciple Pierre Charron (1541–1603). Though his chief work, *La Sagesse*, was largely a systematization of the doctrinal content of Montaigne's *Essais*,[176] in the last edition he tended to soften his scepticism with more dogmatic epistemological views taken from Seneca.[177]

The peak of Seneca's influence is found in the work of the eminent Flemish scholar and philosopher, Justus Lipsius (1547–1606). From as early as 1575, he was a staunch defender of Seneca's literary style, and in 1605 he published what was for long to remain the standard edition of Seneca's prose works. More significantly, he produced a number of books, such as the *De constantia* (1583), the *Manuductio ad philosophiam stoicam* (1604) and the *Physiologia stoicorum* (1604), in which he expounded a version of Stoicism (its metaphysics as well as its ethics) which was based almost entirely on Seneca, and which made few concessions to Christian doctrine.[178] Similar contributions were made to Seneca's ascendancy in Germany by Caspar Schoppe (1576–1649), whose *Elementa philosophiae stoicae moralis* was published in 1606; and in England by Thomas Lodge (1558–1625), who produced the first complete translation into English of Seneca's prose works in 1614, and Joseph Hall (1574–1656), who was so imbued with Senecan Stoicism in his *Heaven upon Earth* (1606) and *Characters of Vertues and Vices* (1608) that he was commonly known as 'our English Seneca'.[179]

By the early seventeenth century, the success of Stoicism was so great that few writers on ethical and even metaphysical questions escaped its influence, and borrowings from Seneca became commonplace. This remarkable phenomenon stands in need of some explanation. I have already mentioned the reaction against Ciceronian literary style and the humanists' preference for ancient philosophers to the scholastics; but these factors hardly suffice to account for the extent to which the Stoics in general and Seneca in particular were revered during the period under consideration. More important are the following reasons. First, the fifteenth and sixteenth centuries had seen not only the revival of virtually all the ancient systems of philosophy, but also a splitting up of scholasticism into a number of opposed factions. This multiplication of unreconciled dogmatisms led to a widespread dissatisfaction with metaphysics in general, encouraging both scepticism, which attacked dogmatic metaphysics on its own ground, and a preference for an untechnical, popular philosophy of life, precisely the area where Seneca had the most to offer. Second, the rise of Stoicism was helped by the bitter wars and persecutions that followed upon the Reformation. Moderates on both sides were shocked by the consequences of religious extremism, and desperately wanted to find a basis for morality which would be essentially Christian, yet independent both of the discredited authority of the Catholic (but no longer universal) Church, and of the subjectively grounded faith of the fanatical Reformers. Christian Stoicism provided an ideal compromise by founding morality on nature. It was still Christian, in that it held nature to be the creation of the God of Christianity, and its laws to be the expression of God's will; and it was effective as a compromise through its assumption that the *codex naturae* could be read more or less directly, thus by-passing any controversial appeals to faith, authority or metaphysical reasoning.[180]

I shall not here embark on even a schematic account of the wide variety of seventeenth-century admirers of Seneca; to say enough would require a study on its own; to say less would mean either a tedious list of names or else a misleadingly arbitrary selection. (For further details of specifically Senecan influence in this period, I can only refer to the work of others, notably that of Fr Julien-Eymard d'Angers.[181]) Besides, few of these admirers had much individual significance in the history of philosophy, and I do not wish to obscure the indirect Senecan influence on more important figures which they helped to transmit. Here too I cannot say much without moving away into the far broader question of seventeenth-century Stoicism in general; but at least a few points can be made.

It is a commonplace to set the beginnings of modern philosophy at the start of the seventeenth century; what is less often recognized is that many of the topics of discussion which distinguish it from what had gone before had their origin in Stoicism. Whether they were to be accepted or rejected, it was the Stoic revival that brought to the forefront of philosophical controversy such topics as pantheism and fatalism; the viability of the concepts of innate ideas, natural law, and the natural light of reason; the ideal of the supremacy of reason over the passions; and so on. Even where there is no direct indebtedness to Seneca, it is he as much as anyone who deserves credit for this, since he was the most important representative of Stoicism during the time of its renaissance. But credit was rarely given even to Stoicism, let alone to Seneca, since these Stoic topics had become such an integral part of the philosophical climate of thought that they ceased to be regarded as specifically Stoic (as had happened in the first century A.D.). It was perfectly possible for a philosopher to be deeply imbued with such ideas, while remaining bitterly opposed to what he regarded as the essence of Stoicism (e.g. the doctrine of the total impassibility of the sage, and the denial of the freedom of the will). For instance, the Platonist Herbert of Cherbury (1583–1648), in his *De veritate* (1624), based his refutation of scepticism on the (Stoic) concept of innate ideas; this was the subject of a detailed attack by Locke (1632–1704) in Book I of his *Essay concerning Human Understanding* (1690), which was in its turn criticized by Leibniz (1646–1716) in his posthumous *Nouveaux Essais*. But though all these philosophers even explicitly used the Stoic technical term κοιναὶ ἔννοιαι, none of the arguments they used were in any way related to their attitudes to Stoicism; the fact that the doctrine originated in Stoicism was simply not considered relevant.

The same goes for Descartes' doctrine of the 'natural light', Spinoza's pantheism, Leibniz's σύμπνοια πάντα, and the predominantly Stoic ethics of all three. This disinterest in the ancestry of their theories is highly significant, in that it is symptomatic of a radical change that had taken place in attitudes to ancient wisdom. Throughout the Renaissance, the ancients were generally regarded as superior in everything but religion, and hence it was natural that their views should be regarded as authoritative. But by the seventeenth century this reverence was being replaced by a confidence that man could and should progress beyond the achievements of the past; and in such a climate of opinion, appeals to ancient authority no longer carried much weight. From now on, there was to be an ever-widening gulf between philosophers, whose starting point was the work of men like Francis Bacon, Descartes and Locke; and classical scholars, who alone centred their interest on the work of the ancients.[182] As a consequence, it was fast becoming an anachronism to campaign either for or against any of the ancient philosophical systems: by the end of the Renaissance their work had largely been done.

This is not to say that none of the philosophers of the seventeenth century were aware of what was happening. Many considered the Stoic movement a profound danger to Christianity;[183] and not without reason: for although few if any of its adherents were consciously anti-Christian, the disassociation of morality from religious doctrine was a crucial step towards the secularism of the enlightenment. Thus we find violent attacks on Stoicism in Pascal (1623–62), La Bruyère (1645–96) and Bossuet (1627–1704), who said of it in his *Sermon sur la providence* (1656): 'But, what truly pompous maxims! What affected insensitivity! What false and delusory wisdom, that considers itself brave because it is hard, and noble because it is puffed up!'[184] When the criticism was more specific, it was invariably Seneca who bore the brunt of it, as being the most influential representative of the school. For instance, the Epicurean Saint-Évremond (*c*. 1614–1703) attacked him (though hardly out of piety) in his *Jugement sur Sénèque, Plutarque et Pétrone* (1664): 'To begin with Seneca: I will tell you with the greatest impudence that I admire his person much more than his writings. I admire the teacher of Nero, the lover of Agrippina, an ambitious man who sought to rule the Empire. I don't think much of the philosopher and writer, and both his style and his thoughts leave me cold.'[185] Less 'impudent' was La Rochefoucauld (1613–80): 'Philosophers, and Seneca above all, have far from cancelled their crimes by their precepts: they have merely used them to bolster up their pride.'[186] Malebranche (1638–1715) devotes a whole chapter of his *Recherche de la vérité* to an attack on Seneca, in the course of which he writes:[187]

> I do not believe one could find a more suitable author than Seneca for demonstrating the nature of the contagion which has infected an infinity of shallow-minded free-thinkers, as they are called, and how people with powerful and vivid imaginations dominate weaker and less enlightened souls, not by the strength or evidence of reasons, which are products of the spirit, but by their turns of phrase and vividness of expression, which depend on the strength of the imagination. I know that this author has a considerable reputation, and that I shall be considered rash for calling him too imaginative and lacking in judgment.

But since the seventeenth century, Seneca has suffered not only from the diminishing relevance of ancient philosophy in general, but from the popularizing nature of his own philosophy, which has never found much favour among those who regard the subject as an independent and technical discipline. He has certainly had his admirers: Hutcheson (1694–1746) and Hume (1711–76) were avid readers of Seneca;[188] the encyclopaedist Diderot (1713–84) wrote a long and impassioned treatise in vindication of his life and work;[189] and Rousseau (1712–78) numbered him among his favourite authors, and even translated the *Apocolocyntosis* into French.[190] But of these only Rousseau can plausibly be said to have undergone any Senecan influence in the formation of his philosophical views; and even in his case the influence was largely mediated by his reading of Montaigne.

Since then Seneca's reputation among professional philosophers has sunk so low that by now he is barely considered a philosopher at all. For instance, Bertrand Russell, in the single page of his *History of Western Philosophy* devoted to Seneca, says not a word about his philosophy; and his opinion of Seneca the man can easily be gathered from the following passage:[191]

> Although, as a Stoic, Seneca officially despised riches, he amassed a huge fortune, amounting, it was said, to three hundred million sesterces (about three million pounds). Much of this he acquired by lending money in Britain; according to Dio, the excessive rates of interest that he exacted were among the causes of revolt in that country. The heroic Queen Boadicea, if this is true, was heading a rebellion against capitalism as represented by the philosophic apostle of austerity.

It would be unfair to leave Russell with the last word, since Seneca has also had his defenders in the present century: a number of writers have vindicated his character and political activity, his literary style, his moral preaching (whether or not as a proto-Christian), and his significance in the history of philosophy;[192] but no one, so far as I am aware, would claim that he has much of value to contribute to philosophy as it is now studied. At the end of his book, Gummere prophesies a revival of Seneca's influence in the future;[193] but this is unlikely to happen unless impatience with the technicalities of metaphysics is once again joined with a general respect for ancient philosophy. Till then we should refrain from making claims for Seneca which his philosophy cannot meet, but give him full credit for what influence he has had on the course of Western philosophy.[194]

Notes

Apart from certain standard abbreviations for titles of classical periodicals, I use the following: *AMN* = *Analecta Mediaevalia Namurcensia*; *CCSL* = *Corpus Christianorum, Series Latina*; *CSEL* = *Corpus Scriptorum Ecclesiasticorum Latinorum*; *MGH* = *Monumenta Germaniae Historica*; *PG* = Migne, *Patrologia Graeca*; *PL* = Migne, *Patrologia Latina*.

Numbers in square brackets refer to the note in which the work is first mentioned.

1 H. R. Neuenschwander, *Mark Aurels Beziehungen zu Seneca und Poseidonios* (Berne, 1951), pp. 7, 10, 97; R. M. Wenley, *Stoicism and its Influence* (London, 1925), p. 61.

2 This is particularly true of the Greek schools until they petered out as institutions in the middle of the first century B.C.; and again after the end of the second century A.D., though then the distinction between the schools was more geographical than doctrinal. The same function was

fulfilled in the Middle Ages by the religious houses, and later by the universities.
3 A. Bourgery, *Sénèque prosateur* (Paris, 1922), p. 158. Martial also mentions Seneca in I.61.7–8; IV.40.1–2; VII.44.9–10; XII.36.8–9.
4 Compare this with what he says of Flavus's last words (*Ann*. 15.67): 'Ipsa rettuli verba, quia non, ut Senecae, vulgata erant...'.
5 J. P. Sullivan, *The Satyricon of Petronius* (London, 1968), esp. pp. 132–9, 186–9, 193–213. He gives a bibliography of the question on p. 195n.
6 Bourgery [3], p. 151.
7 Compare Plutarch II.912B; VI.913E; XIII.915B and XXIX.919B with Seneca 3.21.2, 3.25; 6.13.2 and 7.1–3 and 1.15.1 respectively.
8 P. Faider, *Études sur Sénèque* (Ghent, 1921), pp. 25–8.
9 Bourgery [3], p. 152.
10 M. P. O. Morford, *The Poet Lucan* (Oxford, 1967), esp. p. 46.
11 E.g. Bourgery [3], p. 151: 'Parmi les jeunes son influence fut considérable. Bien peu y résistèrent alors: Perse... est une de ces exceptions.' Cf. Faider [8], p. 14. More positive is R. Verdière, 'Notes critiques sur Perse', in *Mélanges Niedermann* (Neuchâtel, 1954), pp. 339–50.
12 W. V. Clausen (ed.), *Persi et Iuuenalis Saturae* (Oxford, 1959), p. 32.
13 Faider [8], p. 14, argues that Persius was a more orthodox Stoic than Seneca, since he was a pupil of Lucius Annaeus Cornutus (b. *c*. A.D. 20). But so was Lucan a disciple of Cornutus, and we know too little about Cornutus to judge of his orthodoxy or otherwise. Indeed, his name suggests that he may have been a freedman of Seneca's, in which case Cornutus might himself have come under Seneca's influence.
14 The three passages where he mentions Seneca (V.109; VIII.212; X.16) reveal virtually nothing about his attitude towards him. For traces of possible influence, cf. G. Highet, 'Juvenal's Bookcase', *AJP*, 72 (1951), pp. 369–94, esp. pp. 374–5, 383–4, 391.
15 Bourgery [3], p. 158; Faider [8], p. 29.
16 Faider [8], p. 30 argues that since he was an admirer of Lucan, he must have admired Lucan's uncle; but this does not follow. Bourgery [3], p. 158 claims 'Il est célébré à l'envi par les poètes, par Stace (*Silv*. II.7.30)...' But what Statius actually says (*Silv*. II.7.30–3) is: 'Lucanum potes imputare terris!/Hoc plus quam Senecam dedisse mundo/Aut dulcem generasse Gallionem,' which is hardly flattering to Seneca.
17 L. Herrman, 'Autour des Fables de Phèdre', *Latomus*, 7 (1948), pp. 197–207. But the parallels produced are unconvincing, quite apart from the difficulty that Phaedrus was some fifteen years older than Seneca.
18 Bourgery [3], p. 152 gives the author, whom he takes to be Seneca's correspondent Lucilius, as an example of one who 'submitted totally' to Seneca's influence. But see F. R. D. Goodyear, *Incerti Auctoris* Aetna (Cambridge, 1965), pp. 54–9, who concludes that we cannot know who the author was, and that what Senecan parallels there are (with the *Nat. Quaest*.) derive from a common source, probably Posidonius.
19 Donatus, *Vita Vergili*, ed. C. Hardie (Oxford, 1907), ll. 97ff.; Diomedes, *Ars Grammatica*, ed. Putsch, pp. 362, 375; Servius, *Commentarii in*

Vergilii Carmina, VI.154; IX.30. All the quotations are from lost works. Later, Priscian (early sixth century) quotes him in *Inst. Gram.* VI.13.68; VII.15.74, and in *De ponderibus*, III.14. Of these, only the first quotation is from extant works (*Phae.* 710, and *Ag.* 365).

20 Bourgery [3], p. 166.
21 *Sat.* I, *pref.* 5ff., from *Epist.* 84.2ff.; and 1.11.7–15, from *Epist.* 47. W. C. Summers, *Select Letters of Seneca* (London, 1910), p. xcviii, argues that Macrobius' failure to acknowledge his debt is evidence of the extent to which Seneca's work was forgotten; but this is hardly to the point, since there is no reason to suppose that he was deliberately trying to conceal his plagiarism.
22 E.g. 1.6.26 and *Brev. Vit.* 13.5; 1.7.6 and *Epist.* 10.5; 1.7.28 and *Nat. Quaest.* 3.25.8; 1.11.23–4 and *Ben.* 3.23.1–5; 1.12.7 and *Epist.* 47; 1.18.16 and *Tranq. An.* 17.8; VII.1.4 and *Epist.* 29.10.
23 Compare Rutilius' comment on the Jews in *De reditu suo*, 1.397–8: 'Latius excisae pestis contagia serpunt,/Victoresque suos natio victa premit,' with Seneca's in *De Sup.* (*ap.* Augustine, *Civ.* VI.xi): 'Cum interim usque eo sceleratissimae gentis consuetudo convaluit, ut per omnes iam terras recepta sit: victi victoribus leges dederunt.' A. Cameron, 'Rutilius Namatianus, St. Augustine, and the date of the *De Reditu*', *JRS*, 57 (1967), pp. 31–9, argues convincingly (p. 32) that Rutilius *could* have got this from St Augustine rather than from Seneca himself. Less cogent is his argument for saying Augustine is *more* likely to have been his source: since Seneca's 'subject matter laid him under suspicion of being a Christian, he is not at all an obvious candidate for Rutilius' bookshelf'. As I hope to show, Seneca was not regarded as particularly pro-Christian, and even if he was, St Augustine would still be a far less likely candidate for a pagan's bookshelf.
24 Though many would dispute this, I believe that Syme's conclusions are essentially correct. Cf. R. Syme, *Tacitus* (London, 1958), pp. 546, 551–2, 582n.
25 Esp. *Nero*, 52.
26 Esp. 61.10.2.
27 Suetonius, *Caligula*, 53.2. Some have held that Tacitus was critical of Seneca's style. E.g. Syme [24], p. 551 refers to 13.3.1 and 11.2 in support of this view; but in the first passage Tacitus merely says that Seneca's style was popular in his time, and in the second that his motives for writing Nero's speeches might have been suspect. Besides, it is generally admitted that Tacitus was himself influenced by Seneca's style: cf. Syme [24], p. 116; Bourgery [3], p. 155; J. Wight Duff, *A Literary History of Rome in the Silver Age*, 3rd edn (London, 1964), p. 186. For suggestions of Senecan influence on Tacitus' attitudes, cf. P. Grenade, 'Le pseudo-épicurisme de Tacite', *REA*, 55 (1953), pp. 36–57.
28 *The Correspondence of Marcus Cornelius Fronto*, ed. and trans. C. R. Haines (Loeb, 1919–20), vol. II, pp. 100–8. Since Fronto was Marcus Aurelius's tutor, his bitter attack on Seneca may be one of the reasons why the latter ignored him (though Fronto was equally forceful in trying

to deter him from philosophy in general, and was far from successful in that).

29 According to A. Momigliano, 'Note sulla leggenda del cristianesimo di Seneca', *Rivista Storica Italiana*, 42 (1950), pp. 336ff., the first to propose the theory was Giovanni Colonna, *c*. 1332, who was followed by some other Renaissance scholars. Cf. pp. 142–3, *inf.* The theory had a brief revival in the nineteenth century, notably in A. Fleury, *Saint Paul et Sénèque* (Paris, 1953), and it has recently been defended in a highly original way by E. Elorduy, *Séneca*, vol. 1: *Vida y escritos* (Burgos, 1965), pp. 310–53. The classic refutation of the theory is in Ch. Aubertin, *Sénèque et saint Paul, étude sur les rapports supposés entre le philosophe et l'apôtre* (Paris, 1869). For a full bibliography of the question, see J. Haussleiter, 'Literatur zu der Frage "Seneca und das Christentum"', *Bursian's Jahresbericht* 281 (1943), pp. 172–5; J.-G. Préaux, Review of Sevenster, *Paul and Seneca* in *Antiquité Classique*, 31 (1962), pp. 368–9.

30 See esp. J. B. Lightfoot, 'St Paul and Seneca', in *Saint Paul's Epistle to the Philippians*, 4th edn (London, 1908), pp. 270–333; J. N. Sevenster, *Paul and Seneca* (Leiden, 1961).

31 Momigliano [29].

32 C. H. Hay, *Montaigne lecteur et imitateur de Sénèque* (Poitiers, 1938), p. 4, quotes only two passages in support of the theory: Tertullian's 'Seneca saepe noster' (cf. p. 126, *inf.*), and a passage in the *Chronicon* of Flavius Dexter (*fl. c.* 400): 'L. Annaeus Seneca Cordubensis, consularis vir, et in religionem Christianam egregie propensus, cui etiam secreto adhaerebat . . .' (*PL*, XXXI, 211–12). However, this work is a late sixteenth-century forgery (cf. n. 141, *inf.*).

33 In modern times this position has been eloquently maintained in connection with Seneca by F. W. Farrar, *Seekers after God* (London, 1873), pp. ix–xii, 167–85, 318–36.

34 Other pagans have from time to time been called Christians, e.g. Socrates and Heraclitus by Justin Martyr in *Apol.* II.8, 10. But this cannot have been meant literally; and Seneca was never called a Christian in any sense.

35 This has been investigated in detail by J. Stelzenberger, *Die Beziehungen der frühchristlichen Sittenlehre zur Ethik der Stoa* (Munich, 1933), and M. Spanneut, *Le stoïcisme des Pères de l'Église, de Clément de Rome à Clément d'Alexandrie* (Éditions du Seuil, 1957).

36 This is the reason given by R. M. Gummere, *Seneca the Philosopher and his Modern Message* (Boston, Mass., 1922), pp. 53–6. But it can hardly be a sufficient explanation, since at one time or another Christianity has found a home within almost every other philosophical system as well.

37 J. H. Waszink, *Quinti Septimi Tertulliani De Anima* (Amsterdam, 1947), p. 267, says of Tertullian: 'Of course he is familiar with the doctrine *nihil esse in intellectu quod non prius fuerit in sensu* from the Stoics . . .'; and in this he is followed by Spanneut [35], p. 212. But this is a strange comment, since the doctrine is originally Aristotle's (cf. *De an.* 432a),

and the tag itself has never been found earlier than ps.-Bede (early thirteenth century?) (*PL*, LXX, 1017). Cf. P. F. Cranefield, 'On the origin of the phrase "Nihil est in intellectu quod non prius fuerit in sensu" ', *Journal of the History of Medicine and Allied Sciences*, 25 (1970), pp. 77–80.

38 In Clement: H. Chadwick, *Early Christian Thought and the Classical Tradition* (Oxford, 1966), p. 61 and note (p. 147, n. 152); Stelzenberger [35], p. 454. In Origen: P. Barth, *Die Stoa*, 3rd and 4th edn (Stuttgart, 1922), pp. 187–8.

39 Especially Origen, who had the same teacher as Plotinus (Ammonius Saccas). It should be noted that Plotinian Neoplatonism also contains Stoic elements; cf. *Les Sources de Plotin*, Fondation Hardt, *Entretiens*, v (Geneva, 1960), pp. 65–103.

40 Stelzenberger [35], pp. 255–7, 333.

41 Spanneut [35], pp. 42–7, 428–32.

42 E.g. R. Campbell, *Seneca, Letters from a Stoic* (Penguin, 1969), p. 24; Summers [21], xcviii; Gummere [36], pp. 54, 66; Hay [32], p. 4; Waszink [37], p. 98.

43 A. Labhardt, 'Tertullien et la philosophie ou la recherche d'une "position pure" ', *Museum Helveticum*, 7 (1950), pp. 159–80, esp. pp. 173–4. Cf. notes 62, 114, *inf*.

44 Waszink [37], 21*–44*; G. Verbeke, *L'évolution de la doctrine du pneuma du stoïcisme à S. Augustin* (Paris, 1945), p. 415.

45 See the passages listed in *CCSL*, II, 1496. He is favourable in *De an*. XX.1; hostile in *De an*. XLII.2 and *Res*. I.4; ambiguous in *Apol*. XII.6 and L.14. There are also a few unacknowledged parallels with Seneca's writings.

46 F. X. Burger, *Minucius Felix und Seneca* (Munich, 1904).

47 V. d'Agostino, 'Minucio Felice e Seneca' in his *Studi sul neostoicismo* (Turin, 1950), pp. 137–45; J. P. Waltzing, 'Minucius Felix et le Thesaurus Linguae Latinae', *Musée Belge*, 10 (1906), pp. 280ff. If this is true of Minucius, it may well also be true of other writers, pagan or Christian, who had undergone a similar rhetorical training.

48 H. Koch, *Cyprianische Untersuchungen* (Bonn, 1926); Stelzenberger [35], pp. 71, 464–5; Bourgery [3], pp. 163–4; G. Barbero, 'Seneca e la conversione di San Cipriano', *Rivista di Studi Classici*, 10 (1962), pp. 16–23.

49 C. Weyman, 'Novatian und Seneca über den Frühtrunk', *Philologus*, 52 (1893), pp. 728–30; G. Landgraf and C. Weyman, 'Novatians Epistula de Cibis Iudaicis', *Archiv für lateinische Lexikographie und Grammatik*, 11 (1900), pp. 221–49; Stelzenberger [35], pp. 128, 263, 465–6.

50 See the list of passages in S. Brandt's *index auctorum*, *CSEL*, XXVII, 263–4 (though not all on his list are quotations or even parallels). Lactantius is critical in *Inst*. III.15.1; VI.17.28.

51 V.9.19. Cf. V.22.11.

52 *Inst*. VII.7.2. The whole of chapter 7 is concerned to argue that no truths are the exclusive property of Christians, though only Christians can attain the whole truth.

53 See the list of eulogizing references in Brandt's *index nomimum et rerum*, *CSEL*, xxvii, 355–7. For a direct comparison with Seneca, cf. *Inst*. III.15.1: 'Eodem ductus errore Seneca – quis enim veram viam teneret errante Cicerone? . . .' He quotes Cicero roughly seven times as often as Seneca, the Bible four times, Virgil three times, the Sibylline Oracles and Lucretius twice, and Plato, Epicurus, Ovid and Cyprian about the same number of times as Seneca.

54 Despite the claims made, e.g. by Verbeke [44], pp. 470, 472, 475, 480, 482, 527. It is remarkable that all Lactantius' quotations bar the last few words of one (*De ira dei* xvii.13 = *De Ira* 1.3.3) are either from lost works (*Exhortationes, Moralis philosophia, De Immatura Morte*) or from lost parts of extant works: *Inst*. V.22.12 from *Prov*., and *De ira dei*, xvii.13 from the lacuna after *De Ira* I.2.3. (On this lacuna, cf. C. W. Barlow, 'A sixth-century epitome of Seneca *De Ira*', *TAPA*, 68 (1937), pp. 26–42, 29–30; L. D. Reynolds, 'The medieval tradition of Seneca's dialogues', *CQ*, 18 (1968), pp. 355–72, esp. p. 368.) The only part of Seneca's extant writings we have positive proof that Lactantius actually read is *De Ira*, I.1–3 (only about a twentieth of the work). Cf. also p. 131, *inf*.

55 *MGH Script*. I, v.ii, p. 23: 'Dives Seneca nec tamen consul arguetur rectius quam praedicabitur non erudisse indolem Neronis, sed armasse saevitatem.'

56 J. Duhr, 'Une lettre de condoléance de Bachiarius (?)', *Revue d'histoire ecclésiastique*, 47 (1952), pp. 530–85.

57 Stelzenberger [35], pp. 133, 447–8.

58 Ed. C. W. Barlow, *Epistolae Senecae ad Paulum et Pauli ad Senecam (quae vocantur)* (American Academy in Rome, 1938). The nearest to making him a Christian is *Ep*. XIV, when Paul charges him: 'Novum te auctorem feceris Iesu Christi,' but he adds that Seneca is only 'propemodum adeptus' in Christian wisdom. Cf. n. 29, *sup*.

59 R. A. Lipsius and M. Bonnet, *Acta Apostolorum Apocrypha* (Leipzig, 1891) (repr. Hildesheim, 1959), vol. I, p. 24: 'Sed et institutor imperatoris [Seneca] adeo illi colloquio illius [Pauli] temperare vix posset, quatinus si ore ad os illum alloqui non valeret, frequentibus datis et acceptis epistolis ipsius dulcedine et amicali colloquio atque consilio frueretur. . . . Nam et scripta illius [Pauli] quaedam magister Caesaris [Seneca] coram eo [Nerone] relegit et in cunctis admirabilem reddidit.' Cf. O. Bardenhewer, *Geschichte der altkirchlichen Literatur*, vol. I (Darmstadt, 1962), p. 559; Sevenster [30], pp. 10–11.

60 Cf. n. 58, *sup*.

61 Note that most editors apart from Barlow [58] have followed Erasmus in numbering this xi.

62 Faider [8], pp. 97–8. He could have supported this point with Lactantius, *Epitome Div. Inst*. 3: 'Longum est recensere quae de summo deo vel Thales vel Pythagoras et Anaximenes antea vel postmodum Stoici, Cleanthes et Chrysippus et Zenon, vel nostrorum Seneca Stoicos secutus et ipse Tullius praedicaverint . . .,' where *nostrorum* can hardly mean anything other than 'among Latin speakers', or

perhaps 'of more recent writers'. But for a less sceptical view cf. Stelzenberger [35], pp. 433–7; Gummere [36], p. 54. Cf. also notes 43, *sup.* and 114, *inf.*

63 H. Hagendahl, *Latin Fathers and the Classics* (Göteborg, 1958), pp. 111, 141, 150–2, 266, 290–1, 297. On the other hand, see the review of Hagendahl by O. Gigon, *Göttingische Gelehrte Anzeigen*, 216 (1964), pp. 104–124; S. Jannacone, 'S. Girolamo e Seneca', *Giornale Italiano di Filologia*, 16 (1963), pp. 326–38; W. Trillitzsch, 'Hieronymus und Seneca', *Mittellateinisches Jahrbuch*, 2 (1965), pp. 42–54.

64 A. S. Pease, 'The attitude of Jerome towards pagan literature', *TAPA*, 50 (1919), pp. 150–67.

65 E.g. Nourisson and other French scholars; but cf. H. Hagendahl, *Augustine and the Latin Classics* (Göteborg, 1967), vol. II, pp. 678–80.

66 *Epist.* CLIII.14. Cf. *Civ.* VI.10: 'Annaeus Seneca, quem nonnullis indiciis invenimus apostolorum nostrorum claruisse temporibus.'

67 Hagendahl [65], I. pp. 245–9; II. pp. 476–7, 676–80, 694.

68 L. D. Reynolds, *The Medieval Tradition of Seneca's Letters* (Oxford, 1965), p. 84.

69 *Cons.* 1.3.7–11. C. H. Talbot, 'Florilegium Morale Oxoniense, 2a pars', *AMN* 6 (1956), p. 22 claims that he was strongly critical, referring to section 8; but here Boethius is only talking of the Stoics in general, and his remarks on Seneca and some other individuals in sections 9–11 are clearly favourable. He mentions Seneca again in III.5.10–11.

70 *De geom.*, PL, LXIII, 1353B. His pupil Cassiodorus (*c.* 490–*c.* 583) copies Boethius' words *verbatim*, and adds that he is leaving the book to his monastery as worth reading (*Inst.* II.6.4).

71 For Seneca's influence on the *Phil. cons.*, cf. Weinberger's edition, *CSEL*, LXVII.4, *prolegomena*, ix; G. Highet, *The Classical Tradition* (Oxford, 1967), pp. 42–4.

72 In IX.230ff., he distinguishes the Seneca who 'colit hispidum Platona' from the one who 'orchestrum quatit ... Euripidis'. Cf. also XXIII.162–4.

73 *Rescriptorum Honorii Scholastici contra epistolas Senecae ad Iordanem episcopum*, *Anthologia Latina*, I.ii, ed. Riese (Leipzig, 1869), no. 666.

74 G. Sixt, 'Des Prudentius Abhängigkeit von Seneca und Lucan', *Philologus*, 51 (1892), pp. 501–6; Stelzenberger [35], p. 260 and note.

75 E. Bickel, 'De Merobaude imitatore Senecae', *RhM*, 60 (1905), p. 317.

76 E.g. in *Et.* 1.20.2 he mentions Seneca's work on shorthand. Cf. P. Luigi, *Rivista di Filologia*, 41 (1913), pp. 601–7.

77 E. Bickel, 'Die Schrift des Martinus von Bracara formula vitae honestae', *RhM*, 60 (1905), pp. 505–51; C. W. Barlow, *Martini episcopi bracarensis opera omnia* (Yale, 1950); 'Seneca in the Middle Ages', *CW*, 35 (1941–2), p. 257; and [54].

78 Mansi (ed.), *Amplissima collectio conciliorum*, IX (Florence, 1763), col. 795. Cf. F. Haase (ed.), *Senecae opera*, III (Leipzig, 1878), p. 463.

79 C. Pascal, 'Proverbiae Senecae', in his *Letteratura latina medievale* (Catania, 1909), pp. 140–9; Faider [8], pp. 117–22; R. G. Palmer,

Seneca's 'De Remediis Fortuitorum' and the Elizabethans (Chicago, 1953), esp. pp. 20–3; J. L. Heller, ' "Seneca" in the Middle Ages', *CW*, 36 (1942–3), pp. 151–2; Haase [78], pp. xv–xx, 446–75; K.-D. Nothdurft, *Studien zum Einfluss Senecas auf die Philosophie und Theologie des zwölften Jahrhunderts* (Leiden, 1963), pp. 28–34.
80 Cf. n. 54, *sup.*
81 This phenomenon is alluded to, but not explained, by Gigon [63], p. 121, and id., 'Die Szenerei des ciceronischen Hortensius', *Philologus*, 106 (1962), pp. 222–45, esp. p. 224. Cf. M. Lausberg, *Untersuchungen zu Senecas Fragmenten* (Berlin, 1970), esp. p. 5.
82 *Carmen de mundi transitu*, 9–10, in *Opera*, ed. G. S. M. Walker (Dublin, 1957), p. 182. The parallel with *Epist.* 66.6. noted by Walker (p. 58) is unconvincing. Cf. also M. Manitius, *Geschichte der lateinischen Literatur des Mittelalters* (Munich, 1911–31), I, p. 184.
83 *De metris*, CXL, in *MGH, Script.* I.xv, p. 194. Faider [8], p. 129n. quotes Bede (672–735) as saying of Seneca: 'mirabar tantam cuiquam infidelium prudentiam inesse potuisse.' But the *Liber proverbiorum* from which this is taken (*PL*, CXLVI, 299B) was really by Otloh, and Migne reprints it under his name in *PL*, XC. 1089Cff. Cf. pp. 132–3, *inf.*
84 *MGH, Poet. Lat. Med. Aev.*, I, 300, *carm.* LXXXI, 3–6.
85 *Epp.* XXXVII, CLXXXVI. Cf. Palmer [79], p. 11; Manitius [82], I, p. 277.
86 *MGH, Poet. Lat. Med. Aev.*, I, 571, 53–4.
87 *De fide, spe et caritate*, II, in *PL*, CXX. 1442B. He also shows knowledge of Seneca's *Epistles*, *Ben.* and *De morte Claudii* in his *Life of Wala* and his *Comm. on Matthew*. Cf. Manitius [82], I, p. 406.
88 B. Bischoff, 'Eine Sammelhandschrift Walahfrid Strabos (Cod. Sangall. 878)', in *Der Welt des Buches, Festgabe . . . G. Leyh* (Leipzig, 1950), pp. 30–58; and *Carm.* XXXV, 4, in *MGH, Poet. Lat. Med. Aev.*, II.
89 Manitius [82], I, p. 321. Ps.-Senecan sentences were also quoted by Servatus Lupus of Ferrières (805–62) and Remigius of Auxerre (841–908). Cf. Manitius [82], I, pp. 487, 512.
90 *MGH, Poet. Lat. Med. Aev.*, IV, 414–18. The only time he mentions him by name is in his *Species comice, saphicum adonium*, v. 67 (ibid. p. 432).
91 *PL*, CVI, 1132C–D. Cf. Jerome, *De vir. ill.* xii (quoted p. 128, *sup.*).
92 Manitius [82], I, p. 590.
93 *Phronesis, proem.* 7, in *PL*, CXXXV. 374A.
94 *Praeloquiorum libri sex*, in *PL*, CXXXVI, 172B, 173A, 174C, 181D, 220C, 266A, 271B, 323A.
95 *Epistolae Gerberti*, ed. J. Havet (Paris, 1889), p. 204, *Ep.* CCXVII. The relevant part of the letter is omitted as spurious by Migne, *PL*, CXXXIX. 265–6.
96 Manitius [82], II, p. 722.
97 *PL*, CXLVI, 299B. For the ps.-Senecan sentences in Otloh, cf. W. Meyer, *Die Sammlungen der Spruchverse des Publilius Syrus* (Leipzig, 1877), pp. 11f.
98 *MGH, Script.*, VII, 746–7; Reynolds [68], pp. 86–7; id. [54], pp. 355–8.

99 Ibid. p. 356. Cf. *PL*, CXLVII. 1293f.
100 *MGH, Poet. Lat. Med. Aev.*, V, ii, 495–6, *vv*. 19–20, 23–26.
101 F. S. Schmitt, *Anselmus Cantuariensis Archiepiscopus, Opera*, I (Edinburgh, 1946), p. 102n.; J. R. Weinberg, *A Short History of Medieval Philosophy* (Princeton, 1964), p. 66; Nothdurft [79], pp. 192–5.
102 A Senecan passage Anselm is more likely to have read is one quoted by Lactantius (*Inst.* VI.24.12–13): 'Exhortationes suas Seneca mirabili sententia terminavit. "Magnum", inquit, "nescio quid maiusque quam cogitari potest numen est . . ." Quid verius dici potest ab eo qui deum nosset quam dictum est ab homine verae religionis ignaro? Nam et maiestatem dei expressit maiorem esse dicendo quam ut eam cogitatio mentis humanae capere posset . . .' But though he *is* now talking of God's greatness in general (at least as interpreted by Lactantius), he says not that God is the greatest conceivable being, but that he is too great to be conceived at all. Incidentally, it was on the basis of this and Seneca's statement that it is our duty in life to serve God, that Lactantius said in 14: 'He could have been a true worshipper of God . . .' Cf. p.127, *sup*.
103 C. H. Haskins, *The Renaissance of the Twelfth Century* (Cambridge, Mass., 1927), Preface; G. Leff, *Medieval Thought* (Harmondsworth, 1958), chapter 5 and p. 168. On the meaning of 'humanism', cf. P. O. Kristeller, 'The humanist movement', in his *Renaissance Thought*, I (New York, 1961), pp. 3–23.
104 Reynolds [68], pp. 120–2; id. [54], pp. 358–63.
105 J. de Ghellinck, *L'essor de la littérature latine au XIIe siècle* (Paris, 1946), II, p. 301; Reynolds [68], p. 112.
106 Or perhaps because of it: Platonism interpreted pantheistically is not so different from a spiritualized Stoicism.
107 E. Bréhier, *The Middle Ages and the Renaissance*, trans. W. Baskin (Chicago, 1965), p. 51; Nothdurft [79], pp. 186–190.
108 Bréhier [107], p. 70.
109 Nothdurft [79], pp. 162–74.
110 *PL*, CLXXVIII. 197B, 350B, 535D and 567A respectively. Cf. also 593A, 790B, 1033D, 131B.
111 E. Gilson, *Héloïse et Abélard* (Paris, 1938), pp. 65–7, 175–9.
112 Reynolds [68], pp. 115, 122. William was the first to know all the extant *Epistles*.
113 See the indices to the editions by C. C. J. Webb (Oxford, 1909 and 1929 respectively). Some of the quotations are indirect; e.g. the metaphor of the bees (Sen. *Epist.* 84.2ff.) is, as he himself admits, taken from Macrobius, *Sat.* I. pref. 5ff.
114 This should, incidentally, warn us not to read too much into expressions like Tertullian's 'Seneca saepe noster' (cf. notes 43 and 62, *sup*.). Here John contrasts 'nostri' with 'Seneca et alii' [pagan philosophers]; but in VIII.xiii he refers to 'Seneca noster', as contrasted with the Greeks Zeno, Socrates, Plato and Aristotle.
115 *Policraticus*, VIII, xiii (Webb, pp. 318–21); *Metalogicon*, I.xxii (Webb, pp. 51–2); *Entheticus de dogmate philosophorum* (not to be confused with the

Entheticus in Policraticum), vv. 1257–68, *PL*, CXCIX, 992C. This last is little other than a versified paraphrase of the passage in the *Metalogicon*.

116 I.xxii. This chapter is entitled *Quod auctoritate Senece suum tueatur errorem* [*Cornificius*]. However, John is not attacking Seneca himself, but the conclusions 'Cornificius' is supposed to have drawn from Seneca's 'discipline liberales virum bonum non faciunt' (cf. *Epist.* 88.1–2).

117 Ed. P. Michaud-Quantin, *AMN* 8 (1956), vv. 409–412.

118 Ed. R. Bossuat (Paris, 1955), I, 135–6. Cf. J. E. B. Mayor, 'Seneca in Alain de Lille', *Journal of Philology*, 20 (1892), pp. 1–6.

119 For further details, see Reynolds [68], and Nothdurft [79].

120 Ed. J. Holmberg, *Das Moralium Dogma Philosophorum des Guillaume de Conches* (Uppsala, 1929), who identifies 92 Senecan quotations (though there are 181 from Cicero and 104 from Horace). Cf. also J. R. Williams, 'The authorship of the *Moralium Dogma Philosophorum*', *Speculum*, 6 (1931), pp. 392–411.

121 A. Gagnér, *Florilegium Gallicum* (Lund, 1936).

122 *Florilegium Morale Oxoniense, Ms Bodl. 633, prima pars*, ed. Ph. Delhaye, *AMN*, 5 (1955); id., *secunda pars*, ed. C. H. Talbot, *AMN*, 6 (1956).

123 Ghellinck [105], p. 301.

124 *PL*, CLXXVIII, 535D, repeated in 790B.

125 *PL*, CLXXVIII, 1033D, repeated, without the compliment, in 1164C.

126 *Ep.* XIII, in *PL*, CCIII, 110D–111A. The Seneca quotation is from *Clem.* 1.7.2.

127 E. F. Jacob, 'Some aspects of classical influence in medieval England', in *Vorträge der Bibliothek Warburg 1930–31: England und die Antike*, ed. F. Saxl (Berlin, 1932), pp. 1–27, esp. p. 23.

128 Cf. p. 136, *sup*.

129 Gauthier de Saint-Victor, *Contra quatuor labyrinthos Franciae*, ed. P. Glorieux, *Archives d'histoire doctrinale et littéraire du Moyen Age*, 19, 27e année (1952), pp. 187–335.

130 Ed. E. Massa (Turici, 1953). Reynolds [54], p. 361 describes it as 'little more than an abbreviated transcript of the *Dialogues*'. But this is an exaggeration: he does indeed quote Seneca often, at great length, and with full acknowledgment; but much is also his own, or drawn from other authorities (notably Aristotle and Cicero).

131 *Opus tertium*, ed. J. S. Brewer (London, 1859), pp. 55–6.

132 *Apud* É. Charles, *Roger Bacon* (Paris, 1861), p. 411. Cf. also P. Duhem, *Un fragment inédit de l'Opus Tertium* (Quaracchi, 1909), p. 164: '[libri] Senece, qui sunt optimi et rarissime inveniuntur'.

133 Nothdurft [79], p. 20n.; Reynolds [68], p. 121; Bourgery [3], p. 170.

134 Ed. Thor Sundby, *Chaucer Society*, ser. ii, part 8 (London, 1873).

135 See the statistics in J. E. Sandys, *A History of Classical Scholarship*, 2nd edn, vol. I (Cambridge, 1906), p. 614.

136 *Works*, ed. F. N. Robinson (London, 1966), p. 195, line 2497 (*The Monk's Tale*).

137 H. M. Ayres, 'Chaucer and Seneca', *Romanic Review*, 10 (1919), pp.

1–15; R. A. Pratt, 'Chaucer and the hand that fed him', *Speculum*, 41 (1966), pp. 619–42.
138 A. Counson, 'L'Influence de Sénèque le philosophe', *Musée Belge*, 7 (1903), pp. 132–67, esp. pp. 134ff.
139 K. Bartsch, *Denkmäler der provenzalischen Literatur* (Stuttgart, 1856), p. 31.
140 Bourgery [3], p. 171, who gives other examples of the popular survival of Seneca's memory. Cf. also Counson [138], p. 133.
141 J. F. Yela, *Séneca* (Barcelona, 1947), pp. 251–69; J. Gonzalez-Haba, 'Seneca en la espiritualidad española de los siglos XVI y XVII', *Revista de Filosofía*, 11 (1952), pp. 287–302; A. Rothe, *Quevedo und Seneca* (Geneva, 1965). An interesting example of Spanish nationalism is the forgery by the sixteenth-century Jesuit Hieronymus Romanus de la Higuera of a chronicle, allegedly composed by St Jerome's friend Flavius Dexter (printed in *PL*, XXXI, 49–572. Cf. G. Ticknor, *History of Spanish Literature* (London, 1849), III. p. 140n.). In it he set out to glorify the early history of Spain from a Christian point of view, and one of the claims he made was that Seneca had been a secret Christian (cols 189–90, 211–12). Cf. n. 32, *sup*.
142 Bourgery [3], pp. 170–86; Faider [8], pp. 135–52; Summers [21], pp. c–cxiv; Gummere [36], pp. 88–138; Counson [138], pp. 132–67. The same goes for Seneca's considerable influence on Renaissance tragedy. Both are of course indirectly relevant, in that they enhanced his reputation in general.
143 J. E. Seigel, *Rhetoric and Philosophy in Renaissance Humanism: The Union of Eloquence and Wisdom, Petrarch to Valla* (Princeton, 1968). It should be remembered that it was not till the fifteenth century that knowledge of Greek became at all common.
144 Gummere [36], pp. 97–8; P. O. Kristeller, *Eight Philosophers of the Italian Renaissance* (Stanford, 1964), p. 8; A. Bobbio, 'Seneca e la formazione spirituale e culturale del Petrarca', *La Bibliofilia*, 43 (1941), pp. 224–91.
145 *Le traité 'De sui ipsius et multorum ignorantia'*, ed. L. M. Capelli (Paris, 1906), pp. 36–7.
146 C. N. J. Mann, 'Petrarch and the transmission of classical elements', in R. R. Bolgar (ed.), *Classical Influences on European Culture, AD 500–1500* (Cambridge, 1971), pp. 217–24.
147 *Le Familiari*, XXIV.v (*Ad Annaeum Senecam*), ed. V. Rossi (Florence, 1942), vol. IV. His main source was Suetonius; Tacitus' more favourable account was still virtually unknown.
148 *PG*, CLI, 1341–64. Cf. B. Tatakis, *La Philosophie Byzantine* (Paris, 1949), p. 264.
149 E. Garin, *Italian Humanism*, trans. P. Munz (Oxford, 1965), pp. 5–6; W. Dilthey, *Gesammelte Schriften*, II (Leipzig, 1923), p. 23; R. R. Bolgar, *The Classical Heritage* (New York, 1964), pp. 255–6.
150 Momigliano [29], p. 339.
151 Ibid. pp. 336–7.
152 Reynolds [68], pp. 1–4; Faider [8], p. 138.

153 The likeliest candidates are Valla (1407–57) and Pomponazzi (1462–1525); but in both cases their attitude to Stoic ideas is highly ambiguous, and their main source is more likely to have been Cicero than Seneca.
154 W. Trillitzsch, 'Erasmus und Seneca', *Philologus*, 109 (1965), pp. 270–93; M. M. Phillips, 'Erasmus and the Classics', in *Erasmus*, ed. T. A. Dorey (London, 1970), pp. 1–30, esp. pp. 15–17; G. Williamson, *The Senecan Amble* (London, 1951), pp. 11–31.
155 *Opus Epistolarum*, ed. P. S. and H. M. Allen (Oxford, 1906–58), v. 340 (*Ep.* 1390, to John Vlatten, 1523).
156 Ed. cit., II. 53 (*Ep.* 324, to Thomas Ruthall, 1515).
157 *Institutio Principis Christiani*, II, in *Opera Omnia*, ed. Le Clerc (Leiden, 1703–6), IV, col. 587F. Cf. *Ep.* 476 (Allen, II. p. 358).
158 *Opera Omnia*, I.ii (Amsterdam, 1971). Cf. Le Clerc, III. 995B.
159 Amsterdam edn, I.ii.46–7.
160 *Ep.* 2091 (Allen, VIII. p. 27).
161 Ibid. p. 31. For his attack on the authenticity of the correspondence with St Paul, cf. pp. 30–1, 40–1. It should be noted that he made no distinction between the Elder and Younger Seneca, and many of his criticisms are directed against the former.
162 Ibid. p. 34.
163 M. M. Phillips, *The 'Adages' of Erasmus* (Cambridge, 1964), pp. 393–403.
164 L. Zanta, *La Renaissance du stoïcisme au XVIe siècle* (Paris, 1914), p. 82.
165 *Werke* (Zürich, 1828–42), IV. 79–144, esp. 93, 95, 123. Cf. R. Staehelin, *Huldreich Zwingli* (Basle, 1895–7), I. 48–9; II. 192, 457; Zanta [164], pp. 47–73; Dilthey [149], pp. 64–6, 154–61.
166 F. L. Battles and A. M. Hugo, *Calvin's Commentary on Seneca's 'De Clementia'* (Leiden, 1969), 41*–62* (Hugo); F. Wendel, *Calvin*, trans. P. Mairet (London, 1963), pp. 26–35.
167 *Inst.* I.xvi.8.
168 *Moralis philosophiae medulla seu Epicteti Enchiridion cum explanatione Thomae Naogeorgii* [= Kirchmaier] (Strasbourg, 1554). Cf. Zanta [164], pp. 19, 142–3.
169 Ibid. pp. 241–331; R. Radouant, *Guillaume Du Vair* (Paris, 1908).
170 *M. Antonini imp. de rebus suis...* (Cambridge, 1652), *praeloquium*, p. 18.
171 E.g. the euphuism of John Lyly (1553–1606) and the loose style of Robert Burton (1577–1640). For the anti-Ciceronian movement in general, cf. M. W. Croll, *Style, Rhetoric and Rhythm*, ed. J. Max Patrick et al. (Princeton, 1966); W. F. Mitchell, *English Pulpit Oratory* (London, 1932), pp. 107–9; M. L. Clarke, ' "Non hominis nomen, sed eloquentiae" ', in *Cicero*, ed. T. A. Dorey (London, 1964), pp. 81–107, esp. pp. 90–6; Williamson [154]; Highet [71], chapter 18.
172 'C'est un autre Sénèque en notre langue,' said by Étienne Pasquier (1529–1615), *Œuvres choisies*, ed. L. Feugière, vol. II (Paris, 1894), p. 394. For Seneca's influence on Montaigne in general, cf. P. Villey, *Les sources et l'évolution des Essais de Montaigne* (Paris, 1908); G. Pire, *Stoïcisme et Pédagogie...* (Liège, 1958), pp. 159–72; Hay [32].
173 *Essais*, I.xxvi (*De l'instruction des enfans*), ed. M. Rat (Paris, 1962), I. 155.

174 *Essais*, II.x (*Des livres*), ed. cit., I. 453–4.
175 For an excellent account of sixteenth-century scepticism, and its compatibility with religious and moral convictions, see R. H. Popkin, *The History of Scepticism from Erasmus to Descartes* (New York, 1964).
176 J. B. Sabrié, *De l'humanisme au rationalisme: Pierre Charron* (Paris, 1913); E. F. Rice, jr, *The Renaissance Idea of Wisdom* (Cambridge, Mass., 1958), pp. 190–7.
177 M. C. Horowitz, 'Pierre Charron's view of the source of wisdom', *Journal of the History of Philosophy*, 9 (1971), pp. 443–57.
178 J. L. Saunders, *Justus Lipsius* (New York, 1955); Zanta [164], pp. 151–240; Williamson [154], pp. 121–49.
179 *Heaven vpon Earth* . . . , ed. R. Kirk (New Brunswick, 1948), pp. 19–65.
180 This attitude to ethics (knowledge of natural law) is closely analogous to the new conception of science (knowledge of the laws of nature). For a rather different explanation of the renaissance of Stoicism, cf. Zanta [164], pp. 3–26.
181 See the articles listed in Julien-Eymard d'Angers, 'Sénèque et le stoïcisme dans l'œuvre du Cordelier J. du Bosc', *Dix-septième siècle*, 29 (1955), pp. 353–77, p. 353n., and id., *L'Humanisme chrétien au XVIIe siècle* (The Hague, 1970), p. 191. Cf. also R. Pintard, *Le Libertinage érudit dans la première moitié du XVIIe siècle* (Paris, 1943); Zanta [164]; Sabrié [176]; and notes 141–2, *sup*.
182 I am not claiming that ancient philosophers no longer exercised any influence at all, though it was certainly much less than it had been, if only because of the many new developments in philosophy. The change I refer to is that in the exposition of philosophical theories it was no longer fashionable to mention the ancients, let alone appeal to their authority. As a consequence it is normally possible to apportion specific influences only after a detailed investigation of an individual's intellectual history.
183 At the time it was common for the less orthodox to be charged even with atheism. Cf. G. T. Buckley, *Atheism in the English Renaissance* (Chicago, 1932); D. C. Allen, *Doubt's Boundless Sea* (Baltimore, 1964).
184 *Œuvres*, ed. F. Lachet, vol. X (Paris, 1863), pp. 222–3. Cf. Pascal, *Pensées*, ed. J. Chevalier (Paris, 1925), pp. 202–3; La Bruyère, *Œuvres*, ed. M. G. Servois, vol. II (Paris, 1865), pp. 3–4.
185 *Œuvres en Prose*, ed. R. Ternois (Paris, 1962–9), I. pp. 154–5.
186 *Œuvres*, ed. Gilbert, vol. I (Paris, 1968), Maxim 539 (= No. 105 of the first edition, 1665). Cf. the more detailed attack in the anonymous discourse at the beginning of the 1665 edition. Both were subsequently suppressed.
187 II.iii.4, *De l'imagination de Sénèque,* in *Œuvres*, ed. J. Simon (Paris, *n.d.*), III. p. 313.
188 N. Kemp Smith, *The Philosophy of David Hume* (London, 1964), p. 24.
189 *Essai sur les règnes de Claude et de Néron*, first published in 1778, with a second edition, almost twice the length, in 1782. Cf. *Œuvres complètes*, ed. J. Assézat, vol. III (Paris, 1875), pp. 15–407.
190 Pire [172], pp. 173–98; P. Thomas, 'Sénèque et J.-J. Rousseau',

Bulletin de l'Académie Royale de Belgique (Classe de lettres) (1900), pp. 391–420; Highet [71], pp. 870–1.
191 *A History of Western Philosophy* (London, 1946), p. 283.
192 Cf. notes 29, 33, 142 *sup.*
193 Gummere [36], pp. 135–8. Cf. the editor's preface, pp. x–xi.
194 I regret that I was unable to consult W. Trillitzsch, *Seneca im literarischen Urteil der Antike*, 2 vols (Amsterdam, 1971) till after this chapter had been written. Vol. I contains an exhaustive and invaluable collection of references to Seneca in antiquity.

VI

Seneca and English Tragedy[1]

G. K. Hunter

The *Literaturwissenschaft* within which the origins or causes of Renaissance (or 'modern') tragedy have been sought is bound, by its method, to give importance to the tragedies of Seneca. The seminal surveys of Cloetta, Fischer and Creizenach[2] adopted (inevitably enough) a chronological view of the development of a separate genre 'tragedy'. Cunliffe's article on early tragedy in the *Cambridge History of English Literature* (vol. v, 1910) spells out the pattern which emerged, with model simplicity (p. 68):

> The history of renascence tragedy may be divided into three stages, not definitely limited, and not following in strict chronological succession, but distinct in the main: the study, imitation and production of Senecan tragedy; translation; the imitation of Greek and Latin tragedy in the vernacular.

To this pattern one ought to add, to complete the received critical picture, a geographical drift of influence from Italy, to France, to England, which made each subsequent country the inheritor not only of the prime cause, Seneca, but also of the subsequent sub-Senecan developments that happened on the way. Thus M. T. Herrick tells us that Seneca's 'vivid depiction of horrible deeds and black thoughts . . . fascinated the Italians, just as much as the sixteenth-century Italian tragedies of blood and lust and revenge fascinated French and English playwrights' (*Italian Tragedy in the Renaissance*, Urbana, 1965, pp. 2–3).

H. B. Charlton's elaborate and deeply-researched essay on 'The Senecan Tradition in Renaissance Tragedy' (first published as the Introduction to vol. 1 of the Scottish Text Society edition of Sir William Alexander's *Poetical Works*, Edinburgh, 1921) is probably the prime example in English of the charting of these routes, and I shall use this as a model presentation of received attitudes. Charlton sees a powerful Italian influence on Elizabethan tragedy as well as a general Senecan influence. He also sees that the Italian imitators of Seneca made him more horrific and 'romantic' by combining his form with material from the *novelle*, and therefore brought him closer to Elizabethan taste. This means that, in Charlton's view, something called 'the Italian Seneca' is present in Elizabethan borrowings of horrific *novelle* materials. The logical flaw in the argument is perhaps too obvious to require much elaboration. The danger of charting the changes in 'Seneca' as he passes through Dolce or Corraro or Garnier and so reaches England is that elements genuinely Senecan (i.e. characteristically if not uniquely present in Seneca's plays) may cease to be present at all, while elements generally characteristic of late medieval and Renaissance taste (sententiousness, a gloomy sense of overpowering rule by fortune or fate in human affairs, a morbid interest in the limits of human suffering), or indeed characteristic of tragedy as a genre (horror, blood, desolation)[3] come to be labelled 'Senecan' because Seneca also displays them and is thought responsible for the tradition (late medieval tragedy) in which they appear. The Senecan example may have provided the earliest formal model for European tragedy, but it could quickly become (in spite of this status) totally irrelevant to the day-by-day imagination of tragic playwrights.

The same flaw is manifestly present in the use of the chronological sequence: reading and producing Seneca, translation of Seneca, 'Senecan' plays in the vernacular. That these three things happened is abundantly clear, and undoubtedly they usually happened in the order indicated; but the third element in the sequence can only be said to be logically dependent on either the first or the second if the features called 'Senecan' are necessarily derived from the preceding stages of the reception of Seneca and from no other source. The *post hoc ergo propter hoc* argument, which has supported much chronological study and 'explanation' of European or English tragedy, is clearly not enough by itself to establish a detailed and inescapable proof that similar features appearing in some Elizabethan tragedies and some Senecan tragedies are in the former only because they are in the latter.[4] And this is particularly the case when the features in question are available in other (and in some cases more immediate) sources.

Thus stichomythia, ghosts, five-act structure, rhetorical speeches, a devotion to horror, a stress on the ineluctable quality of fate – these 'Senecan' features are equally available in England in vernacular comedy, the *Mirror for Magistrates*, Terence, Ovid, and the Miracle Plays.[5] If we are to talk meaningfully about Seneca and English tragedy it can only be within an awareness of these alternative sources and with some sense of the strainers through which Seneca's plays had to pass if they were to be assimilated into the English scene.

The distinctions we have to make do not, however, concern only the Elizabethan scene. They also involve the multi-faceted quality of Seneca himself. Critics have tended to speak of 'Senecan influence' as if a single and homogeneous quality was being transmitted. I will not dwell here on the problem of excluding from our sense of 'Seneca' the moral treatises that were (in Renaissance England at any rate) his primary source of fame. Even if we suppose that the plays were read in isolation from the treatises and the letters, we are still far from homogeneity. Out of the ten (or nine, or eight) plays in the canon, which are the central texts? When we speak of 'Seneca', do we refer to the doom-laden family histories of the Pelopidae (the *Thyestes* and the *Agamemnon*), or do we refer to the tales of passionate and sorrowful womanhood (*Phaedra* and *Medea*), or are we thinking of the comparatively open atmosphere of the *Hercules Furens*, in which paternal and wifely loyalties are not destroyed and where the father and the friend (Theseus) survive to comfort the hero? The *Troades* offers yet another model: of passive and undeserved suffering caught in the impersonal toils of war, while the *Oedipus* describes the defilement of even the hero in flight from defilement.

If we are to take as 'Senecan' only what is common to the whole body of plays we are left with a residue of pretty obvious features. There is a continuity of style of course, though what I. Scott-Kilvert has recently called 'Seneca's sharply distinct varieties of speech'[6] is often overlooked; and to this I shall return. In formal terms there is the classically simple linear or progressive construction ('arguments ... naked and casual', as Fulke Greville calls them in *Life of Sidney*, ed. Nowell Smith, Oxford, p. 222), usually centred on the woes of the protagonist, showing an attempt to avoid fate or alleviate suffering, with the consequence that misery is only hastened and suffering deepened.

In these formal elements, Elizabethan publicly performed tragedy (the only kind of Elizabethan tragedy to have any aesthetic importance) is notably uninterested. However, in a rigorously progressivist theory the lack of interest may be explained as showing, not the presence of an alternative (Gothic) concept of unity, but the slowness of the Elizabethans to learn the one lesson that is possible. In Brander Matthews's *A Study of the Drama* (1910) we hear (p. 102) that:

> The development of English tragedy ... out of the lax chronicle play, which was only a straggling panorama of the events of a reign, was due largely to the influence exerted by Seneca's tragedies, poor enough as plays, but vigorous in the stoical assertion of man's power over himself and of his right to control his own destiny.

It is difficult to see just what this is saying, but it may be thought to be trying to express a relationship between individual self-assertion and unity of action. If Shakespeare's *King John* is better than Bale's *King Johan* or the anonymous *Troublesome Reign of King John*, it may be implied that this is because Seneca had taught Elizabethan drama to centre action on a single dominant individual.

The trouble with such a theory is that Elizabethan drama shows a total reluctance to unify by other than the thematic interests which had appeared in *Damon and Pithias* (1564), *Cambyses* (?1561) and other pre-Senecan examples of the 'lax chronicle play'. The advance from these plays to the drama of Marlowe, Shakespeare and Webster is not an advance along a line of increasing 'unity of motive', but an advance to an increasingly subtle and brilliantly focused organization of thematic interests. The route to the drama of Scribe and Ibsen could have been shortened by an appropriate attention to the tragedies of Seneca, but quite another route was being followed by the major tragedies of the English Renaissance. Their aim is to crowd the stage and create complex and ironic evaluations. Person is set against person and group against group, so that the validity of alternative positions is allowed to appear. And in this respect (as in others) one must make the point that the formal differences which separate Elizabethan tragedies from Seneca's mark ethical distinctions. All

Seneca's plays stress the malevolent power of fate to bring men beyond what they had thought of as the final limits of cruelty and injustice. In all (except the Hercules plays) the ending is shown without any alleviation of misery: either cruel tyranny is triumphant, or the martyr sinks into further degradation, or both happen together. Elizabethan tragedy's complex structure reflects a different attitude to fate. While allowing the cruelty of tragic destiny, it is also strongly assertive of the redeeming features of a tragic existence: the gratuitous loyalties, the constancy under pressure, the renewed faith. Its variety of moods allows the tragedy to be placed in a context of different and less shadowed lives.

T. S. Eliot has presented Othello,[7] especially at the end of the play when he looks back over his life (*O sors dura!*), as Senecan, but in fact Othello's position is totally unlike anything existing or possible in any of Seneca's plays. Othello does in a sense 'dramatize himself' (and so does the Medea of *Medea superest*), but vivid self-description seems to be an inescapable dramatist's device (surely Sophocles's Oedipus 'dramatizes himself', not to mention Ibsen's Hedda). The quality of Othello's end is derived from the awareness of a normal world existing in his own past and in other people's future, for whom he will be only a name (if that). The perspectives of the ordinary world are essential to Shakespearean tragedy; they are quite absent from Seneca.

The difference I have suggested here may be subsumed under the general rubric that Shakespeare's ethic is Christian, and Seneca's is not. But this distinction has not always been allowed the central importance it undoubtedly has to explain both the attraction of Seneca for the Elizabethans and the inevitability of their failure to be like him. It was often suggested in the late nineteenth and early twentieth centuries that, given the immeasurable superiority of Aeschylus and Sophocles to subsequent tragedies (according to the taste of the nineteenth and twentieth centuries), the Elizabethan drama would have been immeasurably benefited by imitating Sophocles instead of Seneca. The wish that the Elizabethans could have shared modern preferences shows a lack of historical perspective and an unpreparedness for the different (and shocking) revaluation that the past exacts from those attentive enough to it. The Greek drama (except for Euripides in some of his aspects) was necessarily inaccessible to the Elizabethans, not only because the possession of enough Greek to read it properly was rare (after all there were Latin translations), but principally because the Greek drama was embedded in a socio-religious matrix that a Christian writer could not afford not to despise.

It was Seneca's freedom from any real response to the numinous that made him particularly repellent to the nineteenth-century Romantics, for whom his bleak moralism seemed denatured and pedantic. It was his merely intellectual relationship to the 'leaden gods' (as Stephen Bateman called the Roman deities in 1577) that allowed the Renaissance to regard him as a proto-Christian, and enabled them to accept his views without changing their own. In a more credulous age this quality had been expressed by the forged correspondence between Seneca and St Paul, and also by the forged treatises then read as Seneca's, but now attributed to St Martin.

Erasmus was, of course, free of these pious frauds, but he reflects their legacy. As he says in his prefatory letter to his edition of Seneca, sent to the Bishop of Durham (*Opus Epistolarum*, ed. Allen, Oxford, II, pp. 51ff.) (p. 53):

> Et Senecam tanti fecit divus Hieronymus, ut hunc unum ex omnibus ethnicis in Catalogo scriptorum illustrium recensuerit, non tam ob epistolas illas Pauli ad Senecam et Senecae ad Paulum (quas nec a Paulo nec a Seneca scriptas probe noverat . . .) quam quod hunc unum dignum iudicarit qui non Christianus a Christianis legeretur.

> (Indeed St Jerome made so much of Seneca that he included him as the only pagan in his Catalogue of famous authors, not so much on account of those letters of St Paul to Seneca and Seneca to St Paul (which he knew perfectly well to be by neither Seneca nor St Paul) but rather because he judged that he alone among non-Christians was fit to be read by Christians.)

In the new prefatory letter he addresses to the Bishop of Cracow in 1529 (Allen, VIII, pp. 25ff.), he repeats these sentiments and adds a rather crisp and memorable statement of Seneca's ambiguous position (p. 31):

> Etenim si legas illum ut paganum, scripsit Christiane; si ut Christianum, scripsit paganice.

(For if you read him thinking of him as a pagan, then he appears to have written like a Christian; but if you read him as a Christian then he appears to have written like a pagan.)

He also, in this later letter, explains why Jerome included Seneca in his *Catalogus sanctorum* (p. 29): *non admodum probatae sanctitatis* . . . [*sed*] *ob religionis amorem* (not because of proven sanctity . . . [but] on account of his love for religion). In the *Institutio Principis Christiani* he praises Seneca as the most suitable to be read (*Opera Omnia*, Leiden, 1703–6, vol. IV, p. 587):

Qui scriptis suis mire exstimulat et inflammat ad honesti studium, lectoris animum a sordidis curis in sublime subvehit, peculiariter ubique dedocens Tyrannidem.

(Who in his writings marvellously incites us and stirs us up to a zeal for honest action, carrying the mind of the reader into the the heights, far above the base concerns of men, especially where he is warning against tyranny.)

It was thus possible in the Renaissance to think of Seneca as a man wholly acceptable in his moral outlook, and to view the fables of his plays therefore as wholly defensible didactic structures. Dean Nowell defended the *Phaedra* because of its similarity to the story of Potiphar's wife in the Holy Scripture.[8] Indeed the primitive and horrific moral compulsions of the Old Testament provided a natural field for 'Christian Seneca'. Buchanan's *Jephthes* and Jean de la Taille's *Saul le Furieux*, Velo's *Tamar* and Bishop Watson's *Absalom*[9] all reduce Biblical history to quasi-Senecan fable. But the fables of Seneca's plays could be defended at a rather simpler moral level. Philip Melanchthon (*Corpus Reformatorum*, Halle, vol. XIX, p. 787) took out of the *Thyestes*: 'O how much evil does ambition breed':

Proinde spectaculum exemplum damus utile;
Nam cernere licebit hac in tragoedia
Nil esse peius ambitione, quae omnia
Divina humana, iusque et fas vertere solet.

(We present this to the spectators therefore as a useful model; for you will be justified in finding from this tragedy that there is nothing worse than ambition, which commonly overturns all things human and divine, both human law and divine law.)

Below this rather superficial level, at which Seneca could be thought of as quasi-Christian, the problems of true imitation are (and were) more difficult to solve. The ethic of Seneca was, as a unifying factor in his plays, quite hostile to the ethic that is tolerable to a Christian community. The most memorable statement of this incompatibility comes, fortunately enough, from the period of our principal concern and from a 'Senecan' dramatist, Fulke Greville. Greville in his life of Sir Philip Sidney describes his own tragedies and makes in the course of his description a distinction which is curiously overlooked when Elizabethan Senecan imitation is discussed, for it should be central to any such discussion. He speaks first of ancient tragedies which 'exemplify the disastrous miseries of man's life, where Order, Laws, Doctrine and Authority are unable to protect Innocency from the exorbitant wickedness of power, and so out of that melancholic vision stir horror, or murmur against Divine Providence' (p. 221). On the other hand, modern tragedies 'point out God's revenging aspect upon every particular sin, to the despair or confusion of mortality' (ibid.). The central distinction is, as Greville sees it, that the ancient (and he means Senecan) world was, because its gods were unjust, a world of total injustice. On the other hand, the Christian world shows man unable to face up to the justice of God, but hunted down in terms of particular sins, not overall corruption.

The point is not that the innocent do not perish in modern tragedy: Lavinia, Cordelia, and young Macduff perish just as surely as Hippolytus and the children of Thyestes and Medea. But the massacre of those innocents is part of a larger catastrophic movement which is eventually moral: the universe in casting out the particular evil also casts out the good. In Seneca's tragedies the evil are regularly left in manic possession of what their wickedness has achieved: Atreus with his brother (who now incorporates his nephews) in his gloating power, Nero disposing of his relatives, Medea carried off in her magic car, Aegisthus and Clytemnestra in possession of Argos. The impotent chorus can only generalize from these instances that man's lot is indeed hard and (as Greville says) 'murmur against Divine Providence'.

Even a play as concerned to avoid explicit Christianity as Shakespeare's *Titus Andronicus* suggests in the end that justice can return to the world with comfort to the good as well as punishment to the wicked, and decent behaviour all round:[10]

> Some loving friends convey the emperor hence
> And give him burial in his father's grave
> My father and Lavinia shall forthwith
> Be closed in our household's monument.
> As for that ravenous tiger, Tamora
> . . .
> [Then afterwards, to order well the state,
> That like events may ne'er it ruinate.]

Greville's distinction is one that is particularly important when we deal with that strain of Elizabethan tragedy concerned with revenge – a strain often thought to be particularly dependent on Seneca – though often this means no more than that there is horror in both. Shakespeare and other revenge dramatists do, of course, show deeds of horror and violent states of criminal irresponsibility, and in this are like Seneca (and Ovid and the martyrologies). But there is an essential difference. Reuben Brower speaks well of 'the amorality of Seneca's *Agamemnon*, where the heroine joyously gives way to crime' and where – for all the detachment and highmindedness of the choral odes – there is no assurance of a mind or a society outside the criminal mind' (*Hero and Saint*, Oxford, 1971, p. 200). But when Brower speaks of Titus Andronicus joining 'the happy criminal society of Seneca's Clytemnestra or Medea or Aaron, Tamora and her sons' (p. 199), one must regretfully part company from him.

When Seneca's slaves of passion are taken over by inhuman or anti-human emotions they are released from human responsibility, and in this sense 'happy' has its own ghastly appropriateness; they become the vessels or instruments of the *furor* which is personified by the *Furiae* we meet in the infernal prologues. When Medea, contemplating her final crime, begins to relent, the *Antiqua Erynis* snatches her unwilling hand, and forces her into the scream: *Ira, qua ducis, sequor* (Where wrath leads I follow) (953). She is sucked into an infernal and maddening vision (958–68):

> Quonam ista tendit turba Furiarum impotens?
> . . .   quem trabe infesta petit

> Megaera? cuius umbra dispersis venit
> incerta membris? frater est, poenas petit.
> dabimus, sed omnes fige luminibus faces,
> lania, perure, pectus en Furiis patet.
> Discedere a me, frater, ultrices deas
> manesque ad imos ire securas iube.

(Whither goes that mob of Furies, powerless to restrain itself?
... Who does Megaera search for, waving her torch?
What dubious ghost, limbs torn apart, comes forth?
It is my brother; he seeks revenge. He will have it.
But first set all your torches in my eye-sockets
Tear in pieces, set on fire. Lo, my heart receives the Furies.
Now, brother, you may order the revenging goddesses to leave me
and return satisfied to the deep-buried dead.)

What we seem to be given here is a passage of infernal possession, such as Lady Macbeth talks about, but does not display.[11] It is impossible to know just how subjective or how objective Seneca intended *Erynis* or *Megaera* to be, but clearly we are not dealing only with a fluctuation of inner mood. A more objective description of human processes seems to be involved: reason has struggled with *furor* and lost, and thereafter the inner resource of the individual is empty and the infernal passions take its place; as Phaedra remarks (184–5):

> Quid ratio possit? vicit ac regnat furor
> potensque tota mente dominatur deus.

(What can reason do? *Furor* has conquered and reigns over me. The powerful god controls the whole of my mind.)

The Elizabethan model of the human state is more complex than this, and the more complex form of the Elizabethan play reflects it. Revenge as a passion, perhaps as *the* passion, stalks the Elizabethan stage; but in the form of what Greville calls a 'particular sin', as an isolated madness, not as the objective and possessive power of the *ultrices deae*. The *Ultrix Deus* of the Elizabethan world ('Vengeance is mine, saith the Lord, I will repay') is, of course, quite different: not the abrogator of rational order, but its guarantor. Providence, even if only in the form of 'God's revenging aspect', is never wholly withdrawn from the

Elizabethan scene, where potential grace is a condition of being alive. Revengers are absorbed into the horror of their own obsessed imaginings, but they continue to exist inside a world where justice is remembered as a value.[12] Indeed a central point about revenge on the Elizabethan stage is that it is a perverted form of justice.

Of course, the most famous Elizabethan remark about revenge has always told us so: 'Revenge is a kind of wild Justice', says Bacon, where 'wild' (as the imagery following seems to show) means 'fit for the wilderness, run to seed, like a briar'. The madness of Titus Andronicus is a withdrawal into the dream of perfect justice, over which Astraea and not the *ultrices deae* presides as deity. He is the martyr of a world from which the true strain of justice has vanished, in which only the briar is left. Much of his madness turns on the search for justice (IV.iii. 4f.):

> *Terras Astraea reliquit.*
> Be you remembered, Marcus: she's gone, she's fled.

He sends his family to spread nets, to dig into the earth for justice, but he is told that only her 'wild' brother is available (IV.iii.38–40):

> Pluto sends you word,
> If you will have Revenge from hell, you shall.
> Marry, for Justice, she is so employed ...

And in the end his sanity snaps and he grasps at the perverted justice of the 'wilderness of tigers' where he lives. If Seneca is present in the Terean banquet of the final act it is as a kind of antimasque to the central ethic of the play. Tamora and her sons come to Titus's house to playact for his madness the simplifying possession of Revenge, the 'dread Fury' of Seneca's plays. But Titus and the play accept these simplifications only at a level of make-believe beyond that of the actual play-world (v.ii.141f.):

> I knew them all ...
> And will o'er-reach them in their own devices.

He is content (like Hieronimo in *The Spanish Tragedy*) to join their play of revenge, but outside the play he knows well enough what justice is, what its cruxes and problems are (v.iii.34–6):

> My lord the Emperor, resolve me this:
> Was it well done of rash Virginius
> To slay his daughter?

The play ends, not with the 'happy' murderer enjoying his infernal reward and proving (like Medea) that *nullos esse, qua veheris, deos* (wherever you go there will be no gods), but with the brief madness of revenge atoned for in the face of true justice by an expiatory death.

The revenge play of the Elizabethans would have been wholly unacceptable if Titus, or Hieronimo, or Hoffman, or Hamlet had been rewarded for their revenges, as Atreus or Clytemnestra or Medea are. Even if we take an extreme case – that most gloatingly horrific and smugly immoral of scenes, in which Antonio murders the little Julio (Marston, *Antonio's Revenge*, III.i) – we are in a moral world directly opposite to that of Seneca. The difficulties of taste here are often attributed to a surfeit of Seneca, and the quotation from *Thyestes* 151f. (Atreus rejoices in his capture of Thyestes and his children) shows that the corresponding episode was in Marston's mind. In fact, however, the tastelessness of the scene belongs to a quite un-Senecan branch of tastelessness. It sentimentalizes the child in a way that is foreign to the Roman. Julio says (III.i.145–9):

> Brother Antonio are you here, i' faith?
> Why do you frown? Indeed my sister said
> That I should call you brother, that she did,
> When you were married to her. Buss me; good truth,
> I love you better than my father.

Antonio welcomes Julio into his embrace with ironies which recall Atreus, but his motivations are quite distinct (it is indeed difficult to speak at all of Atreus's motivations). He apostrophizes heaven and justice, and declares his devotion to a mad purism of justice which will unambiguously separate guilt and innocence (III.i. 164–6):

> O that I knew which joint, which side, which limb,
> Were father all and had no mother in't.
> That I might rip it, vein by vein,
> In bleeding rases.

Once again revenge is presented as a monstrous mutation of justice, isolating and maddening, in a world still ruled by 'God's revenging aspect upon every particular sin'.

The Senecan ethic was, by a curious paradox, most tolerable when the subject-matter was not the intrigues and passions of individuals but the dynastic quarrels of the modern political world. Greville speaks of these as if somewhere between ancient and modern tragic practices, and reflecting his own interest to 'trace out the high ways of ambitious governors, and to show in the practice that the more audacity, advantage and good success such sovereignties have, the more they hasten to their own desolation and ruin' (*loc. cit.*). Of course the Elizabethan audience did not suppose politics was eventually free of the revenging hand of God, but knowledge of recent history (e.g. the Wars of the Roses) and the Chronicles of those events, showed men that a time-scale longer than any single life was likely to operate before divine justice was seen to be fulfilled. And there was also the awareness that Machiavelli and others had suggested that the political world operated apart from God's providence, and was therefore open to Seneca's interpretation.[13] Shakespeare's *Richard III* deals with a doomed dynasty like those of Argos or Thebes, where the pressure of the past justifies the abrogation of normal standards in the present; but the play is eventually a complex image of a whole world under moral siege, not a linear development of crime and possession. Richard has specific political aims, and a specific social context within which these aims have to be achieved; Atreus has neither.

The wailing queens in Act IV, scene iv, of *Richard III* have often been thought to derive from the wailing ladies of the *Troades*; and so they may, as Clarence's dream seems to derive from Virgil. In both cases a hint of classical material may have triggered off the development of a highly stylized exercise in rhetoric, meant no doubt in its solemn and witty formalism to recall a classical mode (Ovid in particular), but reflecting little or nothing of the meaning of any original. The queens create a joint interpretation of what history means: their repetitive stanzas reflect their repetitive destinies, and the extent to which history can be reduced to royal fate, and fate distilled into formal rhetoric. They create a patch of sombre colour, set against other patches, other interpretations, and beyond all interpretations lies the quite un-Senecan truth of Richmond's virtue and divine right to found the Tudor line.

The ghosts who throng to Richard's or Richmond's tents in Act V of *Richard III* indicate the supernatural world as the guarantor of justice, not its opposite; and in this they are typical of the Elizabethan supernatural. The ghosts who appear in Elizabethan plays may come from heaven or hell, but their interest is not (like Seneca's) in degrading and destroying humanity, but in achieving the satisfaction of justice seen to be done. It is the hunger for justice that drives them to appear and to demand action, whether to Baldwin, the author of the *Mirror for Magistrates*, who gives them satisfaction by telling their sad stories, or later to sons who will destroy their murderers. The ghosts in the *Mirror for Magistrates* offer a clear link between the dream-visions of hell that medieval literature shows and the 'filthy whining ghost/Lapt in some foul sheet or a leather pilch/ . . . screaming like a pig half-stick'd/ . . . Vindicta! Revenge, Revenge!'[14] who provides a stock image of Elizabethan revenge tragedy. The prose links of the *Mirror* carry the burden of evoking the supernatural occasion, and relating the 'history' told to the moral pressures of the individual's timeless fate:

> I waxed drowsy and began indeed to slumber. But my imagination still prosecuting this tragical matter brought me such a fantasy: methought there stood before us a tall man's body full of fresh wounds, but lacking a head . . . And when through the ghastfulness of this piteous spectacle I waxed afeared and turned away my face methought there came a shrieking voice out of the wesand pipe of the headless body, saying as followeth . . . (Prose 12)

> And therefore imagine, Baldwin, that you see him all to be mangled, with blue wounds, lying pale and wan all naked upon the cold stones in Paul's Church . . . (Prose 4)

> I will take upon me the personage of the last who, full of wounds, miserably mangled, with a pale countenance and grisly look, may make his moan to Baldwin as followeth . . . (Prose 1)

The quality of the ghost is thus evoked in terms of description rather than narrative or drama (and I shall return to this point later); the narrator himself is made the principal agent of the pattern which leads from these violent disruptions of silence to the final silence of the conclusion, when all that is required for resolution has been said. The process is strongly reminiscent of a confession and absolution. The ghost is finally satisfied (or exorcized) by having his personal history fitted into an exemplary framework. As James I of Scotland remarks when he begins his tale:

> If for examples' sake thou write thy book,
> I charge thee, Baldwin, thou forget me not.

The fully dramatized ghosts of later drama live, of course, in a world of multiple personal relations, but their motivation is like that of the *Mirror* ghosts and unlike that of Seneca, in that they seek (and achieve) a personal and fully human satisfaction: seeing the criminal destroyed, the usurper brought low. The *furor* which rages unchecked through Seneca's world, the boundless horror and destruction that *Umbra Tantali* is forced to promote: these are held in Elizabethan tragedy within the dimension of a personal or political displacement of the natural equilibrium which justice holds. The Elizabethan playhouse ghosts may begin their reaction to this displacement with screams of 'Revenge, revenge' or '*Vindicta*' (phrases not in the vocabulary of Seneca's ghosts) but end with expressions of family or social stability. Thus Old Andrugio in *Antonio's Revenge* watches the final action from 'betwixt the music houses' and departs saying:

> 'Tis done; and now my soul shall sleep in rest.
> Sons that revenge their father's blood are blest.

At the end of *Locrine* the ghost of Corineus takes his stand to 'stay and see revenge'. This is satisfied, and then Até (the chorus) can pronounce an absolution on the turmoil:

> Lo, here the end of lawless treachery,
> Of usurpation and ambitious pride,
> And they that for their private amours dare
> Turmoil our land, and set their broils abroach
> Let them be warned by these premises.

At the end of Kyd's *The Spanish Tragedy* the ghost of Andrea seems to praise murder with equal enthusiasm whether the victims be innocent or guilty. But justice is assured for the afterlife, where

> ... will I beg at lovely Proserpine
> That by the virtue of her princely doom
> I may consort my friends in pleasing sort
> And on my foes work just and sharp revenge.

And this is the note on which the whole play ends, with Revenge promising a final absolute of punishment:

> For here though death hath end their misery,
> I'll there begin their endless tragedy.

In its distribution of the cast into eternally separated sheep and goats this conclusion is more reminiscent of the Last Judgment sequence in the Mystery Cycles than of Seneca.[15]

The chronological basis of literary history has, in the view propounded here, led scholars to overestimate the force of transmission into an alien culture. The superficial quasi-Christianity of Seneca's morals should not blind us to the real hostility of received English dramatic patterns to the nature of his plays. This is especially important if we concentrate on the popular and public drama of the Elizabethans, putting to one side the plays written for readers or for one specific performance before a noble patron. The force of this distinction is often overlooked.

The Senecan tragedies of the Italian Cinquecento all seem to derive from specific or private production. In this they are like tragedies in England before the opening of the public theatres in 1576, like *Gorboduc* of 1561, or Gascoigne's *Jocasta* of 1566 (from Dolce), like *Gismond of Salerne* of 1567–8, or the Latin tragedies of the universities, such as Legge's *Richardus Tertius* (1573) or Alabaster's *Roxana* of 1592 (from Groto's *La Dalida*), or the later 'closet' (unacted) plays of aristocratic amateurs, the Countess of Pembroke's *Antonius*, Sir William Alexander's *Darius*, Fulke Greville's *Alaham*, etc., written in this way, no doubt, in reaction to the 'vulgar' form of the acted drama. As Greville says: 'be it known it was no part of my purpose to write for them against whom so many good and great spirits have already written' (p. 224).

This whole strain of English tragedy is manifestly close to its Italian and French counterparts, and nearer to Seneca than the popular form. The chronological model would however go further and suggest that the aristocratic plays of the 'sixties should be regarded not only as precursors but also as progenitors of the popular tragedies of the 'eighties and 'nineties, so that Seneca operates on the popular drama at two removes, as well as directly, but with crucial effectiveness. From this point of view there is a continuum of tragedy in England, running unbroken from 1561 – from *Gorboduc*, *Jocasta*, Hughes's *The Misfortunes of Arthur*, through *The Spanish Tragedy*, *Locrine*, *Hamlet*, *The Revenger's Tragedy* and so to Shirley's *The Cardinal* – to 1641. Fansler has put this view succinctly: 'One thing that bound all Elizabethan tragedies together, from *Gorboduc* to *The Traitor* and *The Cardinal*, was the influence of Seneca'.[16] It seems doubtful, however, if the Inns-of-Court private tragedies in fact led directly to or provided the primary stimulus for the public tragedies. David Bevington[17] has documented the connection between the forms of popular repertory entertainment and those of Marlowe. University men writing for professional actors and a paying public had to take note of the popular interest in a crowded stage, a wide variety of passions, a Christian ethic, a patriotic enthusiasm, a joking immediacy of theatrical contact. Seneca, Groto, Thomas Hughes, and the Countess of Pembroke could provide little guidance to deal with such demands, less indeed than the popular strolling theatricals of the English countryside. If Seneca were to be a powerful influence on the tragedy of the English public he would have, it seems, to make a fresh impact. His forms and his outlook could not be carried over, passively, from the private tragedies of the preceding decades.

H. B. Charlton, with his sights fixed eventually on Sir William Alexander, takes the Senecanism of the popular drama to be already proven by others, but the very brevity of his reference to its Senecan inheritance is convenient. He takes Nashe's famous attack on a dramatist (who may be Kyd) as representative of the methods of a school of popular tragedians, who[18]

> busy themselves with the endeavours of art, that could scarcely Latinize their neck-verse if they should have need; yet English Seneca read by candle-light yields many good sentences, as

Blood is a beggar and so forth; and if you entreat him fair in a frosty morning he will afford you whole Hamlets, I should say handfuls, of tragical speeches, But O grief! *Tempus edax rerum*. What's that will last always? The sea exhaled by drops will in continuance be dry, and Seneca, let blood line by line and page by page, at length must needs die to our stage; which makes his famished followers . . . to intermeddle with Italian translations. Wherein how poorly they have plodded . . . let all indifferent gentlemen that have travelled in that tongue discern by their twopenny pamphlets.

Charlton takes Nashe's description of popular tragedians' methods quite literally: 'Seneca . . . was their great storehouse of tragic material' (clxix). However, a quite literal reading of the passage seems impossible: Nashe's contempt is more clear than his argument. The opening gibe (in the section I have quoted) is aimed at those who cannot read Latin and have to read bloodthirsty Senecan *sententiae* in translation. Unfortunately for literalism, no English line 'blood is a beggar' is known, neither from the 1581 nor other translation of Seneca, nor does the line appear in any extant English play. It may be answered that Nashe is talking in particular about a perished play, the so-called *Ur-Hamlet*, and that this play must have had all the characteristics he lists. But it is obviously dangerous to explain a whole movement in terms of a perished and indeed hypothetical play.

What other plays of the supposed movement show these characteristics? The usual answer is, 'Kyd's *The Spanish Tragedy*'. If *The Spanish Tragedy* fitted Nashe's description, then much of the case would be proved, since it was the most popular tragedy of the early period and exercised a profound influence on subsequent plays like *Titus Andronicus*, *Antonio's Revenge*, *Hamlet*, Chettle's *Hoffman*, and others. However, *The Spanish Tragedy* seems to contain not a single line derived from the 1581 translation of Seneca. It has some Senecan lines in Latin and some original lines in Latin, which implies (I take it) some knowledge of that language. And there are no 'tragical speeches' taken out of Seneca in this play. We may wish to continue to believe, however, that Nashe's points, though not true literally, have a general truth, in that Kyd's play is Senecan in its general cast. The evidence for this is hard to find unless we take 'Senecan' to mean things

not found in Seneca, or found in many places.[19] In this context
'Senecan' is sometimes, of course, taken to mean 'having a unified
structure',[20] the assumption being that *The Spanish Tragedy* is
more unified than its predecessors (*Cambyses*, *Horestes*, *Apius and
Virginia*) and that this improvement must be due to Seneca. In
fact, *The Spanish Tragedy* is far from having what has been ascribed
to it: 'unity of action, and . . . also unity of motive, for it all
centres round revenge'.[21] Revenge as a motive, or a psychological propellant to action, only appears half-way through the
play. *The Spanish Tragedy* is unified, far more effectively than the
preceding plays, it is true; but not by motive; rather by the
impersonal but pervasive idea of justice, which appears not only
in the Hieronimo story, but also in the ghostly chorus, in the
Portuguese episode, and the episodes of Pedringano and
Bazulto.[22] And in this mode of organization there is no influence
of Seneca.

It is also true that *The Spanish Tragedy* has, in its interludes, a
ghost (together with a Morality Personification); but this ghost
has the usual non-Senecan characteristics I have described above.
It may be said, on the other hand, that the ghost here is a *protatica
persona* like the ghosts of Tantalus and Thyestes. And this is
true. But the purpose of his eruption from hell and the atmosphere
he brings into the play are quite distinct from anything in Seneca.
Kyd's hell is a place of love and justice (1.i.78–80):

> Proserpine began to smile
> And begged that only she might give my doom.
> Pluto was pleased, and sealed it with a kiss.

Seneca's ghosts are given a causal relationship to all that
follows: they cause the mortal characters to act as they do. The
ghost of Andrea in *The Spanish Tragedy* is, however, only a
spectator and commentator. It might be thought that his companion
Revenge is more like a Senecan *Furia* 'causing' revenge to
triumph in the play. In fact, however, the revenge that takes place
is wholly determined by the natural emotions of the characters:
Revenge is given no direct relationship to Hieronimo, the hero
and revenger. The revenge that Andrea returns to see and that
Revenge is sent to show him, in the manner of a dream, 'through
the gates of horn' (1.i.82), is in fact quite peripheral to the main

dramatic action. The ghost of Andrea is puzzled by what is going on (II.vi.2–3):

> I looked that Balthazar should have been slain
> But 'tis my friend Horatio that is slain

And the ghost's puzzlement is meant to represent, I take it, a natural if simple-minded reaction. Kyd creates, in short, a gap between the supernatural concern in the play, and the more central matter, the individual lives, which exhibit that unexplained capacity to make valid choices which is essential to a Christian view of the world and to modern drama. It is not any Senecan machinery, but this power to show emotion turning into action by the mysterious alchemy of free personal choice that gives *The Spanish Tragedy* and *Hamlet* and *Titus Andronicus* their grip on the audience. The tension between an external set of expectations and an internal set of compulsions ('God's revenging aspect' and 'particular sin') throws the weight of the play on the character of the protagonist in a manner wholly unclassical. Far from being the channel of Senecan influence into Elizabethan popular drama, *The Spanish Tragedy*, in this view of it, forged, in parallel to Marlowe, a dramatic vision of humanity to which Seneca's plays could offer only peripheral decoration.

It may be thought that a description of Seneca's relationship to English drama in terms of his dramatic structures and effects on the one hand and his ethical positions on the other, is too limited. It may be felt, in particular, that more important than any of these is his literary style. The recent Penguin translation of five plays [23] tells us that 'in the effectiveness of the spoken work was all that mattered in Seneca's conception of drama' (p. 25). Certainly the style of Seneca's plays was a point that few English critics of the Renaissance failed to mention: [24]

> the stately style of Senec sage ('H. C. to the Reader' before Studley's *Agamemnon*, 1566)

> ... grace and majesty of style (Preface to Heywood's *Thyestes*, 1560)

> ... endight/with wondrous wit and regal style (Preface to Heywood's *Thyestes*)

> ... penned with a peerless sublimity and loftiness of style (Newton's Preface to *Seneca his Ten Tragedies*, 1581)
>
> ... stately speeches and well-sounding phrases, climbing to the height of Seneca his style (Sidney, *Apology for Poetry*, 1595)
>
> Seneca's tragedies, Plautus' comedies, Virgil's Georgics and Warrior, of the Latins, for the stateliness of the matter and style are most honoured (L. Humphrey, *The Nobles*, 1563)
>
> Albeit he borrowed the argument of his tragedies from the Grecians, yet the spirit, loftiness of sound and majesty of style is merely his own (H. Peacham, *The Complete Gentleman*, 1622).

The terms in which the style is praised remain remarkably constant: high, majestic, regal, lofty, stately; all these seem to be pointing to a single aesthetic category, the sublime.

This categorization tells us about the critics' admiration; it is less helpful in giving us a comparative description of the mode of Seneca's poetry. Seneca's prose style has been described with great exactitude (e.g. succinctly and conveniently in W. C. Summers's edition of *Select Letters*), but it is not clear if his verse belongs to the same class. Certainly some of the features of 'Senecan' prose rhetoric appear also in the poetry. The taste for sharp, compressed and weighty utterance is important here also, especially of course in stichomythia. But we should not forget that Quintilian speaks of Seneca's *ingenium facile et copiosum* (x.i.128). The style of the plays can veer quickly from sharp desiccated 'points' (*harena sine calce*)[25] to flowing and hyperbolic eloquence, as in the following reply of the blinded Oedipus to Jocasta's attempted comfort (*Oed.* 1012–18):

> Quis frui tenebris vetat?
> quis reddit oculos? matris, en matris sonus!
> perdidimus operam. Congredi fas amplius
> haut est. nefandos dividat vastum mare
> dirimatque tellus abdita et quisquis sub hoc
> in alia versus sidera ac solem avium
> dependet orbis alterum ex nobis ferat.
>
> (Who forbids me to enjoy the darkness? Who returns me my eyes? Look, my mother, the voice of my mother! The good

work is thrown away! It is God's law that we should meet no more. Let the vast ocean divide the guilty, let the spaces of the earth yawn between us, bearing away one of us to whatever world hangs beneath this one, looking only at other stars and at a truant sun.)

We do not know how the Elizabethans responded to these polarities of style or how their conception of the sublime depended on one or another pole. We do know, however, that they had a sustained taste for tricksy and conceited writers – Ovid and Lucan as well as Seneca – and that 'height of style' was closely associated in their minds with daring conceits and sustained rhetorical structures. The natures of the Latin and the English languages hardly permit any carry-over of actual details of style, but the Neo-Latin plays of the period show their authors as happy to reproduce Seneca's range of rhetorical effects. Indeed even so considerable a Grecian as George Buchanan[26] shows the extent to which Greek drama was seen through the rhetorical lenses of Seneca's style: translating *Alcestis* 488: κτανὼν ἄρ' ἥξεις ἢ θανὼν αὐτοῦ μενεῖς, he sharpens its rhetoric into a typically Senecan glitter: *Caeso redibis rege, vel caesus cades*.[27]

The 1560–81 translators into English, however, have command of a rhetorical mode which would seem to be directly opposite to Seneca's. They are totally incapable of sharpness or compression; the hobnailed violence of their vocabulary is without self-conscious capacity for variation. To the modern ear, long inured to standards of the 'natural', the 'elegant', the 'easy', the 'conversational', the excesses and obviousness of Seneca's rhetoric may seem like that of his translators. But the sophistication (even decadence) of his repetitive cleverness seems outside the range of their language.

There is one modern frame of reference, however, which may be responsible for creating a greater disparity between Seneca's rhetoric and that of his 1560–81 translators than was seen to be the case in Elizabethan times, and it may be that in this case the modern frame distorts the picture.

Reading Seneca's plays as plays, and thinking of plays as immediate experiences, sharply focused, tensely direct in their confrontations and in the close-up attention they demand, we inevitably find their style grotesquely unreal in its simplified exaggeration and stridency, like posters seen at very short range. In the sixteenth century it was possible to think of a 'tragedy' anywhere along a range of considerable amplitude, stretching from the immediacy of theatrical tragedy to the dreamy and distancing vagueness of late medieval narrative tragedy. We have already noticed the descriptive bias of the *Mirror for Magistrates*. The Elizabethan translators of Seneca (belonging to the same intellectual group as Baldwin) impose a similar bias towards centralizing the narrator and distancing the action behind narrative and description. Jasper Heywood's preface to his translation of the *Troades* sets that work inside the framework of medieval and chivalric narrative of the 'matter of Troy':

> The ruins twain of Troy, the cause of each,
> The glittering helms, in field the banners spread,
> Achilles' ires and Hector's fights they [28] teach,
> There may the gests of many a knight be read:
> Patroclus, Pyrrhus, Ajax, Diomed.

Heywood's versified Preface to *Thyestes* turns this work into the dream-vision of a request to write, in parallel fashion, to the *Mirror for Magistrates*:

> Then dreamed I thus, that by my side
>   methought I saw one stand
> That down to ground in scarlet gown
>   was dight, and in his hand
> A book he bare: and on his head
>   of bayes a garland green.
> Full grave he was, well stepped in years
>   and comly to be seen.
> . . .
> Good sir (quod I) I you beseech
>   (since that ye seem to me
> By your attire some worthy wight)
>   it may your pleasure be
> To tell me what and whence you are.
> . . .
> Spain was (quod he) my native soil:
>   a man of worthy fame
> Sometime I was in former age,
>   and Seneca my name.

Heywood's addition of a final scene at the end of the *Thyestes* has a similar function. It gives narrative expansion to the pressures of the play, takes away the stark finality of the confrontation between Atreus and Thyestes with which Seneca ends. In this added scene Thyestes exclaims against his fate, forecasts his exile (in lines imitated from the end of the *Oedipus*) and suggests the eventual operation of justice:

> Ye scape not fro me so, ye gods,
>   still after you I go,
> And vengeance ask on wicked wight
>   your thunderbolt to throw.

The 'now-read-on' extension of the *Agamemnon* in Studley's translation has a similar effect. The particularity of the single play is absorbed into, and softened by, the longer perspectives of destiny.

The supply of a context or framework of this kind has the effect of making Seneca much closer to Ovid than he seems to be in our modern response to the tragedies. *The Metamorphoses* exhibits the same combination of smug horror and epigrammatic passion that revolts us in Seneca. But those characteristics do not seem to dominate Ovid's telling of his stories. In the tale of Tereus and Procne in Book VI of *The Metamorphoses* (very close in matter to the *Thyestes*) the tragic speeches of the principals are held within a mediating framework of author's narrative and description, and (even more) in the larger perspective of things remote, legendary and exemplary. Seneca's plays may be more like this than their genre suggests; for they are not in any real sense 'imitations of action'. They are comments on the mental states which would be appropriate to action; the interaction they contain is wholly static and sets static positions against one another. At the end of a typical Senecan exchange between *tyrannus* and *satelles*, or *regina* and *nutrix*, the dialogue is not led to a conclusion. A decision is simply taken to move to the next stage of the fable, a decision that could have been taken at any point in the dialogue.

In these terms Seneca's plays are unlike the modern conception of drama, and the style of the Elizabethan translations may be more appropriate than appears at first sight. Moreover, the assumption that Seneca's plays were like narrative tragedies is not one that is confined to the early translators who wrote before the English theatre existed. As late as 1599 Thomas Storer in his *Life and Death of Thomas Wolsey* invokes Seneca as the patron of this *Mirror for Magistrates* image of a tragic fall:

> Now write, Melpomene, my tragic moan
> Call Nero's learned master, he will aid
> Thy failing quill with what himself once said:
>> Never did Fortune greater instance give
>> In what frail state proud magistrates do live.

Samuel Daniel's *Complaint of Rosamond* (1592) shows how the rhetoric of these *Mirror*-type ghosts has advanced towards dramatic sharpness:[29]

> Out of the horror of infernal deeps
> My poor afflicted ghost comes here to plain it.

But though this is sharper than the 1560–81 translators of Seneca, the basis of the rhetoric is still narrative, as is the relationship of the author to his material (64–7):

> Then write (quoth she) the ruin of my youth,
> Report the downfall of my slippery state,
> Of all my life reveal the simple truth
> To teach to others what I learnt too late.

Seneca is not himself, of course, a figure in his own plays (though he quickly figures in his disciple's *Octavia*), but the mode of his rhetoric seems designed to remind us that this is a particular way of telling facts widely known, where the mode of narration or description is at the centre of interest rather than the facts narrated.[30] When Hecuba tells us at the beginning of the *Troades* of the murder of Priam she says that when Pyrrhus drew out his sword, *ensis senili siccus e iugulo redit* (the sword comes out of the the old man's throat still dry). A little later she remarks that: *Priamus et flamma indiget/ardente Troia* (Though Troy is burning Priam lacks a funeral pyre). We seem to be asked to applaud the teller rather than wonder at the tale.

When we turn to the rhetoric of the popular Elizabethan drama, the 'real' drama, we find a very different deployment of rhetoric, for which Seneca can be little except a source of occasional *sententiae*. Kyd's *The Spanish Tragedy* is again a useful text to

display the actual differences between Seneca and the so-called
Senecan drama. The most famous of the many passionately
rhetorical arias in *The Spanish Tragedy* is the speech of Hieronimo
when he discovers his son hanging in his orchard (II.v.1–33):

> What outcries pluck me from my naked bed
> And chill my throbbing heart with trembling fear,
> Which never danger yet could daunt before?
> Who calls Hieronimo? speak, here I am.
> I did not slumber, therefore 'twas no dream.
> No, no, it was some woman cried for help,
> And here within this garden did she cry,
> And in this garden must I rescue her.
> But stay, what murd'rous spectacle is this?
> A man hanged up, and all the murderers gone,
> And in my bower, to lay the guilt on me.
> This place was made for pleasure, not for death.
>
> *He cuts him down.*
>
> These garments that he wears I oft have seen –
> Alas, it is Horatio my sweet son,
> O, no, but he that whilom was my son.
> O was it thou that call'dst me from my bed?
> O speak, if any spark of life remain.
> I am thy father. Who hath slain my son?
> What savage monster, not of human kind,
> Hath here been glutted with thy harmless blood,
> And left thy bloody corpse dishonoured here
> For me amidst these dark and deathful shades
> To drown thee with an ocean of my tears?
> O heavens, why made you night to cover sin?
> By day this deed of darkness had not been.
> O earth, why didst thou not in time devour
> The vild profaner of this sacred bower?
> O poor Horatio, what hadst thou misdone
> To lose thy life ere life was new begun?
> O wicked butcher, whatsoe'er thou wert,
> How could thou strangle virtue and desert?
> Ay me, most wretched, that have lost my joy
> In losing my Horatio my sweet boy.

These lines are specifically designed to make vivid and moving a spectacle visually presented (or imagined) on the stage. A man enters before us; he tells us where he has been and what his state of mind is. He makes a direct appeal to identification. We too have been wakened by night-noises and felt our scalps tingle. Here is no Senecan *nuntius* informing us that his veins freeze to remember a mythological horror for which he is a witness; but instead we have the principal person of the play asking us to participate in his mimesis. Seneca's rhetoric is used to distance from us the highly-charged events described, and continuously resolves them into wit and abstraction. Hieronimo's soliloquy, on the other hand, keeps him close beside us as step-by-step we proceed through the process of discovery, even though by tragic irony we already know what it is he is going to find. He addresses us directly, not simply as an audience, but as if he might expect an answer. To whom is the opening question proposed? Is he addressing himself or us? Are we involved or not? The theatrical situation feeds on these tensions: we are caught in a guilty complicity with the action.

The movement of Hieronimo's speech mimics the movement of circling round and identifying not only the situation but the subject of the situation. Is the call real or imaginary? 'I must find out, I am not a coward, I will name myself. It was not imaginary, it must have been real. It was here and it was to me the call came. I must act.' At the moment of resolve the image of horror is revealed, though still not understood. Kyd skilfully allows a momentary pause on the agonizing brink of recognition, a technique more regular in comedy. Here a powerful effect of pathos is built up by the contrast between what Hieronimo still thinks and what we know, reinforced by the contrast between the bower (and the love-scene we have seen in it) and the present horror. The actual recognition has been delayed till line fourteen, and a series of relationships have been established between us and Hieronimo, and with the place and the object, the body of Horatio. The triple anaphora on 'O' marks the climax of the speech and a return to the opening question, addressed now to a specific answerer, with specific self-definition, 'I am thy father', and a specifically appropriate context, 'these dark and deathful shades'. The remainder of the speech is a circuit of anguished rhetorical questions based on the male *pieta* pose of father and son, aimed (as it were) at the world of values standing behind the audience: 'O heavens... O earth... O poor Horatio... O wicked butcher', and so returning to himself, the only answerer as the only speaker.

The situation of this speech (the discovery of a horror) is paralleled in Seneca, but the mode of its rhetoric is wholly unlike Seneca's. A line like 'O heavens, why made you night to cover sin?' could well have come from Seneca, but the method by which it makes its effect here is un-Senecan. In the *Thyestes*, after the death of Thyestes's children, an unnatural darkness settles over the earth. But this darkness is not conveyed to us as anyone's idea of darkness. The fourth chorus asks: *cur, Phoebe, tuos rapis aspectus?* (Why, O sun, do you hide your face from us?). But the idea of darkness is immediately developed as a general theme. The questions or answers proposed do not reflect on the minds of those speaking. The darkness of Hieronimo's garden acquires importance because we see Hieronimo coming to feel it is important: it is part of the world he creates for us out of the experience he undergoes.

Seneca's characters often describe their own feelings, or their position between alternative feelings. Medea describes the alternation in her mind between guilt and love, her rage for revenge and her desire for peace. But none of this is presented as feeling whose growth we have shared with the character, so that the more extreme moments of rhetoric are backed by a shared humanity. The classical technique of Seneca's plots means that the roots of character are in the distant past, in the habits of ancestors or the crimes of history. Medea presents her emotions as if she were the *nuntius* of her own situation. When we hear (943–4) *ira pietatem fugat/iramque pietas* (wrath chases away affection and affection, wrath), we seem to be hearing about the general qualities *ira* and *pietas* rather than participating in the psychological battle between them. In so far as they have a personal context it is one which requires us to enlarge *ira* to include all the acts of violence that Medea's history has encompassed, and *pietas* to stretch from her own family *pietas* in Colchis to that involving her children by Jason. The individual moment strains always to a generalization that (unlike the generalizations of Elizabethan dramatic rhetoric) lacks any personal, here-and-now dimension in the emotions we see and share with the common humanity of the presented character.

I have suggested that, below the level of cultural generality, the points of contact between Seneca and the public drama of the English Renaissance were small in number, distorted by great (though sometimes obscured) differences of outlook and expectation, and seldom wholly separable from other exemplars of similar taste. But Seneca remained, in spite of all this, an ancient, and praise of his morals and his style could not easily be evaded in an age hungry both for opportunities to reconcile the morality of Christian art with that of classical antiquity, and for models of power and sophistication in language. And this is as true in the England of the seventeenth century as in that of the sixteenth. In some senses the seventeenth century may be said to have increased Seneca's reputation, not only in the neo-Stoic movement associated with the names of Lipsius and Du Vair, Bacon and Feltham, but (in English at any rate) in an increasing sophistication and concision in the use of the language. When Drayton (in his epistle to Reynolds) speaks of 'strong Seneca'[31] he is making the appropriate stylistic connection between Seneca's mode and the 'strong lines' of the Metaphysical poets and the sinewy prose of the early seventeenth century, which we know to exist in terms of the mode of thought and general moral outlook of the period.

It would seem to be no accident that the best English translation of the most translated passage of Seneca (the end of the second chorus of the *Thyestes*) should be the work of Andrew Marvell.[32] The middle of the seventeenth century saw a second wave of English translations of the plays, the first since the 'sixties of the preceding century. Three of the plays (*Medea*, *Phaedra* and *Troades*, the three tragedies centred on female figures) were translated by Sir Edward Sherburn; the *Medea* being printed separately in 1648, the *Troades* in 1679, and all three issued together in 1701. It is a pity that the supposed historical significance of the 1581 volume has caused it to be twice reissued, when Sherburn's much more competent and readable work remains unknown. In addition, Edmund Prestwich translated the *Phaedra* in 1651. The *Troades*, translated by Samuel Pordage, was printed in 1660; and in 1674 came *Thyestes*, translated by John Wright. These remained the last translations of Seneca's plays till the historical interests of this century caused scholars to turn to them again.

With the fading of the Baroque the last connection between the taste of Seneca and that of any possible modern literature was broken. For, though the seventeenth century offered a more sophisticated response to Seneca's style and to the quality of his moral sensibility, the mode of his plays grew less and less acceptable, even to critics. Increasingly the English drama came to judge dramatic rhetoric by standards appropriate to real speech, and think of construction in terms of a fluent *liaison des scènes*.

It is predictable perhaps that Thomas Rymer, as an avowed enemy to non-realistic drama, should despise Seneca:[33]

> It was then a strange imagination in . . . Seneca, to think his dry Morals and a tedious strain of sentences might do feats or have any wonderful operation in the drama.

Dryden says in the *Essay of Dramatic Poesy* that Seneca had the gift to make vulgar things sound lofty (ed. Ker, I.105):

> One would think, *unlock the door*, was a thing as vulgar as could be spoken; and yet Seneca could make it sound high and lofty in his Latin : *Reserate clausos regii postes laris*.

In the context of the defence of rhyme in the Essay, this is clearly an admired gift, but the occasions when it needs to be exercised are allowed to be very few.

And Dryden's defence of rhyme and other 'heroick' appurtenances of tragedy is in any case clearly something of a paradox in the drama of his times. Even in the preface to his own and Lee's furibund *Oedipus* he says much the same thing as Rymer:

> Seneca on the other side, as if there were no such thing as nature to be minded in a play, is always running after pompous expressions, pointed sentences and philosophical notions, more proper for the study than the stage.

The pomposity of Seneca's style offended the canons of naturalness and ease which were to become increasingly the overriding requirements of both stage and study. Theobald in his *Double Falsehood* (1727), alleged to be based on an old play, was still Baroque enough to enjoy (presumably) and paraphrase a typical Senecan conceit (H.F. 84): *Quaeris Alcidae parem?/Nemo est nisi ipse* (You are looking for the equal of Hercules? He has no equal except himself) as 'None but thyself can be thy parallel'. Pope seized on the conceit as typical of Theobald's bad taste and inserted the 'marvellous line' into *The Dunciad* (three-book version), III.271.

The final appearance of Seneca in *The Dunciad* marks very well what happened to his plays in the period of the Enlightenment. After this it clearly needed a complete shift of priorities to bring Seneca's plays back into anything like favour. Today we may be on the edge of some such shift. In 1968 London had what is probably its first ever public presentation of a Seneca play: *Oedipus*, in a translation or rather adaptation by Ted Hughes, produced by Peter Brook with Sir John Gielgud in the title role. Hughes writes (perhaps with memories of Camus's *La Peste*) of a world disintegrated by the Theban plague into separate moments of pain and incomprehension. His style is without sentence-structure, a series of vividly particular phrases expressing separate emotional and sensory responses, the connections unstated, and perhaps unimagined. By this technique the desperateness of man's state is brilliantly exposed; but it is a long way from the dignity and lucidity of Seneca's *senarii*. The 'Senecan style' is certainly one which reduces the power of connectives – 'shattered eloquence' is Dryden's fine phrase for it (in his *Life of Plutarch*) – but his contraction of meaning from large gestures of interpretation, to the privacy and limitation of individual integrity is not a retreat into incoherence and meaninglessness. The taste that lay behind this production goes back to the crazy theatrical theorist Antonin Artaud, who in 1932 was praising Seneca as a model for what he called 'The Theatre of Cruelty'. Writing to Jean Paulhan on 16 December 1932, he says: (*Œuvres Complètes*, Paris, III.303):

> Je suis en train de lire Sénèque ... Quoi qu'il en soit celui-ci me paraît le plus grand auteur tragique de l'histoire, un initié aux Secrets et qui mieux qu' Eschyle a su les faire passer dans les mots. Je pleure en lisant son théâtre d'inspiré, j'y sens sous le verbe des syllabes crépiter de la plus atroce manière le bouillonnement transparent des forces du chaos ... une fois guéri j'ai l'intention d'organiser des ... lectures publiques où je lirai des Tragédies de Sénèque, et tous les commanditaires possibles du Théâtre de la Cruauté seront convoqués. On ne peut mieux trouver d'example écrit de ce qu'on peut entendre par cruauté

SENECA AND ENGLISH TRAGEDY

au théâtre que dans toutes les Tragédies de Sénèque, mais surtout dans Atrée et Thyeste. . . . Dans Sénèque les forces primordiales font entendre leur écho dans la vibration spasmodique des mots.

In these terms Seneca is treasured largely because his plays are an affront to the bourgeois sensibilities of traditional theatregoers. The violence, the *bouillonnement transparent des forces du chaos*, assault and disturb, force the spectators to admit the power of the frightening, the unknown, the disgusting. Artaud planned a version of *Thyestes* (*Le Supplice de Tantale*), but this seems not to have survived. The Ted Hughes version of *Oedipus*, however, shows the same ideals, in its intensification and increased particularity of horror and its avoidance or reduction of both morality and wit, the qualities which were earlier thought of central importance to an appreciation of Seneca the dramatist.

Appendix: *English Translations and Imitations of* Thyestes, *391–403*

> Stet quicumque volet potens
> aulae culmine lubrico;
> me dulcis saturet quies;
> obscuro positus loco
> leni perfruar otio,
> nullis nota Quiritibus
> aetas per tacitum fluat.
> sic cum transierint mei
> nullo cum strepitu dies,
> plebeius moriar senex.
> illi mors gravis incubat
> qui, notus nimis omnibus,
> ignotus moritur sibi.

1. First published 1557; written before 1542.

    Of the same meane and sure estate

    Stond who so list vpon the slipper whele,
    Of hye astate and let me here reioyce,
    And vse my life in quietnesse eche dele,
    Vnknowen in court that hath the wanton toyes.
    In hidden place my time shall slowly passe

> And when my yeres be past withouten noyce
> Let me dye olde after the common trace
> For gripes of death doth he to hardly passe
> That knowen is to all: but to him selfe alas,
> He dyeth vnknowen, dased with dreadfull face.
> <div align="right">(<i>Sir Thomas Wyatt</i>)</div>

2. First published 1560.

> Let who so lyst with mighty mace to raygne,
> In tyckle toppe of court delight to stand
> Let mee the sweete and quiet rest obtayne.
> So set in place obscure and lowe degree,
> Of pleasaunt rest I shall the sweetnesse knoe.
> My lyfe unknowne to them that noble bee,
> Shall in the steppe of secret sylence goe.
> Thus when my dayes at length are over past,
> And tyme without all troublous tumult spent,
> An aged man I shall depart at last,
> In meane estate, to dye full well content.
> But greevous is to him the death, that when
> So farre abroade the bruite of him is blowne,
> That knowne hee is to much to other men:
> Departeth yet unto him selfe unknowne.
> <div align="right">(<i>Jasper Heywood</i>)</div>

3. First published 1681; probably written before 1660.

> Climb at *Court* for me that will
> Tottering favor's Pinacle;
> All I seek is to lye still.
> Settled in some secret Nest
> In calm leisure let me rest;
> And far of the publick Stage
> Pass away my silent Age.
> Thus when without noise, unknown,
> I have liv'd out all my span,
> I shall dye, without a groan,
> An old honest Country man.
> Who expos'd to others Ey's,
> Into his own Heart ne'r pry's,
> Death to him 's a Strange surprise.
> <div align="right">(<i>Andrew Marvell</i>)</div>

4. First published 1668.

>Upon the slippery tops of humane State,
>>The guilded Pinnacles of Fate,
>Let others proudly stand, and for a while
>>The giddy danger to beguile,
>With Joy, and with disdain look down on all,
>>Till their Heads turn, and down they fall.
>Me, O ye Gods, on Earth, or else so near
>>That I no Fall to Earth may fear,
>And, O ye Gods, at a good distance seat
>>From the long Ruines of the Great.
>Here wrapt in th' Arms of Quiet let me ly;
>Quiet, Companion of Obscurity.
>Here let my Life, with as much silence slide,
>>As Time that measures it doth glide.
>Nor let the Breath of Infamy or Fame,
>From town to town Eccho about my Name.
>Nor let my homely Death embroidered be
>>With Scutcheon or with Elegie.
>>An old *Plebean* let me Dy,
>Alas, all then are such as well as I.
>>To him, alas, to him, I fear,
>The face of Death will terrible appear:
>Who in his life flattering his senceless pride
>By being known to all the world beside,
>Does not himself, when he is Dying know
>Nor what he is, nor Whither hee's to go.
>>>>>*(Abraham Cowley)*

5. First published 1676.

>>Let him that will, ascend the tottering Seat
>>Of Courtly Grandeur, and become as great
>>As are his mountain wishes; as for me,
>>Let sweet Repose, and Rest my portion be;
>>Give me some mean obscure Recess, a Sphere
>>Out of the road of Business, or the fear
>>Of falling lower, where I sweetly may
>>My self, and dear Retirement still enjoy.
>>Let not my Life, or Name, be known unto
>>The Grandees of the Times, tost to and fro

> By Censures or Applause; but let my Age
> Slide gently by, not overthwart the Stage
> Of publick Interest; unheard, unseen,
> And unconcern'd, as if I ne'er had been.
> And thus while I shall pass my silent days
> In shady Privacy, free from the Noise
> And busles of the World, then shall I
> A good old Innocent Plebeian dy.
> Death is a mere Surprize, a very Snare,
> To him that makes it his lifes greatest care
> To be a publick Pageant, Known to All,
> But unacquainted with Himself, doth fall.
>
> *(Sir Matthew Hale)*

6. First published 1674.

> While he that loves Ambition's pains
> On the Court's slippery top remains;
> Let me sweet peace enjoy; content
> I am to live where none frequent;
> There shall I fill my longing breast
> With the still blessings of soft rest,
> Free from their knowledge great who are,
> Free from the noise of business, there
> I'll cast my life, and thus shall I
> Rich in an humble fortune die.
> But heavy doth that death befall
> To him who too much known to all
> By fame of his great honours past
> Dies to himself unknown at last.
>
> *(John Wright)*

7. Bodleian MS. Rawlinson 76, second half of the seventeenth century.

> Let him who likes it be stiled great
> Upon the slippery tops of state.
> Give me, O Gods, a quiet life,
> Nor let debate, nor law nor strife
> E'er haunt my cottage, where I find
> All joys can bless a mortal's mind.
> Let time as smooth as swiftly run

And all the craggy roads quite shun
Which lead to honour, which at last
Is lost, and life, in seeking past.
A life I wish wherein I may
Live old, and silent pass away.
Unhappy he who dies, well known
To all but to himself alone,
A man of outside who lives high
Is called a Wit, a Debauchee,
But knows not, vain fool, how to die
                                    (*Anon.*)

8. First published 1732.

   *An imitation of the 2nd chorus, in the second act of
   Seneca's* Thyestes

Whom worldly luxury and pomps allure
They tread on ice and find no footing sure
Place me, ye powers! in some obscure retreat,
O! keep me innocent, make others great;
In quiet shades, content with rural sports
Give me a life remote from guilty courts,
Where, free from hopes or fears, in humble ease
Unheard of I may live and die in peace.
Happy the man, who, thus retir'd from sight,
Studies himself, and seeks no other light:
But most unhappy he, who sits on high,
Exposed to every tongue and every eye;
Whose follies blaz'd about to all are known,
But are a secret to himself alone:
Worse is an evil fame, much worse than none.
               (*George Granville, Lord Lansdowne*)

Notes

1. In 1967 I published an account of Seneca and Elizabethan drama entitled 'Seneca and the Elizabethans: a case-study in "Influence" ' (*Shakespeare Survey*, XX, pp. 17–26). The present study seeks to avoid repetition of the material collected there, and therefore I must begin with some brief summary of what was said. The centre of the study was the suggestion that influence cannot be realistically described as what A gave to B, since the context in which B received A is of vital importance, and thus

201

requires a sense of all that was not A in the *milieu* of B. Seneca was absorbed into an Elizabethan scene in which classical example was treasured within a Gothic framework. *Sententiae* and *exempla* from Seneca were hoarded in *florilegia*, but classical form and 'purity' (in a post-Winckelmann sense) were not involved. In these terms the genetic relationship of Elizabethan tragedy only with previous tragedy comes to seem one strand only among many, and Seneca becomes a minor example of the taste expressed in larger and more accessible terms by Ovid. The conservative vernacular tradition guarded by the guilds of actors kept wholesale innovation at bay, but allowed prestigious classical details to decorate the surface of works which remained at deeper levels true reflections of the non-classical worlds in which they appeared.

2 See R. Fischer, *Die Kunstentwicklung der englischen Tragödie* (Strasbourg, 1898); W. Cloetta, *Beiträge zu Literaturgeschichte des Mittelalters und der Renaissance*, 2 vols (Halle, 1890, 1892); W. Creizenach, *Geschichte des neueren Dramas*, 4 vols (Halle, 1909).

3 The late Victorians, who invented that tautologous genre 'the tragedy of blood', showed their incapacity for tragedy by imagining that blood, cruelty and spectacular horror are optional extras in the tragic experience, only to be explained by Seneca's decadence on the one hand and Elizabethan primitiveness on the other. We should remember that the balanced Horace chose *cena Thyestae* as his type of the tragic episode (*AP* 91).

4 Cf. Jean Jaquot, writing on 'Sénèque, la Renaissance et nous': Si on appelle 'sénéquienne' tout pièce qui a pour ressort la tyrannie ou la vengeance, où les atrocités et les lieux communs abondent, où il y a des rêves prémonitoires, des apparitions, des scènes de magie, on emploie l'épithète dans un sens assez vague, qui n'est pas faux, mais qui ne nous assure nullement d'une familiarité de l'auteur avec le tragique latin. Tout ceci est vite devenu monnaie courante au théâtre et, nous l'avons vu, le sujet des pièces de Sénèque, loin d'être exceptionnel, est dans la bonne moyenne des histoires tragiques susceptibles d'être portées à la scène. (*Les Tragédies de Sénèque, et le théâtre de la Renaissance*, Paris, 1964, p. 282.)

5 See Hunter, op. cit., *passim*.

6 Ian Scott-Kilvert, 'Seneca or Scenario', *Arion*, VII (1968), p. 511.

7 T. S. Eliot, 'Shakespeare and the Stoicism of Seneca', *Selected Essays* (London, 1948).

8 See Hunter, op. cit., p. 25.

9 See John Hazel Smith, ed., *A Humanist's 'Trew Imitation': Thomas Watson's 'Absalom'* (Urbana, 1964).

10 The last two lines quoted are not found in Q1. They were doubtless added to the later texts to make Shakespeare's rather abrupt ending more 'normal'.

11 Cf. I.-S. Ewbank, 'The fiend-like queen', *Shakespeare Survey*, XIX (1966), pp. 82–94.

12 It is interesting that even the translators of Seneca transform this central point so far as they can. Thomas Nuce in his poem before

Studley's translation of the *Agamemnon* changes Seneca's meaningless victory of passion over reason to a demonstration about justice:

> This deed was done by Talion law,
> here blood did blood require,
> And now Thyest hath that revenge
> that he did long desire.
> Whereby thou chiefly mayst be taught
> the providence of god
> That so long after Atreus' fact
> Thyest's revenge abode.

13 Mario Praz in his 1928 British Academy lecture, 'Machiavelli and the Elizabethans', suggested a notable simplification of the map of 'influence' on the Elizabethans. His argument is that the 'Italian Seneca' which reached England had already (mainly through Cinthio) combined the Senecan tyrant with the Machiavellian *principe*. But the 'Machiavel' in English drama is seldom a tyrant: he is an intriguer aiming at power, and enjoying the complexities of intrigue in quite un-Senecan fashion. The maxims of amorality are similar in Seneca and Machiavelli, but 'Machiavellian' amoralism does not carry anything else plausibly 'Senecan' into Elizabethan drama. Cf. W. A. Armstrong, 'Seneca, Machiavelli and the Elizabethan tyrant', *Review of English Studies* (1948), pp. 19–35.

14 Anon., *A Warning for Fair Women*, Induction.

15 See the 'Last Judgment' play (XXIV) in the Chester cycle (*EETS* edn (655–60):

> DEMON PRIMUS Goe we forth to hell in hye;
> Without ende ther shall you lye;
> For you have lost, right as dyd I,
> The Blisse that lasteth ever.
>
> Judged you be to my Belly
> Ther endlesse Sorrow is and nye;
> One thinge I tell you truly:
> Deliverd bene you never.

16 H. E. Fansler, *The Evolution of Technic in Elizabethan Tragedy* (Chicago, 1914).

17 David Bevington, *From 'Mankind' to Marlowe* (Cambridge, Mass., 1962).

18 Nashe, Preface to Greene's *Menaphon* (McKerrow ed., *Works*, London, III, pp. 315–16).

19 I trust there is no need to argue with absurdities like G. B. Harrison's 'from Seneca Kyd had drawn the notion that Tragedy was to be measured by the number of the corpses' (*The Story of Elizabethan Drama*, Cambridge, 1924, p. 23).

20 See above, p. 169.

21 Legouis and Cazamian, *History of English Literature* (London, 1937 edn), pp. 398f.

22 See G. K. Hunter, 'Ironies of justice in *The Spanish Tragedy*', *Renaissance Drama*, VIII (1965), pp. 89–104.
23 Translated E. F. Watling (Harmondsworth, 1966).
24 Derived from J. C. Scaliger, *Poetices*, lib. VI. cap. vi: *Inventiones sane illorum sunt: at maiestas carminis, sonus, spiritus ipsius.*
25 The description of Seneca's style by the Emperor Caligula: see Suetonius, *Caligula*, 53.
26 On Buchanan's 'completely Senecanized' style, see the comments of Charlton, op. cit., pp. xlix ff., and Boas, *University Drama* (Oxford, 1914), pp. 60–1, together with the evidence collected by John Hazel Smith, op. cit.
27 When Roger Ascham translated Sophocles' *Philoctetes*, he did it *ad imitationem quantum potui Senecae* (*Letters*, ed. Giles, Letter XVI, 1.32).
28 Dares, Dictys, Homer, Maro, mentioned in the preceding stanza.
29 A rhetoric copied, it seems, in the academic play, *Caesar's Revenge*: 'Enter Caesar's Ghost: Out of the horror of those shady vaults/ . . . My restless soul comes here to tell his wrongs.' (Malone Society Reprint, Oxford, 1972ff.)
30 See Friedrich Leo, *L. A. Senecae Tragoediae* (Berlin, 1878), p. 148: *novum autem genus, tragoedia rhetorica, inventa est, cuius indoles breviter sic describi potest, ut ἦθος in ea nullum, πάθος omnia esse dicatur.* Cf. H. V. Canter, *Rhetorical Elements in the Tragedies of Seneca* (Urbana, 1925), pp.18–22.
31 See J. E. Spingarn, *Critical Essays of the Seventeenth Century* (Oxford), 1.138.
32 See Appendix.
33 See Spingarn, op. cit., II.211–12.

VII

Seneca and Neo-Latin Tragedy in England

J. W. Binns

A large number of Renaissance plays which were written in Latin survive today from all the countries of Europe.[1] In England, the plays which are extant from the sixteenth and early seventeenth centuries form an interesting by-way of the Elizabethan drama.[2] A number of tragedies in particular remain, which, cast in Senecan mould, constitute an aspect of Seneca's influence which has been little discussed. The extent of Seneca's influence on the popular drama of the Elizabethan age continues to be debated.[3]

On the Latin drama of the age, the drama written by educated men, who were often members of the Universities of Oxford or Cambridge, the extent of Seneca's influence is less open to doubt. Seneca, as the only surviving ancient writer of Latin tragedy, would be familiar to any cultivated man of the times with an interest in literature, especially in view of the pre-eminent position which tragedy then occupied among the literary *genres*. The plays of Seneca were almost certainly on the syllabus at Westminster School,[4] which was attended by two important writers of Academic drama, William Gager and William Alabaster. William Gager, in the prologue to an expanded version of Seneca's *Hippolytus* which was performed at Christ Church, Oxford, in February 1591/2, could assume that at any rate all the men in the audience, even if not the women, would be familiar with the play.[5]

Modern scholars tend to consider that Seneca's plays were not written for performance on the stage. Renaissance critics, however, generally believed that Seneca's plays had been performed;[6] and several performances are indeed recorded at Oxford and Cambridge during the sixteenth century. G. C. Moore Smith records the performance at Trinity College, Cambridge, of a *Troades* in 1551/2 and 1560/1, of an *Oedipus* in 1559/60, and of a

205

Medea in 1560/1 (the 1551/2 performance being certainly of Seneca's play, and the other performances mentioned almost certainly of his plays); of a *Hecuba*, again at Trinity College, in 1559/60 (probably Seneca's *Troades*); and of a *Medea*, perhaps Seneca's *Medea*, at Queens' College, Cambridge, in 1563.[7] G. C. Moore Smith came to the conclusion that 'the original Latin tragedies of Seneca continued to be given on College stages at least down to 1583',[8] and writing of Cambridge Academic plays performed before 1585, he states: 'Judging from the titles of acted plays, Plautus, Terence, and Seneca were the Latin authors most drawn upon'.[9] At Oxford, F. S. Boas lists a performance at Christ Church of *Octavia* (probably the pseudo-Senecan play) in 1588, as well as the performance which I have already mentioned of *Hippolytus* with additional scenes written by Gager in February 1591/2 at Christ Church.[10] Gager himself writing in defence of Academic drama refers to the acting of Seneca as a commonplace event:[11]

> We contrarywise doe it [i.e. come upon the stage] to recreate owre selves, owre House, and the better parte of the *Vniversitye*, with some learned *Poeme* or other; to practyse owre owne style eyther in prose or verse; to be well acquaynted with *Seneca* or *Plautus*; honestly to embowlden owre yuthe; to trye their voyces, and confirme their memoryes; to frame their speeche; to conforme them to convenient action; to trye what mettell is in evrye one, and of what disposition thay are of; wherby never any one amongst vs, that I knowe, was made the worse, many have byn much the better.

Academic acting, then, served the twin ends of amusement and education. It also helped to diffuse a knowledge of and interest in Seneca's tragedies throughout the universities. In all probability, anyone who sat down in the sixteenth century to compose a tragedy written in Latin was thoroughly familiar with Senecan tragedy. Latin tragedies on Senecan lines both are a reflection of the contemporary fascination with Seneca, and help to propagate this interest.

I propose to discuss in this chapter three Latin tragedies to which little attention has been paid, and then to try to see whether it is possible to draw any conclusions which may help us to modify our view of Seneca's influence on the Elizabethan drama.

The first play I shall discuss is *Roxana*, a Latin tragedy by William Alabaster, the minor English poet and writer of works of mystical theology.[12] This play was first published in a pirated edition in 1632, and was followed in the same year by an authorized edition described on the title page as: *A plagiarii unguibus vindicata, aucta, et agnita ab Authore* (claimed from the claws of the plagiarist, expanded, and acknowledged as his own by the author). Alabaster states, in a dedicatory letter to Sir Ralph Freeman,[13] also a dramatist, that the play had, however, been written and acted about forty years previously (at Trinity College, Cambridge, in *c.* 1592), when Elizabethan drama was entering the period of its greatest florescence. As in most of Seneca's tragedies, the action of *Roxana* commences when events are approaching a crisis: much that is important for the narrative had already happened before the play begins, and in the authorized version of the play to which I shall refer in my discussion, a brief summary outlines these events for the reader. In performance these would have been explained by an early speech of the ghost of Moleon, who recounts his past history on his return from the underworld.

When Oxiartes, king of Bactria, lay dying, he entrusted to his brother Moleon the tutelage of his kingdom and his son, Oromasdes, until the latter should be of an age to rule. When Moleon found excuses for not handing over the kingdom, Oromasdes fled to India and married Atossa, the daughter of an Indian king. Returning with a military force, he deposed and executed Moleon. Moleon had a daughter, Roxana, whom, lest she fall into the victor's hands, he had sent away to a secret hideout in the depths of the forest, accompanied by faithful attendants and all necessary supplies. Oromasdes, separated from his companions whilst out hunting, chanced upon Roxana's hideaway, made her his mistress, and had a son and a daughter by her.

Oromasdes has known Roxana for ten years when the action of the play begins with the return from the underworld to Bactria, his old kingdom, of the ghost of Moleon. Moleon had been promised his revenge by the ruler of the underworld. The figure of Death approaches and offers his aid. To him Moleon outlines his tale, maintaining that he had always intended to deliver up the kingdom to Oromasdes when the latter was ready for it, but Oromasdes had acted too precipitately. The seduction of his daughter was a further wrong to be avenged. Roxana too must pay for loving her father's murderer and for bearing children by him. Moleon decides to set his vengeance in motion by use of the figure of Suspicion, who enters, and is briefed by Moleon. A chorus concludes the act, telling of strange omens: the howling of an owl, a wolf entering the court, two snakes entering Atossa's bedroom. Suspicion begins now to poison the minds of the characters.

Act II opens with Oromasdes beset by ill-defined feelings of unease. He wonders whether his wife Atossa has found out about the existence of his mistress Roxana. He sends his counsellor, Bessus, to make sure that all is well with Roxana. Bessus is afraid lest the king believe that he has betrayed his secret. He begins to fall in love with Atossa and to her he recounts his love. Bessus informs Atossa of the existence of Roxana and her two children, and says that the king is thinking of divorcing Atossa. Atossa is outraged at the news, pledges her love to Bessus, and plots vengeance against her husband. In Act III Oromasdes debates with a senator, Arsaces, the advisability of divorcing his wife on the grounds that she has produced him no heir. Meanwhile Bessus has brought Roxana and her children from her forest retreat to the court, under the pretence that she is to be made queen. Atossa, pretending to be Oromasdes's mother, greets Roxana fulsomely. In the next scene, Arsaces soliloquizes on the vices of the court.

At the beginning of Act IV a messenger enters, overwhelmed with the atrociousness of the news with which he is burdened. He proceeds to relate this piece by piece to the chorus. The messenger describes a secret chamber to the north of the palace, shaded by trees of yew and cypress. The chamber is haunted, and used for black-magic rites. When Roxana, who thought she was about to go through a marriage ceremony with Oromasdes, entered the chamber, Atossa had chained her hands together, taunted her, and then had her flogged. The ghost of Moleon now appears and interrupts the messenger's narration with exclamations of delight. Atossa had placed a sword in Roxana's hands and then forced her to kill her own children. In the next scene, Oromasdes, ignorant of what has just occurred, begins to suspect Bessus's loyalty; he hears him speaking of his love for Atossa and kills him, thinking that the secret of Roxana is now quite safe.

In the first scene of Act V Atossa is boasting that she has outdone Medea in monstrous crime. She is preparing a banquet at which she will serve up the bodies of Roxana and her children. She has prepared a poisoned garland for Oromasdes, which will drip into his goblet of wine and cause him to die. Oromasdes is meanwhile plotting to murder Atossa in exactly the same way. The ghost of Moleon arrives to watch the consummation of his vengeance. When they have eaten, Oromasdes reveals to Atossa the head of Bessus. In return, she reveals to Oromasdes that he has eaten from the bodies of Roxana and her two children. Both now begin to die from the poison they had prepared for each other. Atossa looks forward to the glory she will enjoy in the lower world for her deeds. Oromasdes dies, and Atossa dies immediately afterwards.

The prefatory material to the authorized printed version of the play tells us a good deal about its composition. In the dedicatory letter to Ralph Freeman, Alabaster calls the play a *morticinum* . . . *abortum* (a dead, unfinished piece), written in two weeks, and intended, not for immortality, but for one performance only. He had hoped that his play could rest undisturbed, but a plagiarist brought the play to light, and printed it from a corrupt manuscript; the plagiarist was responsible for increasing the number of blemishes caused by the hasty composition of the play. Alabaster had been faced with the choice of allowing this faulty version to be perpetuated, or else of supplicating again his youthful Muses, although he was now nearly seventy. He had therefore chosen to issue under his own name a more correct version of the play.

In fact, the pirated version is a good deal closer to the authorized version than one would think from Alabaster's protestations. The pirated version is indeed rather more handsomely printed than the authorized version. The choruses in particular are set out more elegantly. Moreover, the authorized version contains a long list of *errata* at the end of the play, and the first scene of Act II is headed 'Actus Secundus, Scena Quarta'. There are numerous differences of word order, of accidence, and of punctuation between the two versions, together with many small differences of phraseology, but otherwise it is the same play, virtually line for line. The title page of the authorized version advertises the work as *aucta* (expanded), but the expansions are few and far between. The plot summary of events immediately antecedent to the opening of the play does not appear in the pirated version. On the other hand, the authorized version lacks the scene-by-scene summaries which the pirated version possesses. Otherwise the chief additions to the authorized version are nine lines at the end of the first speech of Death in Act I, scene 2; five lines in the middle of his second speech in the same scene; six lines of stichomythia between Death and Suspicion in Act I, scene 4; a short interchange of seven lines between the chorus and Atossa in Act V, scene 1; and four and a half lines added to Oromasdes's last speech in the final scene of the play. It may be that Alabaster wrote these lines especially for his edition of the play, and that this is what he means when he says that he had to supplicate the Muses of his youth once again. The surviving manuscripts of the play,[14] strangely enough, stand in close relation to the pirated version of the play, not to the authorized version. Alabaster's indignation is undoubtedly overstated in the dedicatory letter which prefaces the play.

He states furthermore that the authorized edition of the play is *crebra linearum interpelatione caperata* (wrinkled with interpellation of many lines), although the additions amount to less than thirty-five lines. Alabaster considered that the style of the play was extravagant throughout. He refers to its *dictionis . . . lolium* (the weeds of its diction). In addition he made a plea for the play to be declaimed in a ranting manner (sig. A5r.):

> cum spuma soni, ut solent poetae tragoedias suas, quia in grandius quodammodo excoluntur, quae cum ampulla oris leguntur.
>
> (with a foaming sound, in the manner in which poets are accustomed to recite their tragedies, because works which are read in a bombastic voice become even more perfect.)

This suggests that Alabaster prized *Roxana* for its grandiose, inflated style, the Latin equivalent, perhaps, of the ranting bombast of Elizabethan popular tragedy.

It may well be that, as I shall suggest below (p. 229), Renaissance Latin tragedies, and the tragedies of Seneca himself, were valued more for their style than for their dramatic qualities. Commendatory verses by Hugh Holland,[15] who also contributed a dedicatory poem to Shakespeare's First Folio, commend the fluency of the inflated style of *Roxana* (sig. A5v.):

> Quis Graium tonat ore tam rotundo,
> Cuius tam cita Musa tamque pressa?

(Which of the Greeks thunders in voice so orotund? Whose Muse is so swift and so concise?)

In another dedicatory poem, Thomas Farnaby,[16] the brilliant Elizabethan scholar, renowned for his editions of Seneca and other classical authors, praised the exalted style of the play:

> Roxana scenae emancipata pulpitis
> Olim, ubi, cothurno nixa, contempsit solum,
> Calcavit astra, condidit coelo caput.

(Roxana is freed from the boards of the stage, where once, supported by her tragic buskin, she contemned the ground, trampled the stars, and hid her head in the heavens.) (sig. A6v)

Modern taste may tend to disparage as inferior imitations the Latin writings of the sixteenth and seventeenth centuries; yet for *Roxana* to merit the praises of such a one as Farnaby was in its day no mean achievement. Moreover, in his *Index Poeticus* (London, 1634), a glossary of poetical commonplaces, giving references to treatments of various themes in ancient and modern Latin authors, Farnaby lists Alabaster as one of the seven modern Anglo-Latin authors on whom he has drawn for illustrative material. Although he refers on occasion to Alabaster's poems, most of his allusions to Alabaster are to *Roxana*. He refers the reader to the chorus at the end of Act III for a description of the power of love; to Act III, scene 4 for the arts of the courtier; to Act II, scene 2 for the mutability of Fortune; to Act II, scene 3 for the Furies; to Act IV, scene 1 for omens; to Act II, scene 4 and Act III, scene 2 for dreams; and to Act II, scene 4 for vengeance. Thomas Fuller too, in his *Worthies of England*,[17] describes Alabaster as 'a most rare poet as any our age or nation hath produced; witness his tragedy of *Roxana* admirably acted in [Trinity] college, and so pathetically, that a gentlewoman present thereat (Reader, I had it from an author whose credit it is sin with me to suspect), at the hearing of the last words thereof, *Sequar, sequar*, so hideously pronounced, fell distracted, and never after fully recovered her senses.'

Dr Johnson too remarked that 'Milton was the first Englishman who, after the revival of letters, wrote Latin verses with classick elegance. . . . If we produced anything worthy of notice before the elegies of Milton, it was perhaps Alabaster's *Roxana*.'[18]

Thus Alabaster himself and those who commend the play seem to stress its stylistic virtues, and we should bear this in mind in any discussion of the play. Although Alabaster complains that a plagiarist has made free with his play, *Roxana* is an adaptation, with some omissions and additions, of an Italian play, Luigi Groto's *La Dalida* (Venice, 1572); Alabaster however reduces by about half the great length (some 4,000 lines) of Groto's play. Alabaster's reliance on Groto for the details of his plot again suggests that his interest in literary composition lay not so much in the invention of his material but in his manner of treating it.

None the less, Alabaster's play, by virtue alone of being written in Latin, can succeed in coming much closer to the Senecan style and mood. The Senecan qualities are not transposed by being rendered into another language, as tends to happen in the Elizabethan translations of Seneca, where the language of the translation takes on a life of its own. *Roxana* is certainly bloodthirsty and horrific; the atmosphere is extravagant and exotic. The setting is the kingdom of Bactria in the Balkans; Oromasdes's wife, Atossa, is an Indian princess; and the names of the other characters too are Oriental: Arsaces, the senator; Sisimithres and Ariaspe, Roxana's children; Damiana, attendant upon Atossa. The whole of the first act is devoted to Moleon's account of his wrongs and his desire for vengeance. He, and the stylized figures of Death and Suspicion, are the only characters to appear in the act. Human characters do not appear until Act II, unless one counts the chorus at the end of Act I. The play is economically constructed with few characters. There is no sub-plot. Bessus and Atossa are balanced by Oromasdes and Roxana, and this symmetry is emphasized by the way in which Oromasdes and Atossa choose to kill each other with poisoned flowers, after having first killed each other's lovers.

That episode provides the horrific climax of the play. Earlier, however, a lengthy and explicit description of the sadistic torture of Roxana by Atossa had been given (sig. D6v.):

>   creber et roseam cutem
> Plagis aravit, lividi vibicibus
> Sulci tumescunt, corpus et totum fuit
> Pro vulnere uno; ...
>   ...   saepe ceu tubulis latex
> Ruptis, aqualis exilit, fusus cruor,
> In ora Atossae purpurae guttas pluit
> Tingens pudore debito invitas genas.
> At illa spumas sanguinis laeta accipit,
> Ut sicca tellus lucidos imbres bibit
> Torrente Cancro.

([the assistant] ploughed frequent blows across her rosy skin; the livid furrows swell with weals, her whole body was as one wound. ... Her blood, spilt like water when it spurts from burst pipes, showers bright drops on Atossa's face, staining her checks with the colour which they ought to have had, but were unwilling to assume. Atossa however happily receives these drops of blood, just as the parched earth drinks up the shining rain at the height of the summer.)

The play dwells lovingly on moments of unnatural horror, on the compelled slaughter by Roxana of her own children, on Oromasdes's feelings when he knows he has eaten his own wife and children. Atossa sees herself consciously acting like a character in a Senecan tragedy. When she hears that her husband has a mistress, she suffers more than Medea (sig. C4v.):

>   non sic ruit
> Medea, laesi stimulo amoris saucia,
> Quando astra, et omnes ad suos gemitus Deos
> Deduxit: hoc maior mihi incumbit dolor,
> Furorque maior.

(Medea, wounded by the goad of her injured love, did not rush thus when she drew down to her groaning the stars and all the gods. I am possessed by a greater grief and a greater madness.)

Atossa decorates the chamber where Roxana is tortured with pictures of, amongst others, Medea dividing the limbs of her brother, Hippolytus dragged along by his father's chariot, and

Thyestes eating his own children. She boasts that she has excelled the crimes of Medea (sig. E2v.):

> Haec dicta Medeae date; haud superbiat
> Cristasque tollat propter antiquum scelus:
> Atossa maius hoc dedit, maius dabit.

(Bear these words to Medea: let her not be proud, let her not preen herself on her ancient crime. Atossa has committed a greater one, and will commit a greater.)

Nor has Atossa relied on supernatural help, as Medea did, but on her own resources (sig. E2v.):

> Hoc quicquid est ab uno, in uno pectore
> Natum et petitum est, nemo laudem hanc dividet.

(Whatever I have done has been conceived and attempted by and in one heart. No one will share the praise with me.)

After Atossa has killed Roxana and her children, and has made from their bodies a dish to be served to Oromasdes, she prepares to kill him too by means of a poisoned garland and replies to the remonstrating chorus (sig. E3r.):

> Nihil Thyestem, Tantalum nihil supra
> Conabor?

(Shall I not attempt more than Thyestes or Tantalus did?)

Oromasdes sees Atossa as worse than Medea (sig. E5v.):

> O Furia Scyllae quoque
> Pudenda vel Medeae, et orci faecibus.

(O Fury of whom Scylla, or Medea, and the dregs of hell would be ashamed.)

The chorus too compares her crime with that of Atreus in *Thyestes* (sig. E1v.–E2r.):

> Ad tua quondam fata Thyestes
> Flexit refugam lampada Phoebus,
> Et caeruleo proluit haustu
> Nondum emeritos fine iugales:
> Non minor haec est causa latendi,
> Et digna tuo Phoebe exilio.

(Phoebus once guided a lamp which shunned to look upon
your fates, Thyestes; and he bathed in the sky-blue draught
the team that had not served their course. There is here no
less cause for hiding away, no less cause for your absence, O
Phoebus.)

The messenger also says that Atossa has equalled the crime of
Atreus (sig. D4r.). The number of such allusions suggests that
the play is to be seen within the Senecan tradition. And this
suggestion is indeed borne out by the play, with its vengeful ghost,
its moralizing chorus, its long speeches on stock themes, its
horrific incidents, its stichomythia and *sententiae*.

The second play I have chosen to discuss is *Nero*, by Matthew
Gwinne.[19] Matthew Gwinne was born in about 1558, and was
educated at Merchant Taylor's school; in 1574 he went to St
John's College, Oxford, later becoming a Fellow there. After
taking the degrees of B.A. in May 1578 and M.A. in May 1582, he
obtained the degree of Doctor of Medicine in July 1593. In
1597 he became the first professor of physic at Gresham College
in London. He died in 1627.

Nero was first printed in 1603. It was entered in the Stationers'
Register on 23 February 1602/3. Later that same year, it was reissued with a dedication to the newly-succeeded King James.
The play was popular enough to be reprinted in both 1638 and
1639. I take my citations from this last edition.

Nero is an extremely long play of some 6,000 lines. The play is a
dramatization of the reign of the Emperor Nero, and is closely
based on Roman historical sources, principally Suetonius's life of
Nero, Tacitus's account of Nero's reign in *Annals* 13–16, and
sections of Dio Cassius's *Roman History*. The play opens with a
long stage direction which outlines a dumb show with which the
action of the play is to begin: to the noise of thunder and light-
ning, Nemesis and the three Furies emerge from the lower world,
walk up and down the stage, and sit down on seats on different
parts of the stage. Music sounds, and Messalina, wife of the
Emperor Claudius, leads a revel, accompanied by Silius her
paramour, his brows bound with ivy. Narcissus the freedman
informs Claudius, who remains unmoved by the pleas for mercy
of Messalina. A band of soldiers at the direction of Narcissus drag
Silius and Messalina on to the stage and kill them. The stage

direction ordains that all this is to be done either in silence, or to the accompaniment of music.

Nemesis then speaks a prologue: she introduces herself and the three Furies, the avengers of sin, and describes and comments on the events which have just been portrayed. The tragedy proper then begins with the ghosts of Messalina and Silius: the ghost of Messalina threatens vengeance in a lurid speech. Act I of the play deals with the events up to the death of Claudius. Claudius chooses another wife, his niece, Julia Agrippina. The senate acclaims Claudius's choice, and, at his command, his son-in-law Syllanus is removed from the roll of senators. Britannicus, Claudius's son by Messalina, begins to be jealous of Nero, Agrippina's son by her former marriage. Pallas the freedman and Agrippina plot to kill Claudius, and when they do so, Britannicus and his sister Octavia lament his death. At the end of the act, Tisiphone the Fury rejoices.

Act II opens with the ghost of Claudius complaining of the punishments of the lower world and prophesying the fate which awaits Britannicus. Nero becomes Emperor, and soon begins, under the influence of Seneca, his tutor, and Burrhus, the praetorian prefect, to exert his independence of his mother. Afraid lest Agrippina try to recover her influence by plotting to put Britannicus on the throne, Nero commands the poisoner, Locusta, to prepare poison for Britannicus. Britannicus dies, and is mourned by Octavia and Agrippina. Agrippina swears revenge on Nero who has now become enamoured of Poppaea. Alecto concludes the act with a moralizing chorus on the greed for power.

Act III opens with the ghost of Britannicus descending to the underworld. Nero's character continues its rapid degeneration. He makes love to Poppaea, and plots the murder of his mother by staging a shipwreck; Agrippina survives the shipwreck, but is dispatched by the henchman Anicetus. Megaera closes the act in a chorus which tells of the savagery of mankind.

Act IV opens with the ghost of Agrippina, who bemoans her fate and threatens vengeance. Nero and Poppaea are now haunted in their dreams and in their waking moments by the ghost of Agrippina. Nero's position becomes insecure. Burrhus disapproves of Nero's plans to divorce Octavia, and is replaced as praetorian prefect by Tigellinus and Rufus. The rebellion of Plautus and Sulla is announced, and Nero sends to execute them.

Helvidius Priscus and Thrasea Paetus begin to resent the subjection of the senate. Nero's tyranny now knows no bounds. Octavia flees for her life, and her servant Pythias is cruelly tortured to make her incriminate her mistress. Poppaea complains that she is hated by the mob, and Nero sends out soldiers to terrorize the populace. The chorus concludes the act by discussing the evils of an uneasy conscience.

Act V is extremely long, and Gwinne suggests in a dedicatory letter to the play that it could form a tragedy complete in itself. The act is itself subdivided into five acts, so that, for example, Act V, scene 2 of the complete play is also numbered Act I, scene 2 of the tragedy within a tragedy. The act opens with the ghost of Octavia telling how she was murdered. As four citizens tell of the burning of Rome and the terror and destruction caused thereby, Nero dressed in theatrical clothes appears on a balcony and sings a song. Conspiracies against Nero's life are now under way, but are betrayed. Piso, Seneca, and Lucan kill themselves by opening their veins. Lucan recites from his *Pharsalia* as he dies. Poppaea, now pregnant, complaining that she has been deserted by Nero, is kicked by him, and as a result she too dies. Petronius commits suicide whilst a slave reads to him from his works. Nero goes through a marriage ceremony with Sporus. The soldiers begin to rebel, led by Galba and Vindex in the provinces. In the last scene of the play, the ghosts of Nero's victims dance around him. Galba is proclaimed Emperor in the camps. Nero stabs himself, and as he lies dying is dispatched by a centurion.

We are able to glean a good deal of information about the play and about Gwinne's attitude towards it from his comments in the dedicatory letter which prefaces the play, addressed to the son and son-in-law of Thomas Egerton, the Lord Chancellor. We learn that the play was not acted; the reason for this was not, however, that the play was not written to be acted, as might be implied by the uneven length of the acts, and the great number of characters (some eighty of them) in the play. Gwinne says that the play had been offered for performance to his college, St John's College, Oxford, but had been rejected.[20] The play was 'caviar to the general', but should please the unlearned.[21] Although aware of the classical rule that not more than three people should appear on the stage at one time, he had decided to ignore it.[22] In this he is like another Oxford dramatist, William Gager, who also claimed for himself a similar freedom from the confining rules of an Art of Poetry.[23] In the first acts, Gwinne felt that he was not at his best; the last act was the most successful, and this was a tragedy complete in itself.[24]

The dedication is dated Ash Wednesday 1603, and Gwinne describes the play as having been written some while previously to beguile his leisure.[25] He had not written a comedy, because comedy was beyond his powers.[26] He was in fact later to write a comedy, *Vertumnus* (London, 1607), which was acted before King James. In the dedication to this, he suggests that comedy could be thought to be below the dignity of a serious man.[27] As for whether he had sufficiently met the requirements of tragedy, Tacitus and Suetonius could be the judges, for he had merely versified their material (sig. A4r.): *ego tantummodo modos feci; ineptus tibicen in comoedia* (I only made the measures, a clumsy piper in the play). The material, Gwinne implies, is essentially tragic; originality of plot was not the prime concern either of Alabaster or Gwinne. The view that the plot is in itself tragic is reinforced by the prologue spoken by Nemesis (sig. B3r.):

> Quod si Tragoedis materia primum malis
> Patheticis turbata lachrymosa, horrida,
> Quaeratur; ullum terra sustinuit, tulit
> Natura, vidit Phoebus, historia edidit,
> Vel par Neroni, vel parallelum malum?

(If subject matter for tragic actors is sought which is in the first place agitated by pathetic misfortunes, tearful, horrid; then has the earth supplied, or Nature borne, the sun looked upon, or history given us a monster equal to or like Nero?)

None the less, Gwinne expected that the play would be criticized. He sees a parallel between Pliny indulging himself in writing verses and himself writing plays,[28] and goes on (sig. A5v.):

At scribi fert: quin legi? et legi; quin edisci? et edisci, quin recitari? et recitari, quin audiri? et audiri, quin agi? quin spectari? Si idem adest animus, de actu parum interest.

(If it is permissible to write a play, then why not to read it? And if to read it, why not to memorize it? And if to memorize

it, why not to recite it? If to recite it why not to hear it? If to
hear it, why not to act it? If to act it, why not to watch the
performance? Performance of the play has little significance if
the mind in which it was written is the same.)

Gwinne defends plays against absent critics who censure them
for indecency.[29] He sees play-acting as an elaborate disguise in
which the living imitate the dead for the sake of giving pleasure:
the spectator remains always conscious of the artifice, however
(sig. A7r.):

> Qui personas induunt, exuunt, se simulare non dissimulant,
> citant ut recitent, dum mortuos viventes repraesentant, quod
> fit in scena histrionibus. Tam putem puerum Octaviam quae
> olim fuit, quam quae nunc non est, foeminam. Ferendi magis
> igitur qui fere fallunt ut delectent, quam qui delectant specie
> ut fallant opere, qui hominem in vulpe quam qui vulpem
> referunt in homine.

(Those who assume parts in a play and then lay them aside do
disguise the fact that they are feigning whilst they represent
dead people as living, as actors do on the stage. I would as
soon think that the historical Octavia was a boy, as that the
Octavia who now has no real existence is a woman. Therefore
those who generally deceive in order to delight, who represent a man in the shape of a wolf, are more to be tolerated
than those who delight by show in order to deceive in their
achievements, who imitate a wolf in the shape of a man.)

In Gwinne's references to the *absentes Momos* (sig. A7v.) who
censure plays at which they are not present, in his denials that
he could ever believe that the boy who would play the part of
Octavia could be a woman, we must see a reference to the
controversy about Academic acting between William Gager and
Dr John Rainolds, the Puritan opponent of academic acting.[30]
Dr Rainolds had criticized the performance of plays by William
Gager at which he had not been present, and had believed that
Gager had caricatured him under the guise of Momus, the carping
critic whom Gager had brought on to the stage at the end of
a performance of *Hippolytus* on 8 February 1591/2. Dr Rainolds
had objected in particular to the playing by men of women's parts,
on the grounds that a boy dressed as a woman furnished an

allurement to lust. Gwinne, who had written dedicatory verses to Gager's *Ulysses Redux*, performed on 6 February 1591/2 at Christ Church, and who, along with Gager, had been a member of the committee charged with the arrangements for the performance of plays before Queen Elizabeth when she visited Oxford in September 1592,[31] could hardly fail to know of this controversy. He appears to be attacking Rainolds's views in this preface to *Nero*, which is an important critical document in the history of Academic drama.

A dedicatory poem by John Sandsbury, the minor poet,[32] addressed to the humanist Justus Lipsius, stresses the affinities between Seneca and Gwinne. *Nero*, says Sandsbury, is to take the place of the pseudo-Senecan *Octavia*, which Lipsius had denied was written by Seneca (sig. A11r.):[33]

> Lipsi, Neronem nunc habe; votis tuis
> Oculisque dignum: quique puerilem putas
> Octaviam illam, quam rudis mundus iubet
> Senecae imputari, Iuste, praesentem loco
> Substitue: Seneca sic enim iratus iubet.
> Μετεμψύχωσιν ille millenam miser
> Sensit, querelas antequam posset suas
> Lingua referre propria; tandem tamen
> Ex ore Gwinni pristinum servat decus.
> Gagere, Buchanane, nec Beza, invide.
> Videte; talis Seneca qui Gwinnus fuit.
> Qui iudicas fatere; qui nescis tace.

(Lipsius, who think that the *Octavia* which the ignorant world attributes to Seneca is puerile, receive this *Nero*, which is worthy of your prayers and notice. Justus, substitute for *Octavia* the present tragedy. Thus indeed Seneca angrily commands. He has wretchedly experienced a thousand-year metempsychosis before being able to give voice to his complaints in his own tongue. Yet in the end he preserves, through the mouth of Gwinne, his former glory. Gager, Buchanan, Beza, do not be envious. See, what a Seneca Gwinne was. You who have judgment confess it; you who are ignorant be silent.)

Gwinne is here seen as a modern writer of Senecan drama, the superior of Gager; of George Buchanan, the renowned Scottish humanist, author of two Latin plays, *Jephthes* and *Baptistes*; and of the French humanist and dramatist Theodore Beza.

What is one to make of *Nero*, with its vast crowd of characters, and its enormous length? Gwinne is surely indulging himself in exploiting to the full the Senecan devices beloved of the Elizabethans. He had discussed in his preface (sig. A8r.) whether the greater art lay in saying a few things in many words, or many things in few words. In *Nero* however he encompasses many incidents at great length. The play is episodic, but it has a loose unity in that it covers all the years of Nero's life from the time when he becomes politically significant as the son by a former marriage of Claudius's wife Agrippina, to his overthrow and death. The device of the vengeful ghost returning from the underworld to threaten vengeance is used to the full, as a recurrent harbinger of doom at the commencement of each act; Messalina's ghost in Act I, Claudius's in Act II, Britannicus's in Act III, Agrippina's in Act IV, Octavia's in Act V. Furthermore, Agrippina haunts Nero and Poppaea intermittently after her death, and just before Nero's death the ghosts of all his victims return to haunt him, as Richard's do in Shakespeare's *Richard III*. Gwinne, having written one enjoyable ghost scene, seems not to have known where to stop, and so repeated himself.

Gwinne similarly exploits an effective scene when Seneca prepares to commit suicide by opening his veins, and this is followed by scenes in which Piso, Lucan, and Petronius die in the same way, the two last to the accompaniment of quotations from their own works. Again, the scene in which Pythias is tortured in an effort to make her betray her mistress Octavia is paralleled by one in which Epicharis is tortured to make her betray details of the conspiracy to depose Nero.

None the less, the play has its effective moments, and would have come off well upon the stage. The dumb show, portraying Messalina's adultery, performed in the presence of the Furies who are stationed in different parts of the stage, is an imaginative opening. Nemesis speaks the prologue and epilogue to the whole play, and Tisiphone, Alecto and Megaera respectively speak the chorus at the end of the first three acts. All of them combine to speak the chorus at the end of Act V. This gives the impression that the events of the play are being stage-managed by the Furies.

A number of lyrics contribute to varying the atmosphere of the play, and give Gwinne an opportunity for displaying his metrical virtuosity. Britannicus and Octavia mourn the death of Claudius in a pathetic song just before Britannicus is poisoned, and Nero sings a splendid song as Rome burns. A messenger sings a happy song in adonics on the occasion of Nero's feigned reconciliation with his mother in Act III, until at the appearance of the Furies his joy is changed to terror.

The character of Nero is a brilliant study in degeneracy. He first appears as a petulant boy, querulously complaining that he is not saluted by his proper title. Once Emperor, the evil traits of his character quickly manifest themselves. He poisons Britannicus, and when Britannicus drops dead at a banquet, Nero callously turns his mind to thoughts of Poppaea's beauty. A long train of deceit, murder, and intrigue begins, and although the play is set in Rome, the atmosphere is also thoroughly of the Renaissance: the stage is peopled by Locusta the poisoner, Paris the tragic actor, torturers and court flatterers. Many of the characters are not, of course, essential to the structure of the play. During the conspiracy scenes especially a great number of characters flit transiently across the stage without leaving any lasting impression.

Seneca himself is a character in this play, and on his first appearance speaks sententiously (sig. C3v.):

> Quicunque parcit improbis perdit probos.
> Probi tenenter praemio, poena improbi
> . . .
> Qui parcit omni ac nemini, est aeque ferus.

(Whoever spares the wicked, destroys the good. The good are held in check by hope of reward, the bad by punishment. . . . The ruler who spares no man and the ruler who spares all men are equally cruel.)

A good many *sententiae* in the play are taken from Seneca's philosophical works (sig. E9v.): *Fortuna magna, servitus magna est* (Great fortune is great servitude), from *De Consolatione ad Polybium* 6.5), as well as two further quotations from *De Tranquillitate Animi* in the same speech. *Sententiae* from Seneca's own plays are also adapted: *Quia conticescit gravis amor, loquitur levis/loqui lubet, pudetque* (sig. C12v.), and *Scelus antevertam scelere: nam sceleri salus/scelus est* (sig. B10r.) based on *Phaedra* 607 and *Agamemnon* 115 respectively. But examples could be multiplied many times.

Some of the *sententiae* about government are perhaps a sign of Gwinne's interest in the problem of power. On one level the tragedy is a political play, a study of ruling, ambition, and greed for power. Agrippina intrigues to try to become the real ruler of the Roman Empire; Seneca and Burrhus manipulate Nero in an endeavour to minimize her influence. When Burrhus is dismissed by Nero from his position as praetorian prefect, Nero appoints two successors in Burrhus's place so that the one will serve as a check on the other. The scenes dealing with the conspiracy of Nero's enemies to overthrow him are also a prominent part of the play. Nero's competence to govern is discussed upon his accession by four Roman knights providing a kind of choric comment in Act II, scene 2.

The language of the play is stylized and formal, typified by lines such as (sig. E9v.–E10r.):

> Est aula ludus; ludit, illudit: vide.
> Est aula Siren; cantat, incantat: time.
> Est aula cavea: claudit, includit: cave.
> Est aula hyaena; comprimit, perimit: fuge.

> (The court is but a game: see, it mocks
>   and ridicules.
> The court is a Syren which sings and
>   bewitches: fear it.
> The court is a cage which confines and
>   imprisons: beware.
> The court is a hyena which oppresses and
>   kills: flee it.)

The highly-wrought and elaborately composed Latin of the dedicatory material also provides an illustration of Gwinne's somewhat florid Latinity.

Basing his story upon the reign of one of the most notorious and sensational Roman Emperors, Gwinne succeeds in weaving together a tragedy centring round the rise and fall of a prince, and containing scenes of violence and torture, love, intrigue, haunting and death. The play has a strong political interest through the scenes which deal with the struggle for power. The language of the play is contrived, artificial and sententious. In his *Nero*, Gwinne succeeds not only in reproducing the traditional elements of Senecan tragedy, but in surpassing them.

The third tragedy which I shall discuss is the anonymous *Perfidus Hetruscus*. This was not printed, and cannot be precisely dated, but was written in the seventeenth century,[34] probably in the early part. Writings still in this era achieved a form of publication by being circulated in manuscript. In spirit and mood, *Perfidus Hetruscus* lies well within the tradition of sixteenth-century Senecan Latin tragedy. The story has no source in history, so far as is known, but deals with imaginary incidents concerning the royal house of Etruria.

Sorastanus, king of Etruria, is on his deathbed. His twin sons, Lampranus and Columbus, together with his brother, Pandolphus, pay their last respects. Sorastanus dies. They mourn his death. Pandolphus resents that he is not made king in succession. He determines to obtain the crown, and attempts to enlist the aid of Cappuchio, a monk. When Cappuchio proves unwilling, Pandolphus kills him. Pandolphus then enlists the aid of Grimalfi, a Jesuit. The two sons of Sorastanus go to lament at their father's tomb. Grimalfi, disguised as the ghost of Sorastanus, attempts to incite them to suicide. The real ghost of Sorastanus enters, and kills Grimalfi.

Lampranus becomes king (off stage) and Pandolphus insinuates that Columbus is treacherous to him. Lampranus orders Pandolphus to fetch Columbus to answer to the charges. Lampranus, alone, thinks of suicide, and swoons. Pandolphus convinces Lampranus and his counsellors, Lansocus and Morelli, in a long scene, that Columbus is false, although the heavens thunder in sympathy for Columbus. Columbus is exiled for life, and in exile, meditates suicide. The ghost of Sorastanus appears and urges Columbus to exact vengeance against Pandolphus. Meanwhile Lampranus repents his action in banishing Columbus. Lampranus summons a priest to tell him of a dream he had had about a giant. At that moment, the ghost of Sorastanus in the shape of a giant appears. He rebukes Lampranus for his treatment of Columbus. Columbus returns, urged on to vengeance by his father's ghost, who appears again. Columbus and Pandolphus fight a duel. Pandolphus prepares poison in a goblet to be drunk by whoever first wounds the other. By mistake Pandolphus drinks the poison he was preparing for Columbus. Seemingly he dies.

A solemn procession with music celebrates the victory of Columbus. They have a banquet. Suddenly Pandolphus appears and they all drop their goblets. It seems that the poison did not kill him after all. He succeeds in throwing suspicion on Columbus once more. Columbus is condemned to death. He kneels to be executed, when a violent storm breaks out and impedes the execution. The voice of Sorastanus is heard protesting against the proposed action. Columbus is taken away to prison; Lansocus begins to doubt the wisdom of what is happening, and says so to Pandolphus, who ignores him. With a rope Pandolphus strangles Columbus, who is still in prison. Collosocus, the murderer whom Pandolphus had engaged to do the job, had swooned when he had made the attempt. Lampranus and Lansocus regret the death of Columbus. Lampranus in a frenzy, now completely full of love towards his brother, threatens to seize him from the jaws of hell itself.

Lampranus falls seriously ill because of his brother's death. A doctor is called, who gives Pandolphus a poisonous plaster to apply to the king. This Pandolphus does, smearing even the crown with poison. Lampranus awakes, and accuses the doctor. Upon Pandolphus's urging, the doctor is made to apply the plaster to himself. The doctor dies. Lampranus then dies and is carried off the stage in solemn procession. Pandolphus is crowned king. In a fit of remorse he confesses his sins. He goes blind. The ghosts of Sorastanus, Capucchio, Grimalfi, Columbus, Lampranus and the doctor appear and torment him. Pandolphus in a frenzied speech prepares for death, saying he will carouse in hell and rule Death herself.

This play has an obvious interest through its parallels with *Hamlet* and other Shakespearean plays. There is in the first place the situation in which a son is urged by the ghost of his father to take vengeance on his uncle. The duel between Pandolphus and Columbus at which Pandolphus drinks by mistake the cup of poison prepared for his opponent has clear similarities to the closing moments of *Hamlet*. The sudden return of Pandolphus, who had been thought dead, to the banquet, calls to mind the return of Banquo in *Macbeth*. The ghosts of his victims return to haunt Pandolphus, just as Richard's do in *Richard III* (and as Nero's do in Gwinne's play).

The prologue to this play announces:

> Tragaedia agetur
> Nigra tumescens bile, madefacta sanguine,
> Non inimico, sed fraterno.

(A tragedy swelling with black bile will be performed, bedewed with the blood, not of enemies, but of brothers.)

It says further:

> Tristior tragaedia agi nequit, vel in
> Infortunatis insulis.

(A sadder tragedy cannot be performed, even in the Isles of the unblest.)

A reference to *hoc tragici cothurni stadio* (this arena of the tragic buskin) suggests that the play was either performed or else written with performance in mind. After alluding in general terms to the horrors that are to come, the prologue warns the audience to expect *plura, sed saeviora* (further crueller events). The prologue thus lays stress on the atrociousness of the incidents, as well as on the inflated style (*nigra tumescens bile*).

In this tragedy one is more conscious of the crowded action of the play than in *Roxana* and *Nero*. *Roxana* is an intense and concentrated tragedy. *Nero* has more incidents, but the structure of the play is expansive; like a chronicle play, it presents on the stage the incidents of a reign that covers several years, and this slackens the dramatic intensity. *Perfidus Hetruscus* is however crammed with bizarre and unusual incidents: the real ghost of Sorastanus interrupting Grimalfi disguised as a ghost; the ghost of Sorastanus appearing in giant form; the duel between Columbus and Pandolphus and the latter's sudden reappearance; the murder by poison of Lampranus; and the sudden remorse of Pandolphus at the end of the play.

The bizarre incidents of the play are matched by the play's extravagance of language, the strained metaphors (Act II, scene 2):

> an apertis cataractis in undosum
> Curarum mare ab oculorum fontibus salsae
> Stillarent guttae?

(Are salt drops to fall in open cataracts from the fountains of the eyes into a surging sea of cares?)

or in Act II, scene 4:

>   tui
> Encomium sphaerarum celebraret harmonia
> Angelicae aemula symphoniae.

(The harmony of the spheres would celebrate your praise, rivalling the angelic symphony.)

or in Act III, scene 1:

> claudantur oculi, olim
> Animae fenestrae, quibus universam naturae
> Machinam intuetur, sed iam maeroris fontes,
> Ex quibus salsugineae destillant limphae:
> Quiescam tandem, vel sit hoc corpus miseriarum
> Emporium, ubi ipsa mors, faeneratorie
> Cauponatur.

(Let my eyes be closed, my eyes, once the windows of my soul through which I looked upon the frame of universal nature, now fountains of grief, from which salt drops drip down. May I at last obtain repose, or else let this body be a market place for misery, where Death herself deals at interest.)

The whole play is written in this extravagant style.

What conclusions can we draw from an examination of these three plays? In them the tragic effect seems to come both from the unrelenting savagery of the action and from the inflated epigrammatic language. We find none of the nobility of the tragic hero in these plays. Oromasdes, the leading male character in *Roxana* – it would be absurd even to call him a hero – is a gloomy suspicious tyrant who ruthlessly kills his counsellor Bessus and his wife Atossa. Atossa herself, who plays a part in that play almost as large, is a cruel woman without a single redeeming feature. Nero in Gwinne's play is shown descending the pathway of degeneracy through a long succession of cruelties and murders. Pandolphus too in the *Perfidus Hetruscus* progresses from wickedness to wickedness. All illustrate the Senecan maxim (*Ag.* 115): *Per scelera semper sceleribus tutum est iter* (through crimes there is always a safe way for crimes).

All the elements which are usually regarded as Senecan can be found in these plays: the vengeful ghost, the moralizing chorus (except in *Perfidus Hetruscus*), the protracted passages of stichomythia, the speeches on stock themes such as the fickleness of fortune, and the evils of ambition, the passages expounding Stoic ideals, the stage horrors, and a profusion of *sententiae*. Examples of these could be given in great numbers, but it would hardly be helpful to do so here. No doubt all these elements could have derived from sources other than Seneca; but since the writers of Academic Latin tragedy could hardly fail to be aware of the plays of Seneca, then it seems legitimate to regard the emphasis given to these traditional Senecan elements in these Academic plays as a sign of Senecan influence. I believe that the writers of these plays are trying to out-Seneca Seneca. And so Gwinne is not content with one vengeful ghost, but must have five, in addition to Nemesis and the Furies; Alabaster devotes the whole first act of his play to the ghost of Moleon and the supernatural figures of Death and Suspicion; the *Perfidus Hetruscus* has a ghost which appears in the shape of a giant. And, similarly, the stichomythia is exploited to excess in lengthy passages of up to sixty and seventy lines at a time; the horrors can excel those of Senecan tragedy (as Atossa, in *Roxana*, pointed out); the *sententiae* glitter, so many paste diamonds, on the page.

The authors of these plays manipulate the conventions in a bravura manner and indulge their taste, with the aim, surely, of pleasing themselves and their audience. Gwinne wrote, it seems, for pleasure; and Alabaster spoke slightingly of his play as destined for one performance only. Great aesthetic pleasure is undoubtedly to be derived from the manipulation of well-worn conventions.

It may not be too far-fetched to see a similarity between these plays and what is perhaps their equivalent today, the Gothic horror films of Roger Corman.[35] In his films an audience takes pleasure in the manipulation of the stock ingredients of the genre; the old house surrounded by mist, and in the end destroyed by fire, the mysterious recluse, the secret room, the bodies mouldering in the family vault; and a good deal of the effect of these films comes from the manner in which the director lovingly reproduces these cinematic clichés.

So it is, I believe, with the Senecan elements in these plays. They serve as a virtuoso display for the authors' talents, and the enjoyment we derive is the enjoyment of the familiar. In the film the camera follows the heroine up the stairs to meet the nameless horror which lurks in the corridors above; in the play, it thunders and lightens, and through the din the ghost emerges from hell with lurid imprecations. In the film and the play, the *frisson* of delight is similar.

And, in the play, given the framework of the story, what opportunities there are for the dramatist to compose a highly coloured speech: 'We'll have a speech straight. Come give us a taste of your quality: come, a passionate speech' (*Hamlet*, Act II, scene 2). Herein lies one of the differences between Seneca and these sixteenth-century imitations. The atmosphere of these plays is after all not quite the same as that of a Senecan play. Seneca lived in an age of jaded rhetoric; when the drama had already died, when to be above all else clever, to strain after effect, to invent dazzlingly brilliant epigrams, to be super-subtle in reiterating the old *sententiae* was to merit the highest praise in literature. But the authors of these plays are writing in an age when there is a new delight in verbal wit, when there is a fresh and lively interest in the drama, and they reflect the vitality of the new age of Elizabethan drama, transmuting and revitalizing what they borrow from Seneca. The language of these plays is indeed not purely imitative. It would, I believe, be wrong to see all Renaissance Latin as being merely a mechanically correct imitation of the classical Latin of the Golden Age. The style of the *Perfidus Hetruscus* is highly individual, using many words and phrases from late Latin writers, and making great use of highly wrought metaphors. *Nero* is florid and almost euphuistic in style, and the Latin of *Roxana* is strange too. But detailed studies of sixteenth-century Latinity are needed before we can draw any firm conclusions.

Renaissance critics, however, seem to have valued Seneca's plays quite as much for their language as for their dramatic qualities; and we may fairly consider that a contemporary audience would judge these Renaissance imitations by the same aesthetic criteria. Julius Caesar Scaliger, drawing a distinction between plot and words, praises Seneca's style:[36]

> [Senecam] nullo Graecorum maiestate inferiorem existimo: cultu vero ac nitore etiam Euripide maiorem. Inventiones sane illorum sunt: at maiestas carminis, sonus, spiritus ipsius.

> (I consider Seneca inferior to none of the Greeks in grandeur: greater even than the Euripides in ornamentation and splendour. His plots are indeed theirs: but the majesty, the sound, the spirit of his verse are his own.)

Scaliger indeed believed that *sententiae* contributed largely to the tragic effect of a play:[37]

> Sunt enim quasi columnae, aut pilae quaedam universae fabricae illius.

> (They are as it were the pillars and columns of its whole construction.)

We should not forget in this context that Scaliger considered that *sententiae* were one of the means by which a poet could achieve *efficacia* (or *enargeia*), the vivid concretization of experience which was no small part of the appeal of poetry.[38]

Justus Lipsius, giving his opinion of Seneca's tragedies, emphasized their qualities of style:[39]

> Sonus in iis et granditas quaedam Tragica, fateor: sed nonne adfectatio saepe et tumor? Verba et dictio an usquequaque electa? Iam sententiae probae, acutae, interdum ad miraculum. Sed nonne saepe et sententiolae? Id est, fracta, minuta, quaedam dicta, obscura aut vana.

> (I confess that they have sonorousness and a certain tragic sublimity. But are they not also affected and bombastic? Are the words and the style everywhere well chosen? On occasions the *sententiae* are excellent and acute, sometimes miraculously so. But are they not also often 'sententiolae' i.e., the words are obscure, or devoid of meaning, weak and feeble?)

A grandiose style is then admired. Bartolomaeo Ricci too, stated as a commonplace that *sententiae* were an essential part of the tragic effect; they were not simply extrinsic ornamentation:[40]

> Tragoediae vero gravitatem, de qua nunc agitur, adiuvari
> inprimis gravitate sententiarum, nemo non intelligit. quis
> autem unico Seneca in sententiis est crebrior? quis etiam
> gravior? ... in eo quot versus, tot pene gravissimae
> sententiae.
>
> (Everyone knows that the weightiness of tragedy, which we
> are now discussing, is increased by the weightiness of the
> *sententiae* in particular. And which author is more studded with
> *sententiae* than peerless Seneca? Who is more dignified
> even? ... In him, there are almost as many over-weighty
> *sententiae*, as there are lines.)

In his discussion of Seneca's tragedies, Ricci states that the three qualities specially appropriate to tragedy are suspense, the action, and the outcome of the action. Ricci finds that Seneca's tragedies lack nothing in suspense. The action is either acted out before the eyes of the audience or else narrated. A sad ending is appropriate to tragedy. Even the slightest suggestion of happiness would detract from the tragic effect. Seneca's language harmonizes with the dreadfulness of the incidents he is describing. And, says Ricci, the tragic effect is enhanced in proportion to the atrociousness of the action.[41]

> Quanto tragoediae scriptor magis misericordiam auditori
> commovebit, quanto rem crudeliorem, ac magis atrocem
> faciet, tanto ab hoc maiorem sibi plausum excitabit, tanto
> eius gratiam inibit aequiorem.
>
> (The more a writer of tragedy moves pity in an audience, the
> crueller and more atrocious the nature of his theme, the more
> applause will he gain for himself, the more will he obtain the
> audience's favour.)

William Gager too was familiar with this doctrine.[42] The choruses should furthermore, says Ricci, condemn crime and extol virtue in their *sententiae*. Ricci's precepts are indeed exemplified by the three tragedies I have discussed. And, seen in this light, a tragedy such as *Roxana*, far from being a 'gruesome story', which 'no graces of style could redeem' and which 'outdoes even *Titus Andronicus* in its accumulation of the crudest horrors',[43] would pass muster as a truly tragic drama.

Renaissance Latin tragedy is, then, another channel through which the influence of Seneca distils itself. Written in Latin, free from the inevitable distortions which the constraints of another language imposed upon Senecan tragedy in the vernacular, these tragedies constitute a neglected but important aspect of Seneca's influence in the sixteenth century. When performed at a university they would come to the notice of an influential section of educated men. These tragedies would both meet and help to shape the assumptions of such an audience about tragedy, assumptions which they would then carry away with them from the university to regions far beyond.

Notes

1 A list of original Neo-Latin plays printed before 1650 is given by Leicester Bradner in 'The Latin drama of the Renaissance (1340–1640), *Studies in the Renaissance*, IV (1957), pp. 31–70.
2 The best accounts of this drama are Frederick Samuel Boas, *University Drama in the Tudor Age* (Oxford, 1914), and George Charles Moore Smith, *College Plays Performed in the University of Cambridge* (Cambridge, 1923). Plot summaries of most of the important plays were given by George B. Churchill and Wolfgang Keller, 'Die lateinischen Universitäts-Dramen Englands in der Zeit der Königin Elisabeth', *Shakespeare Jahrbuch*, XXXIV (1898), pp. 221–323. There is a brief account of Seneca's connections with University drama in Henry Buckley Charlton, *The Senecan Tradition in Renaissance Tragedy* (Manchester, 1946), pp. clxxi-clxxii. Ghost scenes in Elizabethan drama, including those in Alabaster's *Roxana* and the *Perfidus Hetruscus* are discussed by Gisela Dahinten, *Die Geisterszene in der Tragödie vor Shakespeare* (Palaestra, 225) (Göttingen, 1958).
3 For a recent article arguing against the influence of Seneca, see G. K. Hunter, 'Seneca and the Elizabethans: a case study in "Influence"', *Shakespeare Survey*, XX (1967), pp. 17–26.
4 See Thomas Whitfield Baldwin, *William Shakspere's Small Latine and Lesse Greeke* (Urbana, 1944), II, p. 560. From the evidence he concludes: 'It looks as if Westminster was the grammar school center of propagation for Seneca in the sixteenth century.'
5 'Tragoediae summam eloqui, non est opus; Quem Seneca, vestrum lateat?' (Prologue, lines 29–30). Gager's addition to *Hippolytus* are edited in my 'William Gager's additions to Seneca's *Hippolytus*', *Studies in the Renaissance*, XVII (1970), pp. 153–91.
6 See e.g. George Puttenham, 'The Arte of Englishe Poesie', *Elizabethan Critical Essays*, ed. George Gregory Smith (London, 1950), II, p. 27; Martino Antonio Delrio, 'Prolegomena De Tragoedia', esp. chapters

SENECA AND NEO-LATIN TRAGEDY IN ENGLAND

vi–viii in L. *Annaei Senecae Tragoediae*, ed. Joannes Casper Schröderus (Delft, 1728), sigs f3v.–g3v.; Daniel Heinsius, *De Tragoediarum Auctoribus Dissertatio*, also in Schröderus's edition, esp. sig. b4v.
7 G. C. Moore Smith, *College Plays* . . ., pp. 53–7, 106, and 'Plays performed in Cambridge Colleges before 1585', *Fasciculus Ioanni Willis Clark dicatus* (Cambridge, 1909), pp. 269–70.
8 *College Plays*, p.5.
9 'Plays performed in Cambridge Colleges before 1585', p. 272.
10 Boas, op. cit., p. 389.
11 See Karl Young, 'William Gager's Defence of the Academic Stage', *Transactions of the Wisconsin Academy of Sciences, Arts and Letters*, xviii (1916), pp. 593–638. The extract quoted is on p. 614.
12 See *DNB* s.v., 'Alabaster'; the introduction to *The Sonnets of William Alabaster*, ed. George Morley Story and Helen Gardner. Oxford English Monographs (London, 1959); and Louise Imogen Guiney, 'William Alabaster 1567/8–1640', *Recusant Poets* (New York, 1939), I, pp. 335–46.
13 See *DNB*, s.v., 'Freeman, Ralph'.
14 Cambridge University MS. Ff, 11.9; Lambeth Palace MS. 838; Emmanuel College, Cambridge MS., III.1.17; Trinity College, Cambridge MS. R. 17.10. There is a further MS. which I have not seen in Yale University Library. Alfred Harbage, *Annals of English Drama 975–1700*, rev. by Samuel Schoenbaum (London, 1964), p. 307 records also a MS. of an English translation which I have not seen: Folger Shakespeare Library MS. V b. 222.
15 See *DNB* s.v. 'Holland, Hugh'.
16 See *DNB* s.v. 'Farnaby, Thomas'.
17 (London, 1840), iii, 185.
18 'Milton', *Lives of the English Poets* (London, 1959), I, p. 65.
19 See *DNB*, s.v. 'Gwinne, Matthew'.
20 'At cur non acta? Non dico, quod non apta; forte nec scripta in hunc finem: etsi utrumque innuat et personarum multitudo et longitudo inaequalis actuum; et modus tractandi non plausibilis. Nec dico quod non oblata: nec enim debui, qui multum, qui me debeo Collegio in primis Ioannensi, . . . quod apud illos exaratum certe non debui non offerre: etsi sic (fateor) obtulerim, ut quam acceptam, melius repudiatam tulerim. Repudiatam dico' (sig. A8r. and v.).

This suggests that the play may have been written when Gwinne was still in permanent residence at the College, perhaps before 1595.
21 He quotes Pliny *Letters*, ii, xix: 'Tanto maiorem . . . apud doctos habere debet gratiam, quanto minorem apud indoctos habet' (sig. A9r.).
22 'Quin ad leges poeticas . . . ne quarta loqui persona laboret?' (sig. A7v.).
23 In his epistle 'Ad Criticum' in *Ulysses Redux* (Oxford, 1592).
24 'Dormivi forsitan in primis actibus: at non defeci in extremo, qui per se compleat non absonam tragoediam' (sig. A8r.).
25 'Hoc mihi in otio negotium, ne otiosus' (sig. A3v.).
26 'Quin ergo comice? Demum non decuit. Etsi et sciam quiddam altius poetice, et acutius ut scribam comice, quam ego quidquam sapiam (sig. A4r.).

27 'Medicus num prostat comicus?... Vix cogitare levia vir gravis debuit; sic cogitata scribere, scripta in vulgus edere Doctorem medicum non decuit (sig. A2r.).
28 'Pro me sic Plinius, acsi de se loquatur, et Studiosus et Senator. Facio nonnumquam virsiculos, severos parum facio, comaedias audio, specto mimos, lyricos lego, satyricos intelligo, rideo, iocor, ludo.' (sig. A5r.)
29 'Plus indecori, inhumani, illiciti, (quod unquam senserim) vident qui absunt, imaginantur qui obtrectant, memorant qui maledicunt, quam qui interfui, vidi, audivi, cogitavi, vel (vigilans si somniaret) somniavi' (sig. A6r.).
30 For an account of this controversy see Boas, op. cit., pp. 229–48 and Karl Young, op. cit.
31 Boas, op. cit., p. 252.
32 See *DNB* s.v. 'Sandsbury, John'.
33 Justus Lipsius, 'Animadversiones in Tragoedias quae L. Annaeo Senecae tribuuntur', *Opera Omnia* (Wesel, 1675), 1. pp. 872–3.
34 The date assigned to the paper on which it is written by Churchill and Keller, op. cit., n. 2, p. 250. The MS. is in the Bodleian Library: MS. Rawlinson C. 787. The work has now been edited by R. G. Wittmann in an unpublished Ph.D. dissertation (St Louis University, 1969).
35 On the films of Roger Corman see Peter John Dyer, 'Z films', *Sight and Sound*, XXXIII (1964), pp. 179–81.
36 Julius Caesar Scaliger, *Poetices Libri Septem* (Lyons, 1561), p. 323.
37 Ibid. p. 145.
38 Ibid. p. 117.
39 'Animadversiones in Tragoedias quae L. Annaeo Senecae tribuuntur', *Opera Omnia*, I, p. 873.
40 Ricci, *De imitatione libri tres* (Venice, 1545), p. 22v.
41 Ibid.
42 He says in a critical preface to his *Meleager* that he has introduced the suicide of Oeneus into the play 'ut Tragoediae argumentum, maiore cum varietate, tum atrocitate pertexeretur' (*Meleager*, Oxford, 1592, sig. A5r.).
43 Boas, op. cit., p. 287.

Subject Index

Acts of the Apostles, 11
adultery, 30, 121
adversity, 49–54, 85–7
Aetna, 120
Africa, 126
Agamemnon, 97, 120, 132, 168, 174, 185, 189, 223
anger, 44–7, 54–8
antilabe, 101
antiquity, Seneca's influence in, 117–31
antithesis, 101
Antonio's Revenge, 177, 180, 183
Apius and Virginia, 184
Apocolocyntosis, 19–20, 29, 30, 151
aristocratic plays, 181–2
Aristotelians, 124–5, 140
Armenia, 17
asceticism, 5, 7, 31, 33, 90
atheism, 164

Baetica, 3
Baroque, 195
beauty, 105–6
Beneficiis, De, 8, 16, 26, 27, 29, 30, 32, 65
Bible, The, 11, 172
biographical details of Seneca, 3, 5, 6–30, 80–1
boredom, 88

Brevitate Vitae, De, 13, 29, 41
Britain, Seneca and, 2, 152

Cambyses, 169, 184
Carolingian Renaissance, 132
Chartres, school of, 135
chorus, dramatic, 106–8, 231
Christian antiquity, Seneca in, 122–31
doctrine, 124–5, 137–8
philosophy, 124–5
Christianity Seneca and, 122–3, 126–9, 133–4, 137–9, 142, 144, 171–3
civil war, 27
Clementia, De, 12, 13, 22–3, 29, 30, 32, 43, 65, 146
Consolatio ad Helviam, 6, 9, 10
Consolatio ad Marciam, 29
Consolatio ad Polybium, 8, 10, 19, 29, 222
conspiracy against Nero, 24–8
Constantia Sapientis, 8, 14, 29, 30, 42, 59–64
Controversiae, 5–8 passim, 99–100
contumelia, 62–3
Corduba, 3–4, 40
Corsica, 10
court life, 12, 21, 24

SUBJECT INDEX

crimes, Nero's, 17–18, 22–5 *passim*, 31, 121
critics, Renaissance, 205, 219, 229
Cynics, 45, 50

Damon and Pithias, 169
death, 87–9, 112–14; *see also* suicide
of Seneca, 24–5, 27–9, 86, 93, 139, 142
declamation, 42–3
declamatory drama, 98–101, 104–5, 109–10
deification, 20–1
despair, 88
dialectics, 48, 52, 102
dialogue, 43, 45, 60, 98, 101–3
Dialogues, 65, 133, 135
diatribe, 45
dissuasoria, 57
dithyramb, 107–8
divisio, 41, 49–51, 56, 61–2
drama, declamatory, 98–101, 104–5, 109–10
Elizabethan, 167, 169, 171–93, 201–2n, 207, 229
Greek, 97–8, 107, 170–1, 187
neo-Latin, 187
Renaissance, 205
see also plays; tragedy
Dunciad, The, 196

education, in Middle Ages, 140–1, 143–4, 206
in rhetoric, 98–100, 121
Elizabethan era, drama, 167, 169, 171–93, 201–2n, 207, 229
literary taste, 187
epigrams, 42–3, 62, 97, 101, 104
Epistulae ad Paulum, 130, 137–8, 139, 144, 171; *see also* Paul, St
Epistulae Morales ad Lucilium, 6–8 *passim*, 14, 24, 27–30

passim, 33, 44, 60, 70–94, 108, 121, 131, 132, 135, 147
ethics, 173; *see also* morality
Exhortationes, 131
exile, 9–11, 87, 97, 119
exordium, 41, 47, 48–9, 55–6, 59–60

fatalism, 51–2, 114, 145, 149
Florilegium Gallicum, 137
Florilegium morale Oxoniense, 137
form, literary, 41, 48–65, 73–4, 90–1
Forma Mundi, De, 130, 132
furor, 174–5

Gallia Narbonensis, 14
games, 65
ghosts, 179–81, 184–5, 190, 207–9, 215–17 *passim*, 221, 224–6
Gismond of Salerne, 181
God, definition of, 134–5
Golden Age, 91, 93, 229
good and evil, 49, 51–2
Gorboduc, 181, 182
grammarians, 121
Greek drama, 97–8, 107, 170–1, 187
Greek philosophers, 118, 123, 133, 143

Hamlet, 183–4, 225, 229
Hebrew prophets, 123
Hecuba, 206
Hercules Furens, 97, 101–4 *passim*, 109, 168
Hercules Oetaeus, 97, 108–10
heresy, 123
Hippolytus, 97, 205, 206, 219; *see also Phaedra*
Hoffman, 183
Horestes, 184

SUBJECT INDEX

horror, 110, 167–8, 174, 192–3, 197, 202, 204, 208–9, 212–15, 228, 231
films, 228–9
humanism, 135–9 *passim*, 141, 143, 148
humour, 19–21
hypochondriacs, 80
hypocrisy, 1, 12, 31, 33, 121, 129, 146, 152

iambic trimeter, 98
illness, 7, 80
Immatura Morte, De, 131
incest, 11, 17
inconsistency, 55
iniuria, 61–3
interlocutor, 45–6, 59
Ira, De, 8, 10, 12, 14, 26, 43, 44, 46–7, 54–8, 61, 121, 130
Italy, 166–7, 181

Jephthes, 172, 221
Jocasta, 181–2
Judaism, 7, 123–4

King John, 169

Latin, drama, 187; *see also* tragedy Renaissance, 229
letters, literary, 73; *see also Epistulae*
Liber de moribus, 131
Locrine, 180, 182
luxury, 31–2, 84–5, 92, 139
lyrics, 105–7

Macbeth, 225
matricide, 17–18
Matrimonio, De, 30, 129, 131
Medea, 97, 98, 101–4, 106–7, 109, 168, 174–5, 193, 194, 206
Metamorphoses, The, 189

metaphor, 94
metre, 98, 107–8
Middle Ages, education in, 140–1, 143–4, 206
Seneca in, 128, 130–40
miracle plays, 168
Mirror for Magistrates, 168, 179–80, 188, 190
Monita Senecae, 131
Moral Essays, 39–69
moralis philosophia, 71–2
moralist, Seneca's influence as, 120, 121, 127, 135–6, 141–5 *passim*
morality, 1–2, 9, 30, 33, 34, 51–3, 121–2, 174, 177–8, 181, 195
Moralium dogma philosophorum, 137
Moribus, De, 132
Morte Claudii, De, 132

natural beauty, 105–6
Naturales Quaestiones, vii, 7, 8, 9, 14, 29, 30, 71–2, 75, 119–21 *passim*, 130, 134, 135
Neoplatonism, 143
Nero, 215–24, 226–9 *passim*
Neronians and Flavians, viii

Octavia, 2, 97, 120, 190, 206, 220
Oedipus, 97, 101, 107–8, 110, 114–15, 168, 170, 186, 189, 195, 196–7, 205
Officiis, De, 130
Old Testament, 172
oratory, 8, 44–5, 55
Othello, 170
Otio, De, 14, 29, 71

pagan antiquity, Seneca in, 117–22
papyrus roll, 48
patronage, 17
Paupertate, De, 131
Perfidus Hetruscus, 224–9
Peripatetics, 56–7, 58

SUBJECT INDEX

peroratio, 42, 49, 63
Phaedra, 97, 98, 101, 103, 104, 106, 110, 168, 172, 194, 223; see also *Hippolytus*
philosophical influence of Seneca, 116–52
  in Christian antiquity, 122–31
  in Middle Ages, 128, 130–40
  in pagan antiquity, 117–22
  since Renaissance, 128, 137, 140–52, 171–2
philosophy, 5–7, 11, 13, 29–30, 39–65, 71–2, 84–5, 87–93
  Christian, 124–5
  disestablishment of, 117–18
  Platonic, 118
Phoenissae, 97
Platonism, 118, 124–6; see also Neoplatonism
plays, aristocratic, 181–2
  miracle, 168
  revenge, 174–85, 189, 207–9, 212, 215–16, 221, 224, 228
  stage, 100, 109, 182, 205, 207, 217, 221
  see also drama; tragedy
poetry, 186
political behaviour, 1–2, 13, 14–20, 22–4, 29, 71
popularity of Seneca, 119, 135, 143
poverty and wealth, 31–2
praeteritio, 48
predestination, 145
principate, 22–4
propositio, 41, 49
Proverbia, 131–3
Providence, 48–9, 51, 54, 178
Providentia, De, 15, 42, 43, 48, 71, 75
Pyrrhonian scepticism, 147

recitatio, 48
reform, 15

Reformation, 148
Remediis Fortuitorum, De, 131
Renaissance, Carolingian, 132
  critics, 205, 219, 229
  drama, 205
  Latin, 229
  Seneca since, 128, 137, 140–52, 171–2
  tragedy, 166, 169, 194, 205–32
repetition, 46–8, 50, 52, 54, 58–9, 61, 64, 187
retirement, 24, 32, 80–2
works of, 71–2
revenge plays, 174–85, 189, 207–9, 212, 215–16, 221, 224, 228
rhetoric, 39, 40–5, 47–8, 56–7, 59, 74, 100, 109, 187, 190–4, 229
  education in, 98–100, 121
rhyme, 195
Richard III, 178–9, 221, 226
Richardus Tertius, 181
Rome, reconstruction of, 31
Roxana, 181, 207–15, 226–9 *passim*, 231

satire, 10, 19–20, 45
scepticism, 147–9
scholasticism, 135, 140–2 *passim*, 148
self-portraiture, 79
senate, 12, 21, 23
sententiae, 100, 114, 131, 136, 183, 222–3, 228, 229–31
slaves, 33
soliloquy, 102–3
Spain, 3, 130, 141
Spanish Tragedy, The, 176, 180–5 *passim*, 190–2
speech writer, Seneca as, 18–19, 21, 23, 119
stage plays, 100, 109, 182, 205, 207, 217, 221
stichomythia, 101, 168, 186, 228

SUBJECT INDEX

Stoicism, 9, 12, 13, 22, 29, 30, 32, 33, 34, 40, 44, 45, 51–3, 59–64, 86, 89–90, 108–9, 117–18, 120, 124–6, 142, 145, 147–50
style, 2, 5, 6, 8, 39–40, 44, 64–5, 74, 84–5, 109, 119, 121–2, 143–4, 146, 148, 185–6, 194–6, 210–11, 227, 229–30
pointed, 44, 101
Suasoriae, 5, 99
suicide, 24–5, 49, 52, 86, 88, 139
Superstitione, De, 121, 129, 131
swimming, 81

technological progress, 92
temples pillaged, 24
theology, 88–9
Thyestes, 97, 101, 110–12, 168, 172, 177, 185, 188–9, 193, 194, 197–201, 214
Titus Andronicus, 173–4, 176–7, 183, 185, 231
torture, 86–7, 212–13, 216
Tragedies, 96–115, 132, 168–70, 173–5, 176–7, 186–90, 193, 194, 196–7, 231
tragedy, English, 166–201, 96
  Latin, 98, 170, 181
  neo-Latin, in England, 205–32

Renaissance, 166, 169, 194, 205, 210
Tranquillitate Animi, De, 12, 13, 29, 30, 32, 34, 41, 145, 222
translations, 187–90, 194, 197–203, 212
travel, 82–3
Troades, 97, 103–4, 112–14, 168, 178, 188, 190, 194, 205–6
tuberculosis, 7
tutor, Seneca as, 12, 14, 33–4, 151
type-figures, 109
tyrannicide, 25, 27–8

Ur-Hamlet, 183
usury, 152

vegetarianism, 5, 7, 79
vice, 33, 121, 122, 144
  death penalty for, 26–7
violence, 196–7
Vita Beata, De, 1, 29, 32, 33, 42
viticulture, 82
volumen, 48

wealth, 31–2
Westminster School, 205
wise man, Stoic, 59–64, 91–3

Name Index

Abel, K., 65n
Abelard, Peter, 135–6, 137
Accius, 98
Acte, 16
Aeschylus, 97–8, 170
Agrippa, 3, 16
Agrippina, Julia, 10, 11, 13, 14, 16–17, 18, 20, 22, 23, 30, 119
Alabaster, William, 205, 207, 209–12, 218, 228
Alan of Lille, 137
Albertanus of Brescia, 140, 141
Albertini, E., 65, 68, 72
Alcuin, 132
Aldhelm, 132
Alexander, W. H., 37–8
Alexander, Sir William, 166, 181, 182
Ambrose, St, 127
Angers, Fr Julien-Eymard d', 149
Anicetus, 18
Annaeus, L. Junius Gallio, 5
Annaeus family, 3, 5
Anselm of Canterbury, 134–5
Antonia, 27
Aquinas, 124
Aristides, 80
Aristotle, 40, 55, 56–7, 58, 129, 141
Artaud, Antonin, 196–7

Artemon, 73
Asper, Sulpicius, 25, 26
Attalus, 7, 31, 90
Augustine, St, 129–30, 131, 134, 154
Augustus, 16, 18, 19–20, 21, 22, 29
Ausonius, 127

Bachiarius, 127
Bacon, Francis, 150, 176, 194
Bacon, Roger, 140
Baldwin, William, 179, 188
Barker, E. P., 34, 94, 96
Barlaam, 142
Basil, 126
Bateman, Stephen, 171
Bede, 159
Bevington, David, 182
Beza, Theodore, 220–1
Binns, J. W., 205–34
Bion the Borysthenite, 45
Boadicea, see Boudicca
Boas, F. S., 206
Boccaccio, 142
Boethius, 29, 130
Bonner, S. F., 67, 115
Bossuet, J. B., 150
Boudicca, 2, 152
Bourgery, A., 119, 120

NAME INDEX

Bradner, Leicester, 232
Britannicus, 11, 12, 17, 18, 20, 22, 31
Brower, Reuben, 174
Brutus, 129
Buchanan, George, 172, 220–1
Budé, Guillaume, 145
Burger, F. X., 127
Burrus, Sextus Afranius, 14–18 *passim*, 23, 24
Burton, Robert, 163

Caesar, Julius, 4, 7, 22, 27, 28
Caligula, 8, 20, 21, 27, 39, 43, 63, 121, 143
Calvin, John, 145
Cambrensis, Giraldus, 137
Cantor, Petrus, 137
Cassiodorus, 132, 158
Cato, 44, 49, 52, 60–2 *passim*, 64, 85–6, 89
Charlton, H. B., 166–7, 182–3
Charondas, 92
Charron, Pierre, 147
Chaucer, Geoffrey, 141
Chekhov, Anton, 110
Chrysippus, 44
Cicero, 9, 29, 41, 43, 74–5, 77, 84, 98, 127, 129, 133, 135, 140, 141, 143, 145, 146
Claudian, 121
Claudius, Emperor, 9–12, 13, 16, 17, 19–20, 119
Clement of Alexandria, 126
Cloetta, W., 166
Cluvius Rufus, 15
Coccia, M., 68
Coffey, M., 37
Colonna, Giovanni, 142, 155
Columbanus, 131
Columella, 118
Corbulo, Cn. Domitius, 17
Cordus, Cremutius, 8
Corman, Roger, 228

Cornutus, Lucius Annaeus, 153
Costa, C. D. N., vii–viii, 96–115
Cotta, Aurelius, 31
Cowley, Abraham, 199
Creizenach, W., 166
Cunliffe, 166
Currie, H. MacL., 66–7
Cyprian, 127

Daniel, Samuel, 190
Dante Alighieri, 141
Demetrius, 50, 73
Descartes, René, 150
Deschamps, Eustache, 141
Desiderius, Abbot of Monte Cassino, 133
Diderot, Denis, 151
Dio Cassius, 2, 9, 10–11, 15, 17, 19, 25, 30, 31, 119, 121, 146, 215
Dio Chrysostom, 94
Diomedes, 120
Domitius, 12
Donatus, 120
Drayton, M., 194
Dryden, John, 195, 196
Du Vair, Guillaume, 146, 194

Eliot, T. S., 96, 170
Elorduy, E., 155
Ennius, 98
Epicharis, 25–6, 27
Epictetus, 40, 117, 145–6
Epicurus, 40, 62–3, 74–5, 78, 85, 88, 108, 125
Erasmus, 143–5, 171
Euripides, 96, 97–8, 106–7, 109, 170, 230

Fabianus, Papirius, 9, 42
Fabius Rusticus, 2, 15, 26, 27, 28
Faenius Rufus, 24–5, 28

Faider, P., 153, 159
Fansler, H. E., 182
Farnaby, Thomas, 211
Faustus, 127
Feltham, O., 194
Fischer, R., 166
Flavius Dexter, 155, 162
Flavus, Subrius, 25-6, 29
Freculphus, 132
Fronto, 44, 122
Fuller, Thomas, 211-12

Gaetulicus, Cornelius Lentulus, 8
Gager, William, 205-6, 217, 219-20, 221, 231
Gaius, *see* Caligula
Galerius, C., 6, 7
Gallio, L. Junius, 5, 7, 11-12, 28
Gascoigne, George, 181-2
Gataker, Thomas, 146
Gellius, Aulus, 78, 120, 122, 143
Gerbert of Rheims, 132
Germanicus, Nero Claudius Drusus, 12
Giardina, G. C., 115
Gilbert of Poitiers, 135
Godfrey of St Victor, 136, 138
Graecinus, Julius, 8, 15
Granville, George, 201
Gregory of Nazianzus, 126
Gregory of Nyssa, 126
Greville, Fulke, 168, 173-4, 175, 178, 181
Griffin, Miriam T., 1-38
Grimal, P., 66, 67
Groto, Luigi, 182, 212
Guaiferius of Salerno, 133
Gummere, R. M., 152, 155
Gwinne, Matthew, 215, 217-24, 228

Hale, Sir Matthew, 200
Hall, Joseph, 148
Harrison, G. B., 203

Heinsius, Daniel, 97
Helvia (Seneca's mother), 3, 5, 6
Herbert of Cherbury, Edward, 149
Hercules, 108-9
Herrick, M. T., 166
Heywood, Jasper, 185, 188-9, 198
Holland, Hugh, 210
Honorius Scholasticus, 130
Horace, 64, 107
Hucbald of St Amand, 132
Hughes, Ted, 196-7
Hughes, Thomas, 182
Hume, David, 151
Humphrey, L., 186
Hunter, G. K., 166-204
Hutcheson, F., 151

Ibsen, H., 170
Isidore, 130

Jaquot, Jean, 202
Jerome, 128-9, 131, 132, 138, 139, 171-2
John of Salisbury, 136, 138
John of Wales, 141
Johnson, Samuel, 212
Juvenal, 2, 26, 31, 104, 120

Kirchmaier, Thomas, 146
Kraft, K., 37
Kyd, Thomas, 180-5 *passim*, 190-2

La Bruyère, J. de, 150
Lactantius, 55, 127, 131, 157-8, 160
Lansdowne, Lord, 201
La Rochefoucauld, F. de, 151
Laurence of Durham, 138
Liebniz, G. W., 149, 150
Lepidus, Aemilius, 8
Lewis, C. S., 76
Linus (ps.-), 128

NAME INDEX

Lipsius, Justus, 39, 97, 147, 194, 220, 230
Liutprand of Cremona, 132
Livilla, Julia, 9, 10
Locke, John, 149, 150
Lodge, Thomas, 148
Lucan, 5, 6, 17, 28, 100, 120, 137, 187
Lucilius, 9, 24, 33, 54, 75, 84, 153
Lucilius Junior, 14
Lucretius, 84
Lyly, John, 163

Machiavelli, 178, 203
Macrobius, 121, 160
Maecenas, 3, 16, 84
Malebranche, N., 151
Marcellinus, 78
Marcellinus, Ammianus, 121
Marcellus, Eprius, 24
Marcia, 8
Marcus Aurelius, 44, 75, 117, 146
Marlowe, C., 182, 185
Marston, John, 177
Marti, B., 108
Martial, 2, 31, 119, 120
Martin, St (of Braga), 130, 133, 171
Marullus, 4
Marvell, Andrew, 194, 198
Maternus, Curiatius, 100
Matthews, Brander, 169
Maurus, Hrabanus, 132
Mela, L. Annaeus, 5–6, 11, 25, 28
Melanchthon, Philip, 172
Merobaudes, 130
Messalina, Valeria, 9–11, 20
Metellus, 85
Milton, John, 212
Minucius Felix, 127
Modoin of Autun, 132
Momigliano, A., 123
Montaigne, M. E. de, 146–7, 151

Mucius, 85
Muret, Marc-Antoine, 146

Namatianus, Rutilius, 121
Narcissus, 9
Nashe, Thomas, 182–3
Natalis, Antonius, 25
Nero, 12–31
Nerva, Cocceius, 24
Newton, Thomas, 96, 186
Niger, Petronius, 24
Novatian, 127
Novatus, Annaeus, 5, 7, 8
Nowell, Dean, 172
Nuce, Thomas, 202–3

Octavia, 11
Oltramare, A., 67
Origen, 126
Otho, L. Salvius, 17, 21
Otloh of St Emmeran, 132–3, 159
Ovid, 10, 29, 52, 109, 137, 141, 168, 178, 187, 189, 202

Pacuvius, 98
Pallas, 16, 17
Panaetius, 32
Papias, 132
Pascal, B., 150
Pasquier, Étienne, 163
Paul, St, 123, 127–30 *passim*, 133, 137–8, 171
Paulinus, Pompeius, 13, 17
Peacham, H., 186
Pembroke, Countess of, 181, 182
Persius, 28, 120
Peter, Hermann, 72
Petrarch, 142–3
Petronius, 27, 83, 119
Pfennig, R., 65n
Phaedrus, 120
Pharius, 82
Philip of Harvengt, 138
Piso, C. Calpurnius, 25–7, 31

244

NAME INDEX

Plato, 1, 27, 40, 43, 64, 74, 90
Plautus, 206
Pliny the Elder, 15, 27, 118, 119
Pliny the Younger, 10, 19, 36, 73, 74, 84, 140, 218
Plutarch, 13, 17, 119, 129, 142, 143, 146–7
Pollio, Asinius, 4
Polyaenus, 25, 27
Polybius, 10–11
Pompeia Paulina, 30
Pompey, Sextus, 4
Pomponazzi, 163
Pope, Alexander, 196
Popkin, R. H., 164
Poppaea, 18
Pordage, Samuel, 194
Posidonius, 44, 91–2
Praz, Mario, 203
Prestwich, Edmund, 194
Prudentius, 130
Pythagoras, 92

Quintilian, 2, 32–3, 41, 57, 68, 118, 121, 136, 143, 186

Radbertus, Paschasius, 132
Rainolds, Dr John, 219–20
Ratherius of Lüttich, 132
Regenbogen, O., 110
Reynolds, L. D., 130, 133, 161
Ricci, Bartolomaeo, 230–1
Romanus de la Higuera, H., 162
Ross, G. M., 116–65
Rossbach, 36
Rousseau, J.-J., 151
Russell, Bertrand, 151–2
Russell, D. A., 70–95
Rutilius, 85
Rymer, Thomas, 195

Saint-Évremond, C. M. de, 150–1
Sallust, 137

Salutati, Coluccio, 142
Sandsbury, John, 220
Saturninus, L. Volusius, 21
Scaliger, J. C., 96, 229–30
Schoppe, Caspar, 147
Scott-Kilvert, I., 168
Scotus, Sedulius, 132
Seneca, L. Annaeus (Seneca's father), 3–6, 40, 79–80, 99–100, 163
Seneca Rhetor, 4
Serenus, Annaeus, 13–14, 17, 23, 60
Servius, 120
Sextius, Q., 7, 47
Shakespeare, William, 169, 170, 173–8, 221, 225
Sherburn, Sir Edward, 194
Shirley, James, 182
Sidney, Sir Philip, 186
Sidonius Apollinaris, 130
Silanus, L. Junius, 11, 26
Smith, G. C. Moore, 205–6
Socrates, 1, 28, 63, 85, 145
Sophocles, 97–8, 170
Sotion, 7, 67
Spinoza, B., 150
Statius, 120
Stelzenberger, J., 126
Stilpo, 61
Storer, Thomas, 190
Strabo, Walahfrid, 132
Studley, John, 185, 189
Suetonius, 2, 13, 26, 119, 121, 137, 162, 215, 218
Suillius Rufus, 1–2, 30, 31
Summers, W. C., 154, 186
Sylvester II, Pope, 132
Syrus, Publilius, 131

Tacitus, 1–2, 9–28 *passim*, 31, 32, 100, 119, 121, 215, 218
Taille, Jean de la, 172
Talbot, C. H., 158

NAME INDEX

Terence, 168, 206
Tertullian of Carthage, 126
Theobald, Lewis, 195–6
Thierry of Chartres, 135
Thrasea Paetus, 27, 28, 29
Tiberius, 7
Tibullus, 64
Tigellinus, Ofonius, 16, 23, 24
Trachalus, P. Galerius, 17
Trimalchio, 83
Turrinus, Clodius, 6

Valla, L., 163
Velo, 172
Veranius, Q., 21
Vincent of Beauvais, 140
Virgil, 84, 142, 178
Vitellius, Aulus, 23–4

Vitellius, Lucius, 16, 18
Vulgarius, Eugenius, 132

Walter of St Victor, 138–9
Waszink, J. H., 155
Watling, E. F., 115
Watson, Bishop, 172
Weber, H., 67
William of Conches, 135, 137
William of Malmesbury, 136
William of St Thierry, 137
Wright, John, 194, 200
Wright, J. R. G., 36–69
Wyatt, Sir Thomas, 198

Zaleucus, 92
Zwingli, Huldreich, 145